ER'S ENTIRE.
GEORGE
NT FURNISHING
AUCTION & ES
DRAWING, DINING,
& BEDROOM SUITES.
BEDSTEADS
& BEDDING.
NITURE
EHOUSED
HT, SOLD OR
CHANGED.
FURNITURE
STUFF'D
BEDDING
FUNERALS
AF593809

A Pictorial Record of SOUTHERN SIGNALS

FRONTISPIECE
'THE SOUTH WESTERN SCENE'. An up goods, hauled by 0-4-2 loco No. 537, trundles through New Milton (between Bournemouth and Brockenhurst).

Photo courtesy National Railway Museum

A Pictorial Record of SOUTHERN SIGNALS

By G. A. PRYER

Oxford Publishing Co · Oxford

© Oxford Publishing Co. 1977

SBN 902888 81 1

Typesetting by Getset Ltd, Eynsham
Photo reproduction by Oxford Litho Plates Ltd
Printed by Blackwell's in the City of Oxford
Bound by Kemp Hall Bindery, Oxford

Wool signal box and level crossing *Photo B. L. Jackson*

Published by
Oxford Publishing Company
8 The Roundway
Headington
Oxford

Contents

Bibliography and Acknowledgements

Information and illustrations for this book have been drawn from a wide variety of sources. It is not practical here to name the many who have contributed photographic material, but the appropriate credits are given under each illustration. The author wishes to express his gratitude to all these, without whom the photographic content of the book would have been tame indeed. However, thanks of a special nature are due to several who have put themselves to considerable trouble on my behalf. Firstly, Brian Jackson of Weymouth, who has travelled hundreds of miles to photograph such interesting items as still exist. Peter Rutter and Graham Bowring have put in hours of hard work at the drawing table, and their scale drawings of signals and signal box buildings will, I'm sure, be greatly appreciated by modellers with an interest in the Southern. The work of obtaining reasonable prints from old and faded negatives has been undertaken by Colin Caddy of Weymouth and Michael Tattershall of Bridport, whilst further assistance in this matter has been received from David Bampton of Southampton.

Printed sources of information are as follows:-

The South Eastern & Chatham Railway by O. S. Nock.

The London, Brighton & South Coast Railway by C. Hamilton Ellis.

The London & South Western Railway by O. S. Nock.

The Southern Railway Magazine, published as a staff journal by the S.R.

A History of Southern Signalling, a series of articles by D. A. Collins in the Newsletter of the Signalling Record Society.

History of the Southern Railway (Revised Edition) by C. F. Dendy Marshall.

Other information has been drawn from the archives of the Signalling Record Society, with the kind assistance of Martin Elms, who holds the records relating to the South of England. The drawing office of the same society has supplied the layout diagrams.

Thanks also go to Mrs. E. Wallis, wife of the late E. Wallis, for permitting me to use many photographs from her husband's collection. The co-operation of British Rail, Southern Region, is also much appreciated. With their permission, the operational sketches and operating instructions for the various types of block instruments, other quotations from the Train Signalling Regulations Book, and the 1913 signal diagram of Victoria are reproduced. The Public Record Office, Ashridge Park, has also been of great assistance, allowing me to use tracings of the early 'low-pressure' signals between Andover and Grateley for reproduction in this book. Finally, thanks go to the Public Relations and Publicity Officer of the Westinghouse Brake and Signal Company and to the Bluebell Railway for facilities and assistance.

AUTHOR'S NOTE: This book has been produced at an unfortunate time, when the Signal Engineers Department of the Southern Region has been heavily committed with the resignalling of London Bridge, and therefore unable to render much assistance with research. The obtaining of old material has further been hampered by the movement of all the Southern's historical items to the National Railway Museum at York, where it has yet to be sorted before it becomes available. The record is therefore not as complete as it might be, and there must be many items of interest which receive no mention whatsoever. However, in view of the unfavourable circumstances, I would ask that readers bear with me. What I have tried to produce is not a signalling history as such (as this ground has been covered before) or a technical manual. It is a PICTORIAL record of many things appertaining to signalling which were once commonplace, and have now vanished for ever. It is in this light that I trust that all readers will find the book interesting.

G. A. Pryer.
Redbridge Station,
Southampton.
1977

Branch home signal at Weybridge, 'pulled off' for the bay platform.

Photo: J. Scrace.

Foreword

At the Grouping of 1923, the newly formed Southern Railway was faced with no mean task. It inherited a motley assortment of locomotives, rolling stock, and, of course, signalling equipment from three, and originally four, independent companies, much of it in a rather run-down state as the result of heavy usage and reduced maintenance during the 1914–18 War.

The human aspect must have been equally delicate. Railwaymen of the 'old school' were very proud of the companies for whom they worked. Thus a former L.B. & S.C.R. man would continue to staunchly champion everything connected with his old employers, and bitterly resent the introduction of 'imported' ideas from the L. & S.W.R. or 'South Eastern'. Seen in this light, it is hardly surprising that the Southern Railway made little difference to the outward appearance of its empire for several years. It is perhaps a pity that its period of development and consolidation, terminated by Nationalisation in 1947, was too short to permit the building up of much true 'Southern' tradition. Such traditions as they possessed tended to be left-overs from one or other of the pre-grouping concerns, such as the ability to organise dozens of extra trains at very short notice to cater for race meetings, military manoeuvres, and various other events, which had long been a feature of the old L. & S.W.R.

This could explain why the Southern has never enjoyed the popularity it deserves amongst railway enthusiasts. Its neighbour, the G.W.R., was a 'traditional' railway in every sense of the word, with a long record of safe public service, and a certain continuity in the design of its locos and other equipment. For many years, photographers have flocked to every vantage point on the Great Western system, to capture on film the stately 'Kings' or 'Castles' in action, but the Southern has been badly neglected. In the West Country, views of trains on the 'sea wall' around Dawlish are so common as to become almost a bore, but photographs taken on the old S.R. route between Exeter and Plymouth are rare indeed. Somehow, the Southern has always been regarded as the 'other railway' in the West.

In this book, I hope to prove that there is, or has been, much of interest on the Southern. Regrettably, there is much that cannot be included as the system was so unstandardised, that to do true justice to one subject alone—signal box architecture—would involve covering virtually every box individually. If your favourite box makes no appearance in these pages, it is not because it is considered to be of no interest, but because of lack of space.

The Southern today, although ranking as Britain's premier passenger-carrying system, tends to be taken rather for granted. The trains are frequent, and for the most part, punctual, to the extent that adherents of other lines view it as something akin to an electrified tramway. I hope that this book will stimulate more interest in the lines of Southern England. There is still much to be seen. Go and look at it before modernisation sweeps it away!

'THE BRIGHTON SCENE'. The old 'box on stilts' at Keymer Junction, (Brighton line), photographed in June 1886.
Photo courtesy National Railway Museum.

'THE SOUTH EASTERN SCENE'. Signalman's view of Charing Cross station in 1910.

Photo courtesy National Railway Museum.

1. The Early Years

The Southern Railway, and the Southern Region of today, was made up of the lines of three major companies. Largest of these was the London and South Western Railway, which served most of Surrey, Hampshire, East Dorset, South Wiltshire, and East Devon, continuing beyond Exeter to stretch out long tentacles into the remotest parts of North Devon and Cornwall. The company also possessed a considerable mileage of suburban railway in and around London.

Next came the London, Brighton and South Coast Railway, who reigned almost supreme in Sussex, and came as far west as Portsmouth, where they met the 'South Western'. Kent had been originally in the hands of two continuously warring concerns — the London, Chatham & Dover Railway, and the South Eastern Railway. The numerous disputes and rivalries between these two companies succeeded in covering the south-east with a veritable network of lines, many routes being duplicated — a feature not readily appreciated until the outbreak of World War One, when there was tremendous pressure on the lines leading to the Channel ports. These two companies eventually buried the proverbial hatchet, (out of financial necessity), to become amalgamated as the South Eastern & Chatham Railway on 1st February, 1899. Each of these four companies was highly individualistic in outlook, and in the equipment they provided — factors which tend to complicate the story of the early years. However, one or two remarks of a general nature, applicable to all the lines that were to form the Southern Railway, are in order before looking at the various railways in turn.

When our railway system was new, traffic was sparse on most lines. It was only the wealthy who travelled, and a handful of daily trains was quite sufficient to meet their needs. True, with only the horse-drawn carrier's cart for competition, the railways quickly obtained a virtual monopoly of goods traffic, but it must be remembered that Britain was more thinly-populated and less industrialised in those days, and that the South of England has never been an area of heavy industry. It follows, then, that the number of goods trains required to run over any particular section of line was quite small. If a line carried twelve trains a day, of all types, it was considered quite busy by the standards of the day. Because of this, signalling of any sort was thought to be unnecessary at first, but as traffic increased, and with it the risk of accident, what is known as the 'Time Interval' system was adopted.

The operation of this system was extremely simple. 'Policemen' were stationed at regular intervals along the line, who were required to exhibit a flag-signal to the driver of each passing train, which, in theory, conveyed to him the state of the line ahead. As a general rule, a 'Policeman' was required to exhibit a 'Danger' signal for five minutes after the passage of a train, after which a 'Caution' signal was displayed for a further five minutes. When this had elapsed, the 'Clear' signal could be given. These intervals varied slightly according to location, local conditions such as severe gradients, tunnels, or density of traffic giving rise to amended instructions at some places, but the intervals quoted serve to illustrate the working of the system. As these Policemen had no communication with each other, it can be seen that this was a very negative approach to the control of traffic. In fact, all that a Policeman's 'Clear' flag meant was that no train had passed that spot within the last ten minutes! The possibility that the previous train may have broken down or become derailed only a few hundred yards ahead, concealed perhaps by a tunnel or curve, never seems to have occurred to those who devised the system. It was, of course, better than having no signalling system at all, but as traffic and speeds continued to increase, its hit or miss nature became a matter of public concern.

Fixed signals first appeared on the London and Greenwich line as early as 1839. These consisted of large boards, which, when turned parallel to the track, denoted 'Clear'. Night indications were given by oil hand lamps. Of course these still operated in conjunction with 'Time Interval' working.

About 1840, what was almost certainly the first 'signal box' in the world was erected at the junction between the

Plate 1.
The earliest form of railway signalling. A 'Policeman' gives the 'All Clear' signal at the entrance of a tunnel.
R. H. Clark collection

'Greenwich' and the London and Croydon, known as Cobbett's Lane. This strange edifice, dubbed 'The Lighthouse', operated a disc, painted reddish-orange. When the points were set for Croydon, the disc was turned to face London, but when the points were set for Greenwich, it was turned edgeways to traffic. Night indications were even more odd. A white light was shown in all directions when the road was set for Greenwich, and a RED light, also shown in all directions, when set for Croydon. Sir Frederick Smith, when he inspected the line in July 1841, was very critical of this unusual application of red as an 'All Clear' signal.

Plate 2.
A Gregory type signal showing arms applicable to both lines of traffic. One is in the 'Caution' position, and the other as 'Danger'. Signals of this type were introduced in 1841.
R. H. Clark collection

However, primitive discs and boards were not to last long. In 1841 Mr. (later Sir) Charles Gregory introduced a semaphore signal on the London and Croydon Railway at New Cross Gate. The arm had three positions – horizontal to indicate 'Stop', lowered to 45 degrees for 'Caution', and vertical (concealed within a slot in the signal post), for 'Clear'. The arms themselves were slotted, probably in an attempt to reduce wind resistance. At night, a lamp attached to the post and revolved through a bevel gear, gave the required indication.

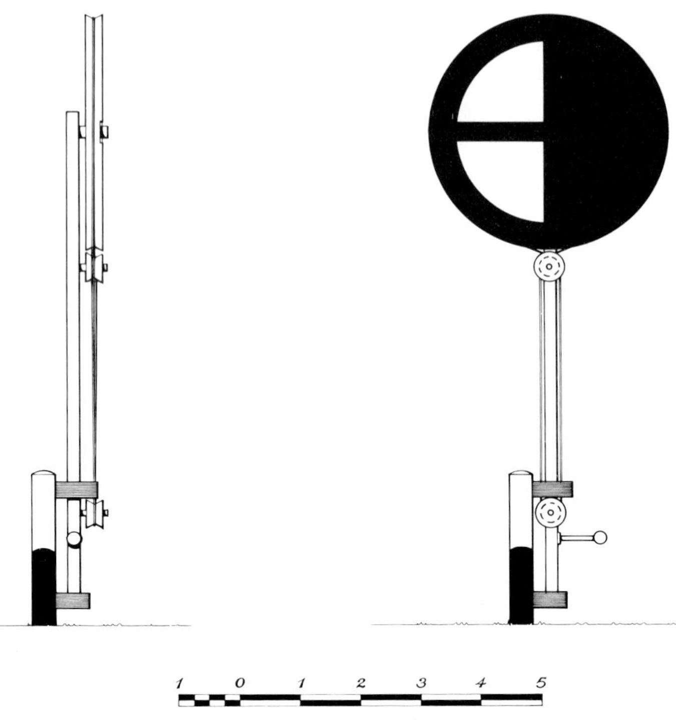

Plate 3.
Scale drawing of an early L. & S.W.R. signal as designed by Albinus Martin. On double lines, the discs were coloured red on both sides when used as 'Station', (Home), signals, and when used as 'Auxiliary', (Distant), signals, the working face was red, and the back white. The disc was revolved by means of a rope, and the indications were as follows:-
Apertures on left—Left-hand line only clear.
Apertures on right—Right-hand line only clear.
Apertures at bottom of disc—Both lines blocked.
Disc turned edgeways to line—Both lines clear.
Drawing P. D. Rutter.

Signals of the Gregory type must have proved successful, as they soon became standard on the L.B. & S.C.R. and several other railways, notable exceptions being the G.W.R. and L. & S.W.R. The former preferred Brunel's 'Disc and Cross-bar' signals, whilst the South Western installed large revolving discs to the design of Albinus Martin, so constructed as to control traffic in both directions. One of these signals is illustrated in Plate 3. The very destructive accident at Abbots Ripton on 21st July 1876, caused the design of the semaphore signal to receive some close scrutiny, as a result of which, several modifications were made. The arms no longer vanished within slotted posts to indicate 'Clear', but dropped to an angle of 45 degrees. The 'Caution' position, rendered virtually redundant as 'Distant' signals spread, was dispensed with. The question of counter-weighting was also examined, so that, in the event of any part of the controlling mechanism failing, the arm would

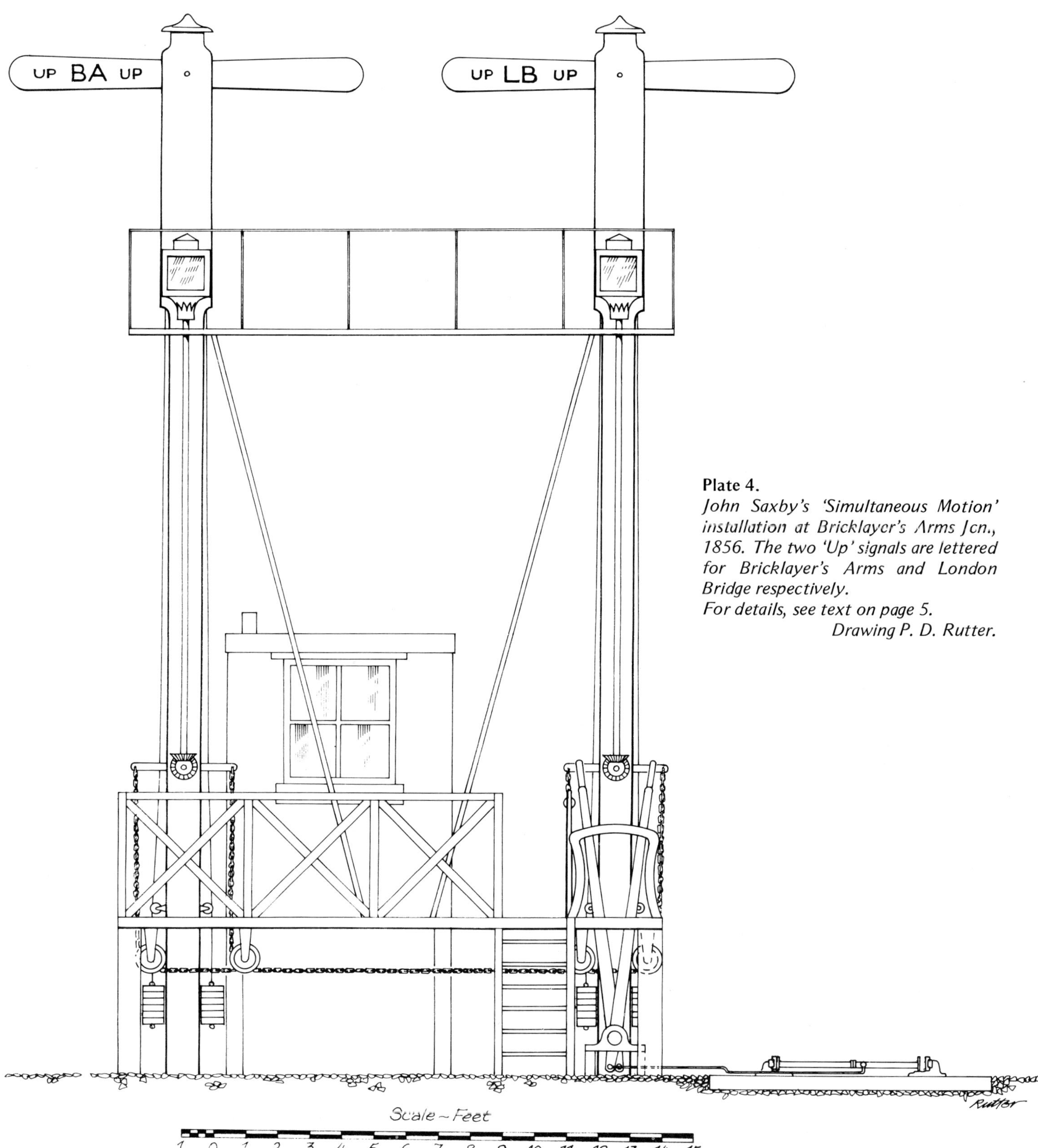

Plate 4.
John Saxby's 'Simultaneous Motion' installation at Bricklayer's Arms Jcn., 1856. The two 'Up' signals are lettered for Bricklayer's Arms and London Bridge respectively.
For details, see text on page 5.
Drawing P. D. Rutter.

return automatically to the 'Danger' position. It was to be many years before signals with slotted posts vanished completely from the signalling scene, but the mounting of arms was modified so that they did not enter the slot.

Although signals were provided to control trains, telling the Drivers when to stop and when to proceed, in the early days they did not tell him exactly WHERE to stop. The signals were not positioned clear of conflicting movements, but were grouped together at the signal box, often sprouting through its roof. It was left entirely to the discretion of the Driver, and the knowledge he possessed of his route, to halt his train in a safe and suitable place. This kind of arrangement was first installed on the Brighton Railway, and later appeared at both Waterloo and Cannon Street. (See Plate 4.)

The speed attained by trains had been steadily increasing ever since the invention of the steam locomotive. In fact, railway officials seemed to be highly aware of the prestige of sustained high-speed runs, but less so of the dangers of inadequate brake power and poor signal siting, which combined to make rail travel a rather hazardous business. A Driver could suddenly come upon a signal displaying 'Danger', and would be expected to stop his train at it with only the aid of wooden brake blocks on the engine, applied by a hand wheel, and reversing his engine. There must have been many a run-by in those days! The first recorded use of a 'Distant' signal, (then referred to as 'Auxiliary' signals), was on the L. & S.W.R. in 1848, when one was installed at Kingston (today called Surbiton). The Brighton company also provided 'Auxiliary' signals at a very early date. At first, the arms were the same shape and colour as 'Stop' signals, Drivers requiring a very thorough knowledge of the road in order to observe them correctly. The 'Time Interval' system was still the method of working, and the idea was that a Driver finding an 'Auxiliary' signal at Danger, must stop his train at it, then proceed with extreme caution up to the 'Stop' signal under protection of the 'Auxiliary'. The distinguishing of 'Auxiliary' signals by means of the 'Fish-tail' notch in the end of the arm, was the idea of W. J. Williams, the Brighton company's Outdoor Superintendent, who had one installed at Norwood Junction in August 1872. The arms, though now of a different shape, were still painted red as for 'Stop' signals, and at night, exhibited a red light in the 'Caution' position. Drivers still had a difficult task at night, but they were later aided by a device known as the Coligny-Welch lamp, which displayed a small white chevron to the right of the main signal light. These lamps only found general use on three British railways, the 'Brighton', the L. & S.W.R., and the Furness Railway, other companies continuing to put their trust in the ability and expertise of drivers.

Until the 1890s, the night indication for clear had been a white light (Green being used originally as a 'Caution' signal). However, more lights were appearing in towns and at other places along the line, and the comparatively feeble glow of a white signal lamp must have become very difficult to spot. In any case, green was a much better 'clear' signal than white, as in the event of a spectacle glass falling out or becoming broken, a white light would automatically be revealed regardless of the position of the signal arm. Speaking generally, green had replaced white as the 'clear' signal by 1893.

Plate 5.
Early 'Brighton' signal box at Brighton Yard, showing the grouping of signals above the box roof.
R. H. Clark collection

2. Brief Signalling History of the Independent Companies

THE LONDON, BRIGHTON AND SOUTH COAST RAILWAY

We have already seen in Chapter One how the Gregory type semaphore became standard throughout the lines of the Company at an early date. A form widely used by the 'Brighton' was that shown in Plate 2, having an arm on each side of the post, one applying to 'Up' and the other to 'Down' trains. The arms worked in the lower quadrant, and gave three indications:— 'Stop' when horizontal, 'Caution' when lowered to 45 degrees, and 'Clear' when invisible within a slot cut in the post. They were, of course, operated by 'Policemen' in conjunction with the time interval system.

'The Lighthouse' has already been described, but this strange arrangement lasted only until 1843, when it was replaced by semaphore arms of a more conventional nature, operated by a row of stirrups mounted on a wooden platform. The 'Policeman' depressed the stirrups with his feet, and they were so arranged that they fouled each other when depressed, thereby preventing the signalling of conflicting movements. It was, indeed, an early attempt at interlocking, although there was no locking or detection between the points and signals.

In the early 1850s, C. F. Whitworth invented a so called 'Automatic' signal, although the only automatic action was that the arm was returned to the 'Danger' position by the train passing over a mechanical treadle. Once this had been actuated, the signal had to be pulled to the 'Clear' position by the Policeman. Two of these contraptions were installed on the 'Brighton's' main line, one at each end of the 2,266-yard-long Clayton Tunnel, the line through the tunnel becoming the first Block Section. The Whitworth signal consisted of a revolving banner, and it was through the failure of the Policeman to observe that the returning mechanism had not operated after the passage of a train, that the worst disaster in the history of the Company occurred on 25th April 1861, when an up express ran into the rear of a crowded excursion train in the smoky blackness of the tunnel.

More sophisticated signalling was installed at Bricklayers Arms Junction in 1856, consisting of John Saxby's 'simultaneous motion' system, in which the signals acted as point indicators. In its original form, this would have meant that the signals would automatically have exhibited 'Clear' for whichever route was set through the points, but Saxby fitted 'Slotted Link' handles, which enabled all signals to show 'Danger' irrespective of the lie of the points. In 1860, Saxby made a locking frame for the Hole-in-the-Wall box at Victoria.

The firm of Saxby and Farmer was formed in 1863, and from that year until 1904 they provided all the signalling for the L.B. & S.C.R. The first box to be equipped with a Saxby and Farmer frame was Brighton North, which had thirty-seven levers. In 1866, three frames totalling seventy-two levers were provided for London Bridge (South, East and North Boxes). These incorporated the new 'Striking Mechanism', in which the levers pushed against inclined notched plates attached to the locking bars.

As already mentioned, the notched, or 'fish-tail', arm was introduced for Distant signals in 1872, the use of these being made obligatory by the Board of Trade for all new works after 1877. It appears to have been the G.W.R. who first painted the white chevron on these arms, an idea adopted by the L.B. & S.C.R. about 1900.

The 1870s saw the final abolition of time interval working throughout the 'Brighton' system. All the company's lines were equipped with the Block System as early as 1874, Tyer's or Harper's two-position instruments being the rule on double lines. Following the initial trials of Sykes' Lock and Block in the London area, this equipment superseded the two-position instruments in much of the suburban area, and, in 1880, was extended down the main line as far as Balcombe Station, south of which Tyer's three-position one-wire instruments were introduced.

In 1878 came the first permissive use of platform lines at termini. At the approach to the platform, there would be a 'Stop' signal with a 'Distant' arm beneath it. To admit a train to a partially occupied platform, the 'Stop' signal only would be lowered, but if the line was clear to the buffer stops, the 'Distant' arm would also be operated. This arrangement was Saxby's own invention, and was first in service at London Bridge North Box, the largest on the L.B. & S.C.R., having two lever frames of 140 levers each. By this time, Rocker Locking had generally replaced the somewhat primitive 'Striker' frames. Permissive platform working was later introduced at Victoria and Brighton.

As early as 1883, the L.C. & D.R. installed some electrically-operated shunting signals at Victoria, in full view of the Brighton management! Not to be outdone, the Brighton installed some of their own soon after.

On single lines, the electric train staff became standard in 1892. There were, however, a few exceptions where 'Staff & Ticket' working was employed. These were:—

Christ's Hospital to Baynards
Dyke Jcn. (Hove) to Dyke
Havant to Hayling Island
Connecting line to S.E. & C.R. at Tunbridge Wells.

In connection with the reconstruction of Victoria Station in 1906/07, one of Sykes' many inventions, the 'electro-mechanical' signalling system, was introduced. This system retained mechanical levers for the operation of points, but the signals were worked electrically by slides mounted above the lever frame. All points were electrically detected, so that a signal could not be cleared unless the route was correctly set and the point blades firmly closed against the stock rail, and any subsequent movement of the points would immediately return the signal to 'Danger'. When used in conjunction with Sykes' 'Lock and Block' instruments (see S.E. and C.R. section), it will be appreciated that the system offered a very high degree of safety.

The L.B. & S.C.R. used their own method of block working; quite different from that used by most railways that were parties to the Railway Clearing House. There were no 'Is line clear?' bell signals, the first signal for a train being known as the 'Warning', which was acknowledged by exact repetition whether the Signalman in advance could accept the train or not. If he could, he replied with one extra beat, and lowered the arm of the block instruments. Where Sykes' instruments were in use, he simply gave the required electrical release, without sending the one extra beat. Instead of the 'Train entering section' signal used on other lines, the 'Warning' was given a second time as the train passed the signal box. The 'Train out of section' signal was called the 'Arrival', and consisted of three consecutive beats on Tyer's and Harper's instruments, and one beat on Sykes'. This sounds rather confusing, but it should be added that the Company had, for the most part, an excellent record of safety.

The Dyke branch, near Brighton, was used for trials of an Automatic Warning System developed by A. R. Angus of Sydney, Australia. This had been previously tried out on the West Somerset Mineral Railway, between Watchet and Washford, as well as in Sweden and Russia, and appeared on the Dyke line shortly after the First World War. The warning was given by whistle.

THE SOUTH EASTERN RAILWAY AND THE LONDON, CHATHAM & DOVER.

The South Eastern was one of the first British companies to install the Block System. Charles Vincent Walker was the Company's first Telegraph Superintendent, and in 1851 he introduced single-stroke bells that enabled messages to be sent by a series of codes. This method, though crude by the standards of today, proved extremely effective, and by the beginning of 1863 the whole line, with the exception of a few branches, totalling 280 route miles, was protected with the invention. Several hundred sets of bells were then in service, many of them fitted with an index pointer, (also designed by Walker), which showed the number of beats sent. The pointer had to be manually re-set to zero when answering. This fitting was particularly favoured where the Signalman might have other duties to perform, that took him outside the signal box between trains —which was often the case in those days when traffic was much lighter

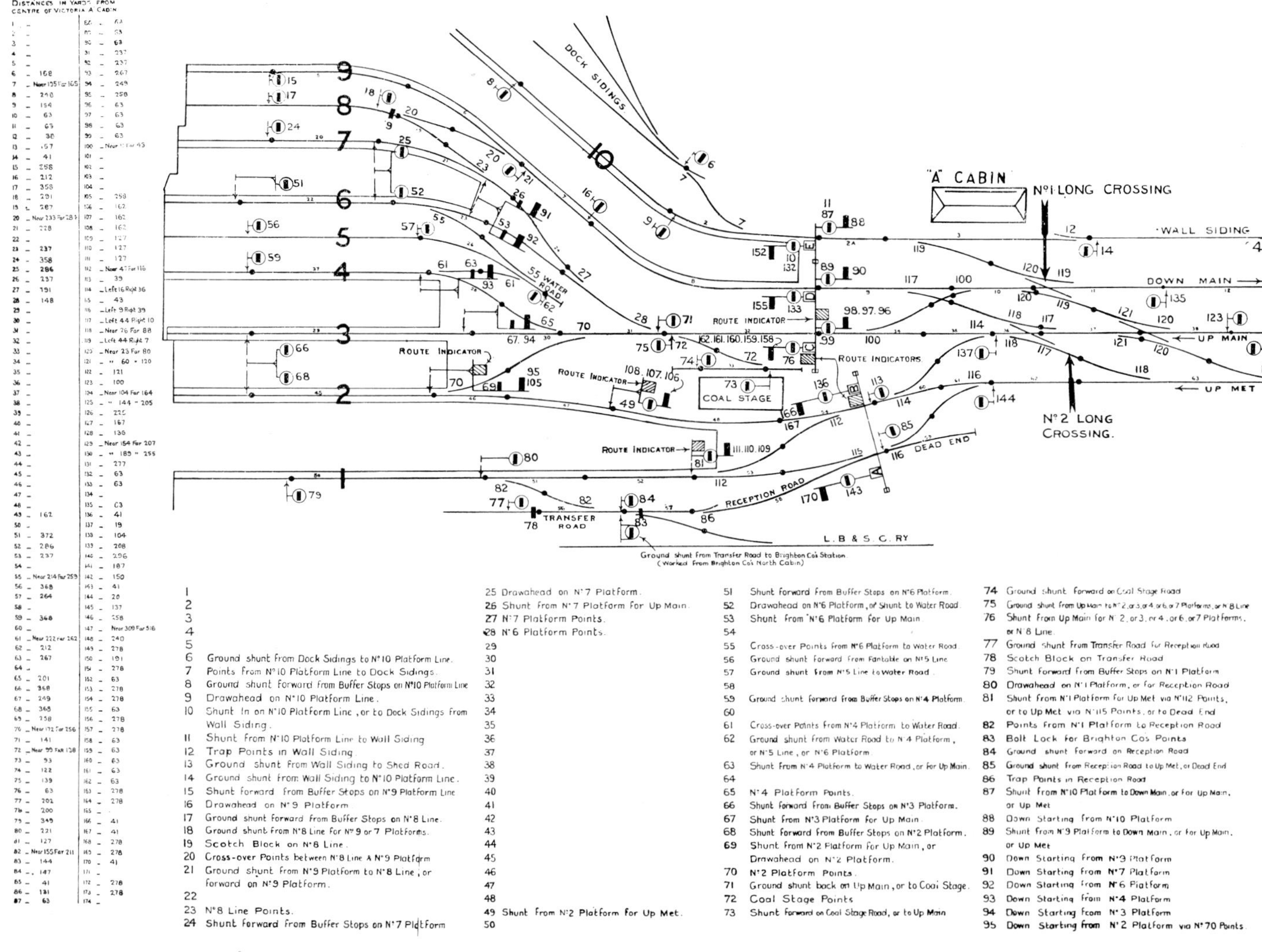

than it became later. Walker's bell codes were very simple, the whole range being as follows:—

.	Up Train	'Out'. (This had to be given, and repeated back, before a train might start from, or pass, a signalling point).
. .	Down Train	
. . .	Train 'In'.	(This meant that train had arrived. Equivalent to the 'Train Out of Section' Signal).
. . . . .		Obstruction on Line.
. . . . . .		Obstruction Removed.
. . . . . .		Testing Signal.
. . . .		Cancelling Signal.

It is worthy of note that at every S.E.R. level crossing, without exception, repeater bells were inserted in the signalling circuit, so that Crossing Keepers were informed of the position of trains.

Both Walker and the S.E.R. General Manager, C. W. Eborall, were satisfied with this system, but the Traffic Department wished it to be supplemented by some form of visual indication. To meet this demand, Walker designed his first Block Instrument, which he called his 'Electro-magnetic Semaphores', first used with the opening of the line to Charing Cross in 1864. Within eight years, over 200 sets of these instruments were in use, and the Company had decided to extend them to cover the entire system. The only other Company to adopt Walker's instruments was the Stockton and Darlington Railway. Edward Tyer, (1830—1912), another well-known name in the signalling world, designed a similar instrument that required fewer line wires, and by 1873 the whole systems of both the S.E.R. and L.C. & D.R. were protected by either these, or Walker's original equipment. Both are still in use at a number of locations today, the latter with a modified bell key and commutator, but are rapidly being replaced by more modern instruments. Walker also invented a rotary Train Describer, (see Plate 187, Signal Box Equipment section), and these were used not only by the S.E.R., but also on the 'Brighton' and L. & S.W.R.

On the London, Chatham, & Dover Railway, J. S. Forbes was appointed General Manager in 1873. Whatever other short comings he may have had, he was keenly interested in the operating side of his line. He appointed a Mr. Rudall to

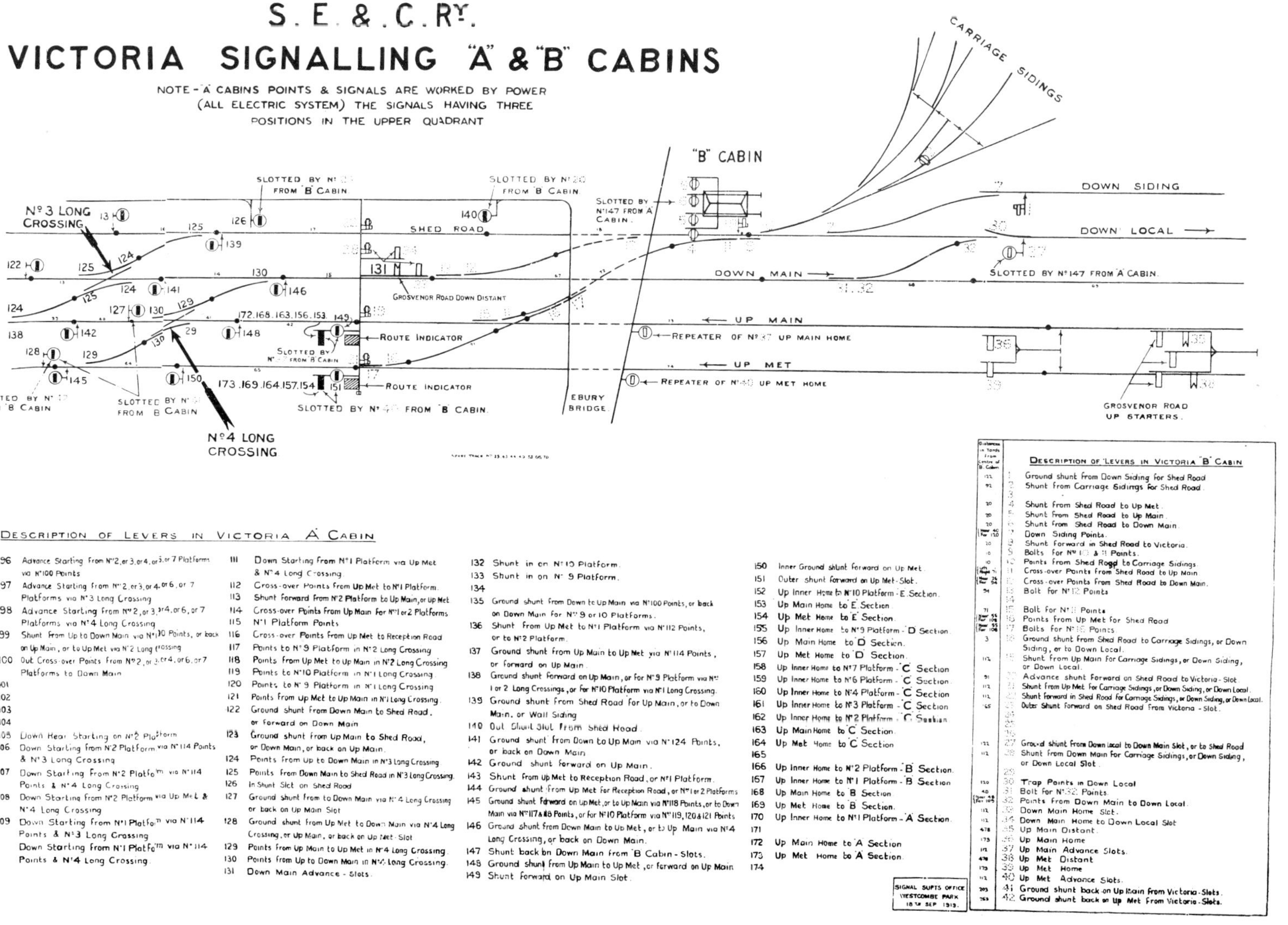

Plate 6.
A group of early L. & S.W.R. signals standing at Eastleigh, having been replaced by conventional semaphore types.

Photo courtesy National Railway Museum.

Plate 7.
The early 'Brighton' signal box at Old Kent Road Junction, photographed in 1886, shortly before being replaced by the more modern structure in the background.

Photo courtesy National Railway Museum.

the post of 'Electrical Superintendent', and it was he who employed W. R. Sykes as a maintenance man. Sykes proved to be a man of great ability, inventing many items which contributed greatly to increased safety on our railways, and his most famous invention, the 'Lock and Block' system, was produced as early as 1874. He horrified Forbes by suggesting that his new equipment be tested on one of the busiest stretches of line in London! Forbes could see the benefits of Sykes' invention, and had a desire to see it thoroughly tried and tested, but would have preferred this to have been done in a quieter area, where a failure of the instruments would have a less devastating effect on the running of traffic. However, the Board of Trade Inspecting Officers were so enthusiastic about 'Lock and Block', that they virtually over-ruled the dismayed Chairman. Sykes' new system was promptly installed in three busy London signal boxes—Shepherds Lane, Brixton, and Canterbury Road Junction. The patent was granted to Sykes in February, 1875.

One can sympathise with Forbes in his cautionary attitude when we realise what a revolutionary idea 'Lock and Block' was. Up to that time, safe working was entirely dependent upon the signalmen correctly observing the rules and regulations, but with this new invention, every step of the signalling sequence had to be carried out in the correct order, the passage of the train over a series of treadles re-setting the instruments and freeing the signals for a following train. With such comparatively complex equipment, any failures would be the cause of considerable delay.

Not content with introducing a completely new concept in signalling, Sykes also conducted experiments with track circuits. In 1876 he installed some at Crystal Palace, and although results were not very promising, he continued with the experiments, and by 1886 sufficient progress had been made to permit a permanent installation at St. Paul's (Blackfriars).

The great advance in safety offered by 'Lock and Block' was appreciated at once, but it was an expensive system to install, particularly to an impecunious concern like the 'Chatham'. It was not until after the Sittingbourne accident of 1878, which Forbes realised would have been prevented by the system, that its use began to spread. Within quite a short time, it was extended to cover the majority of L.C. & D.R. territory.

Locking frames on the 'Chatham' at that time were mostly the manufacture of Stevens and Sons, (who were also main contractors to the L. & S.W.R.), but in later years, Evans O'Donnell and Saxby and Farmer frames were used to some extent. The Company also possessed their own signal works at Cold Blow, Deptford, and made locking frames to their own designs.

Working fusion between the S.E.R. and L.C. & D.R. took place on 29th June, 1898, and thereafter there was a certain amount of standardisation of signalling equipment.

During the First World War, the volume of traffic handled by the S.E. & C.R. was truly enormous, to the extent that it was decided to speed up the working at Victoria by introducing some form of power signalling. The contemporary practice in America was the use of three-position upper quadrant signals, and an installation of similar type was decided upon in this instance. As no British firm could supply the necessary equipment, much of it was ordered from the General Railway Signal Company, of Rochester, New York. In the event, however, the power signalling was barely completed when the War ended, as the ship carrying the original frame was torpedoed and sunk, and another had to be manufactured.

It was a large installation by the standards of the time, the locking frame having 200 levers. These were of the standard G.R.S. pattern, being horizontal pull-out slides instead of miniature levers. Of the 200 levers, 107 were for signals, indicators, and releases, and 47 were for points.

THE LONDON & SOUTH WESTERN RAILWAY

This company was perhaps the most diverse of those that were later to form the Southern Railway. It possessed not only many miles of heavily-used main line and an extensive suburban network around London, but also stretched out long fingers into the far West, eventually reaching Padstow. Incidentally, that part of the 'South Western' beyond Exeter has always been known as the 'Withered Arm'. Mostly single track, and served by slow and infrequent trains, it was quite unlike the rest of the Southern system. To this remote area were banished all the oldest locomotives and rolling stock to spend their last years of service, and lower quadrant signals survived in many places long after they had become a rarity elsewhere. Well into British Railways days, the remote lines of North Devon and Cornwall were unmistakably L. & S.W.R. in appearance.

The earliest fixed signals of the Company have already been dealt with in Chapter One, and these were of course operated in conjunction with the 'Time interval' system. The task of installing block working lay with W. M. Williams, and it is interesting to observe that he was one of the first to issue diagrams of new works to train crews and signalmen. His notices went into great detail, to the extent that the issue covering the opening of the Kensington to Richmond and Kingston to Wimbledon lines covered twenty-seven foolscap sheets!

Of course, the L. & S.W.R. kept abreast of the other companies when it came to installing interlocking. Its most famous signal box was Waterloo 'A', opened in March 1867, which contained a Stevens 'Hook' frame with twenty-three levers for the Windsor lines, and twenty-four for the Main. However, this structure had a short life, being replaced in 1874 by a much larger box with a Saxby 'Rocker and Grid Iron' frame of 109 levers—a large installation by the standards of the time. A separate box was erected to control the 'Windsor' side of the station, which contained a frame of forty-seven levers. Four years later, even this was added to—another thirty-five levers being squeezed into the main box. This work was carried out by Stevens and Sons, by now firmly established as the South Western's main signalling contractors. Waterloo station was enlarged still further in 1885, and the box was extended once again to a total of two hundred levers arranged in two frames back-to-back connected by intermediate locking, and manned by four signalmen during the day, and two on nights. In 1889, 350 Sykes' fouling bars were installed to improve safety. Waterloo 'A' had one more replacement before the present power box—an enormous edifice fitted with a Stevens

'Special' frame of 220 levers, with tappet locking, triple working, and gear levers, the latter devices permitting 247 signal arms to be controlled by 102 levers. Even this was extended in 1911, when it was enlarged to contain 250 levers plus six slides, doing the work of 410 levers.

But we must not dwell too long on the story of Waterloo, for all it was the signalling show-piece of the Company. As already stated, Stevens and Sons carried out the vast majority of work on the L. & S.W.R. In elevated signal boxes, their standard frames with levers at $4\frac{1}{8}$ inch centres were the rule, whilst for ground-level boxes, special frames with short levers and the locking encased above floor level were supplied. Railwaymen generally referred to these as 'Knee frames', the locking casing coming up to about knee height.

In an attempt to reduce the overall length of lever frames, many of those supplied by Stevens and Sons contained 'push-and-pull' levers for the operation of signals. These stood half-way in the frame when 'Normal', being pushed to work one signal, and pulled to work another. The wire adjustment on these was on the delicate side, and extremes of temperature could sometimes affect the working quite badly.

Block instruments on the L. & S.W.R. were mainly of the Preece one-wire or three-wire type, (illustrated in the Signal Box Equipment section on page 147) except in the areas where Sykes' 'Lock-and-Block' was installed. On single lines, Tyer's electric train tablets ruled the roost. Usually these were of the 'No. 6' pattern, or the non-returnable version, 'No. 3', but there were exceptions. Tyer's 'No. 1' instruments were introduced in 1878, the last example remaining in use between Shillingstone and Sturminster Newton until 1950. More unusual still, the section between Shillingstone and Blandford was worked with a McKenzie and Holland square tablet.

Incidentally, it was the L. & S.W.R. who pioneered the locking of the section signal with the tablet at Farnham in 1893—an important contribution to the safe working of single lines.

Signal boxes and equipment with a definite 'South Western' appearance could also be found on two cross-country lines that were not, strictly speaking, the property of that Company. The L. & S.W.R. and Midland Railways acquired a joint lease of the Somerset and Dorset lines with effect from 1st November 1875, (although this was not sanctioned by Parliament until the following year), and the task of supplying and maintaining the signalling fell to the former. Thereafter, much of the equipment was identical to that found on the L. & S.W.R. in general.

A certain 'South Western' influence could also be detected in the design of some of the signal boxes on the old Midland and South Western Junction line from Andover to Andoversford Junction (near Cheltenham). As this was an independent concern, and finally passed into the hands of the G.W.R. the reason for this is not so obvious, but can probably be found in the fact that an L. & S.W.R. man, Sam Fay, was its General Manager from February 1892 to 1899. As a result, this Company was on excellent terms with the 'South Western', and the latter were almost certainly asked for assistance with new works.

The signalling of the L. & S.W.R. changed very little over the years, the original Stevens frames in their small brick-and-timber signal boxes surviving in some places to the present day. However, at the turn of the century the Company took a massive stride forward with a completely different form of power signalling—the 'low pressure pneumatic'—a phase of such interest that it is dealt with in the following chapter as a separate subject.

Plate 8.

The giant overhead structure of Waterloo 'A' signal box as it appeared following extension in 1911.

Photo courtesy National Railway Museum.

3. The London & South Western Railway and the 'Low Pressure' Era

In the Autumn of 1900, the Company's Chief Engineer, Jacomb-Hood, and Sam Fay visited the United States of America to inspect some of the pneumatic signalling installations in use there. They returned home full of enthusiasm, determined to see similar ideas brought to fruition on their own railway. Little time was wasted. The way-side station at Grateley, between Andover and Salisbury, was selected as the site for initial trials of the new equipment, possibly because traffic was less heavy over this section of line than on much of the L. & S.W.R. system, so failures in the signalling would have less serious consequences on the time-keeping of the railway as a whole. Unlike the story of Sykes, and his experiments with 'Lock and Block' right in the thick of London's suburban traffic, the L. & S.W.R. management were ever cautious, and preferred to try out new ideas in quieter areas.

The contract for the plant at Grateley went to the British Pneumatic Railway Signal Company, of Palace Chambers, Westminster, and a large brick signal box was erected on the Up platform to receive the pneumatic lever frame, which consisted of seventy 'Levers'. The 'Levers' were in fact pull-out slides, set at 3 inch centres, with handles painted in the usual distinctive lever colours. The overall length of the frame was 24 feet, and it was estimated that a mechanical frame to operate the same track layout would have required almost exactly 50% more space. Interlocking was of the usual tappet form, and was laid out along the front of the frame to provide easy access for oiling and maintenance. The Signal Engineers began connecting up to the new frame on the evening of Saturday 20th July, 1901 and the entire system, including some experimental pneumatic automatic signals covering the six-and-a-quarter miles between Andover Junction West Box and Grateley, was complete and ready for Board of Trade inspection on Sunday 13th October. The L. & S.W.R. gave an undertaking to the Board of Trade that they would supply detailed reports on the working of the system at monthly intervals, and it is interesting to note from these reports that, after several months of operation, the number of failures had been extremely small, with not one instance of an 'Automatic' failing to return to Danger behind a train. There had been a couple of occasions when a signal had failed to 'clear', the faults being traced to such things as broken bond wires, but as these only resulted in minor delays to traffic, such teething troubles were definitely not of a dangerous nature.

Having proved itself at Grateley, it was natural that other such installations would follow. At about the same time, the ramshackle and inconvenient station at Salisbury was being rebuilt, which necessitated a complete remodelling of the signalling and track layout, so it is not a matter for surprise that the 'Low Pressure' system was also installed there. Two new signal boxes, Salisbury East and West, containing pneumatic frames of sixty-four 'levers' each, were brought into use in November 1902. As with the Grateley signalling, air at a pressure of 15 lb per square inch was used, the pressure being maintained by compressor engines housed in specially-constructed buildings well away from the signal boxes.

At that time, Staines was controlled by no fewer than *five* mechanical boxes, and was therefore an obvious candidate for the pneumatic treatment. Two 'low-pressure' boxes were opened in the spring of 1904.

But the most ambitious application of the new system was over the twenty-four miles of quadruple track between Woking Junction and Basingstoke, including the station area at the latter. Altogether twelve signal boxes and ground frames were fitted with pneumatic frames, and the fairly long sections between boxes divided by automatic signals at 1,500 yard intervals. This scheme again used air at a pressure of 15 lb per square inch, the supply being maintained by power houses at Basingstoke, Fleet, and Woking. The automatic signals took 'Clear' as the normal indication, unlike similar equipment in use on the North Eastern Railway between Northallerton and York, which stood normally at 'Danger'.

By 1911, the trend on the L. & S.W.R. was firmly towards pneumatic power signalling. That year another such signal box, supplied with air at the much greater pressure of 30/40lb per square inch, was opened at Clapham Junction. This was later modified to become 'electro-pneumatic', the valves controlling the supply of air to signals and points being opened and closed through electrical circuits, and in this form it remained in service until the area was re-signalled with colour lights in 1936.

The 'low-pressure' system was in advance of its time, and proved to be very reliable under the most taxing conditions such as at Clapham Junction. It is therefore rather strange that most of these installations have now vanished, the notable exception being that at Salisbury. The original pneumatic plant at Grateley was taken out of use as long ago as 1919, a 66-lever Westinghouse frame replacing the low-pressure one. This is not an indication that the experiment was a failure, as the reason for its early demise was the opening of a new box at Red Post controlling a wartime connection with the Midland & South Western Junction line. This interfered with the automatic sections, and it was decided that the cost of abolition was less than that of large-scale alterations.

Staines also reverted to mechanical working, one box taking control of the entire layout. The layout involved a triangular junction, and was therefore of considerable length, and several sets of electrically operated motor points had to be provided.

The Woking-Basingstoke equipment lasted rather longer. There were a number of alterations over the years, such as the closure of Pirbright Junction box, where control of the points was transferred to Brookwood. Latterly, some of the old semaphore automatics were replaced by colour-light signals, but much of the old signalling remained intact until the introduction of the panel box at Basingstoke in 1966, which took control of the whole area. Even today, some of the points controlled by this panel are pneumatically operated.

Salisbury, on the other hand, has changed little over the years, apart from the usual crop of siding redundancies which have rendered more of the levers 'spare'. As first installed, there were no track circuits, but these were provided to cover the entire layout at both boxes in 1928. That year also saw the modernisation of the East Box, making it 'electro-pneumatic', but similar plans for the West Box, although prepared, have never been carried out. The 'out-door' fittings have, of course, changed considerably since installation in 1902, the lower quadrant signals having all been renewed as upper quadrants.

Plate 9.
L. & S.W.R. low-pressure pneumatic signals at Basingstoke. The shorter arms at the bottom of the picture act as repeaters for the signals.
Photo J. Scrace.

Plate 10.
A set of pneumatic automatic signals on the Woking-Basingstoke Section, as originally installed. Note red distant arms as painted in the days before the white 'chevron' became universal. The air cylinders can be seen at the base of each signal doll, built into the iron-work of the gantry.

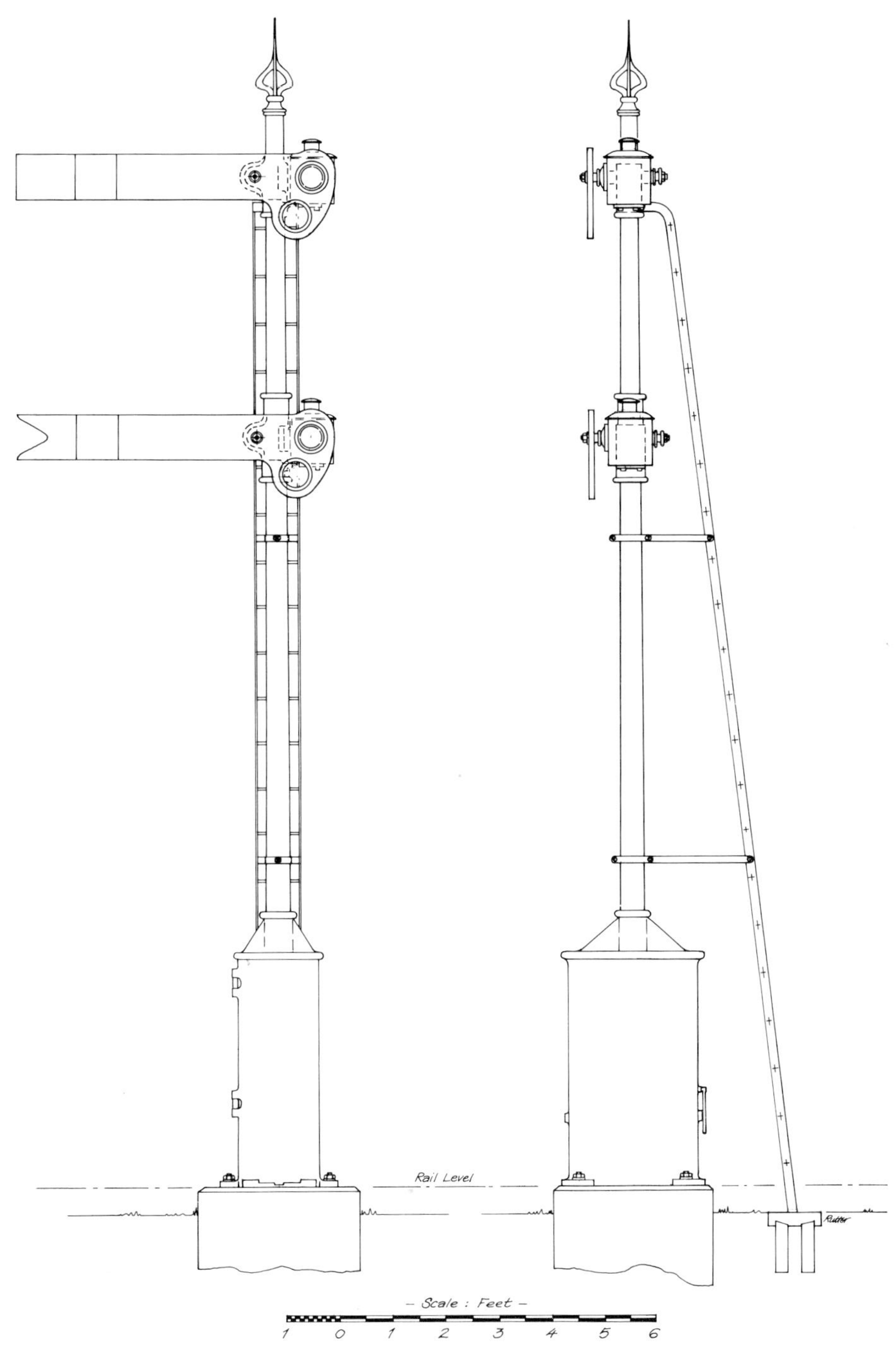

Fig. 1.

Scale drawings, (front and side elevations), of the experimental pneumatic automatic signals, installed between Andover Junction West and Grateley in 1901. The lower distant arm acted as the 'Distant' for the next automatic signal, and it will be noted that in those days the L. & S.W.R. painted a straight band on Distant arms. The air pistons and valves were encased within the base of the signal post, the operating rods between there and the arms running up inside the hollow post itself.

Drawing P. D. Rutter

Published by permission of the Public Record Office.

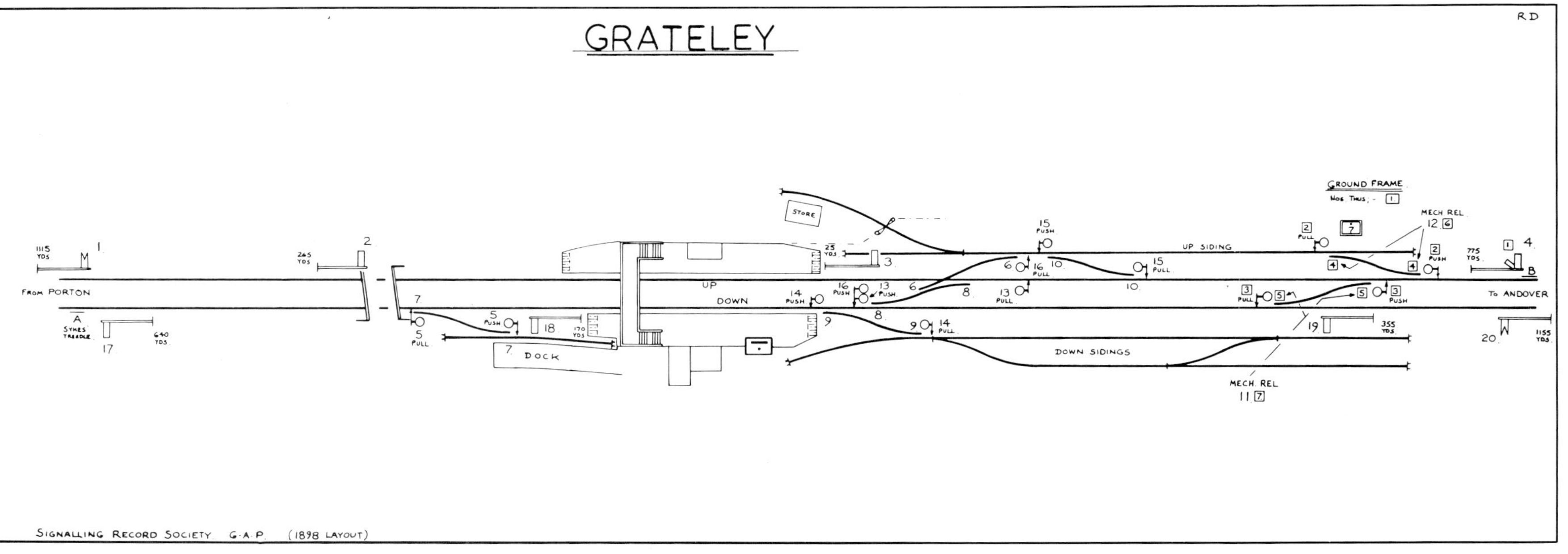

Fig. 2.
Shows the track layout and signalling at Grateley in 1898—before the introduction of the 'Low Pressure' system.

Fig. 3.
Shows the new layout as installed in 1901 for the L. & S.W.R.'s first pneumatic signalling.

GRATELEY

APPARATUS
37 LEVERS FOR 46 SIGNALS
17 LEVERS FOR POINTS AND F.P. LOCKS
16 SPARE LEVERS

DISCS AND SIGNALS SELECTED:- 7 11 12 13 16 20 56 58 61

SPARE 4 21 22 23 24 25 37 38 39 40 47 48 49 50 51 52

GROUND FRAME 'B' ELECTRICALLY RELEASING POINTS 26 & 27

SIGNALLING RECORD SOCIETY G.A.P. (L.P. LAYOUT)

Plate 11.
The west end of Salisbury in L. & S.W.R. days. The approaching train obscures the West Box, but the G.W.R. box can be seen on the right. Lower quadrant signals such as those in the foreground were of the type originally installed with the 'Low Pressure' equipment.

Photo Lens of Sutton.

Plate 12.
Pneumatic ground disc signal at Salisbury West. The air cylinder is in the base of the signal. Behind it can be seen a pneumatic point machine, (partly boarded over), and its associated F.P.L. assembly.

Photo G. F. Gillham

Plate 13 *(above).*
The neat interior of Salisbury East Box. On top of the wooden casing are the Sykes' instruments to Tunnel Junction (Bell Block is used to the West Box). Below are the bell plungers, and a little lower, the point and signal repeaters. The 'pull-out' slides can clearly be seen, below which are the brass description plates.
Photo A. Vaughan.

Plate 14.
Close-up of the air cylinder and drive mechanism on the Up Outer Home Signal at Salisbury West.
Photo G. F. Gillham.

Plate 15.
A section of the low-pressure pneumatic frame at Salisbury West Box. Some of the casing has been removed, showing the locking and miniature air cylinders behind the 'Pull-out' type slides.
Photo A. Vaughan.

Plate 16.
Salisbury West Up Outer Home Signal. Note the air cylinder and drive rod to the counterweight arm. The signal is also worthy of note as being one of the few Upper Quadrants to be fitted with a siting shield.
Photo G. F. Gillham.

Plate 17.
The Up Starter for Salisbury East, with lower Distant arm for Tunnel Junction. Note the air cylinders, and rod drive to the counterweights.

Plate 18.
The same signal, showing clear for the Romsey line. If the other Distant was 'Off', the line at Tunnel Junction would be set for Andover and Waterloo.
Photos A. Vaughan.

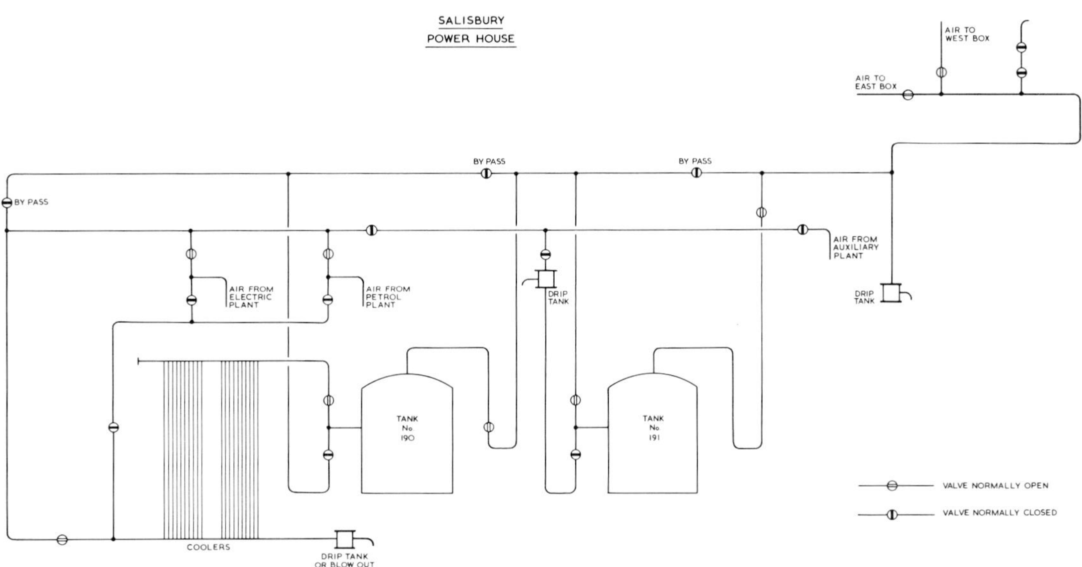

Fig. 4.
Diagram of air supply for low-pressure pneumatic signalling—Salisbury Power House. *Drawing P. D. Rutter.*

Plate 19.
A typical gantry of low-pressure pneumatic 'Autos' on the Woking-Basingstoke section.
Photo Maurice Earley.

PRE-GROUPING POWER SIGNALLING INSTALLATIONS
LOW-PRESSURE PNEUMATIC

AT OR BETWEEN	LEVERS					Signals	Points	AUTOMATIC		
	Signal	Points	Control	Space	Total			Station Distants	Sections	Signals
Grateley	37	17		16	70	46	31			
Grateley Ground Frame		2		6	8		4			
Grateley & Andover									12	22
Salisbury East	26	17	3	18	64	33	30	2		
Salisbury West	22	20	7	15	64	34	30	2		
Salisbury Ground Frame	2	1	1	4	8	2	2			
Basingstoke East	24	20		16	60	32	36	4		
Basingstoke West	31	23	1	13	68	37	40	4		
Basingstoke Ground Frame	1	1	1	1	4	1	2			
Barton Mill	12	8	1	11	32	19	14	4		
Barton Mill & Hook									16	28
Hook	16	11	2	11	40	23	22	4		
Hook & Winchfield									4	4
Winchfield	21	14	1	12	48	34	28	4		
Newnham Siding Ground Frame	2	1	1	4	8	2	2			
Winchfield & Fleet									8	12
Fleet	16	10	1	5	32	24	20	4		
Fleet & Farnborough									8	12
Farnborough	19	11	1	9	40	23	22	5		
Sturt Lane Jcn.	10	4	1	5	20	12	4	7		
Sturt Lane & Pirbright									4	4
Pirbright Jcn.	6	2	1	3	12	7	2	6		
Brookwood	18	15	2	5	40	26	28	5		
Brookwood & Woking									10	4
Staines East	15	10	1	6	32	20	19	3		
Staines West	22	13	1	4	40	25	21	3		
Staines Ground Frame	2	1	2	3	8					
Clapham Jcn. West Main	5	3		4	12	8	5	5		
Clapham Jcn. West Windsor	18	13		5	36	21	22	12		
Clapham Jcn. East Windsor & Main	43	28		13	84	56	46	13		
West London Jcn.	23	15	2	8	48	33	26	14		
West London Jcn. Ground Frame	3	4	2	3	12	5	5	4		

SYKES' ELECTRO-MECHANICAL

SIGNAL BOX	LEVERS		
	Mechanical	Electrical	Total
Victoria North	21	77	98
Victoria South	106	163	269
Victoria Shunting Box	11	11	22
Grosvenor Road	6	24	30
Battersea Pier	11	29	40
Battersea Park	21	49	70

Plate 20.
Four-aspect colour-light signals as installed by the Southern Railway in 1926—the first installation of its kind in the world. This signal at Blackfriars Junction has a distinctly American appearance, and differs from modern practice in two ways. Firstly, this is a junction signal, and NOT one applying to two parallel lines. The position junction indicators of today had yet to be invented! The other difference is not obvious from the photograph, as it concerns the positioning of the aspects. The order was, (from the top) Green, Yellow, Red, Yellow, whereas modern signalling places them Yellow, Green, Yellow, Red. In the Waterloo re-signalling, floodlit discs were used to control shunt movements, but here a miniature two-aspect colour light, mounted on the main post of the signal, has been used.

Photo courtesy National Railway Museum, York.

4. The Southern Railway

PART ONE – THE NEW COMPANY TAKES CONTROL

As already stated in the introductory chapter, when the 'Southern' took control of the independent companies at the 1923 Grouping, it did not embark immediately on a programme of sweeping changes. The railways it absorbed were safely signalled, although some of the equipment was rather elderly, so with the sound common sense, expenditure was saved for the busiest routes.

21st March 1926 was a 'red letter' day in the history of Signalling, for it was on that date that the SR introduced the first four-aspect colour-light signals in the world between Holborn Viaduct and Elephant and Castle. A new 86-lever Siemens' power frame (with mechanical locking) was installed in the old mechanical box at Holborn Viaduct, and a completely new box with a 120-lever power opened at Blackfriars Junction. These two signal boxes took over the work previously done by SEVEN mechanical boxes.

June 27th of the same year saw new signalling in use at both Cannon Street and Charing Cross, and again seven mechanical boxes were replaced by two power installations–(Charing Cross with 107 levers, and Cannon Street with 143)–and one mechanical box at Metropolitan Junction, where the 60-lever frame was adapted to the control of the colour-light signals. This re-signalling was extended through London Bridge on 17th June 1928. The old 'South Eastern' box at Borough Market Junction was equipped with a 35-lever power frame–the busiest frame of its size in the country–whilst London Bridge received a Westinghouse style 'K' miniature lever frame of 312 levers in which the locking was carried out mechanically using miniature tappets. The London Bridge frame weighed twenty-three tons, and the manufacture of the locking caused many a headache at the Westinghouse works! A further seven mechanical boxes were abolished with the opening of two new boxes, (both mechanical), at Parks Bridge Junction and St. John's, together with colour-light signalling, on 30th June 1929.

The Westinghouse Brake and Signal Company became established as the main signalling contractors to the Southern Railway, and were associated with all new works whether electrical or mechanical.

During this hectic period of alterations in the London area, several new schemes of a lesser nature were carried out on other parts of the system. Bournemouth received a new signal box to control the Central Station. It replaced the old 'A' and 'B' boxes, and had a 60-lever mechanical frame, and was opened on 8th July 1928. Further west on the same line, Wareham had been re-signalled in May of the same year, a new box being opened adjacent to the level crossing. On the West of England line, Seaton Junction was remodelled on a lavish scale, with loop lines to serve the platforms and greatly increased siding accommodation, a new 55-lever signal box being opened on 3rd April 1928. In fact, the SR had high hopes of Seaton as a 'working-class' resort, in sharp contrast with the other watering places of East Devon which strive even today to remain 'select'. As things turned out, traffic over the Seaton branch never reached the volume anticipated, and the money invested in Seaton Junction would have been spent to better advantage at Sidmouth Junction, where the branch was considerably busier.

Speaking generally, re-signalling schemes were something of a rarity in the West, so it is interesting to note that one of the Southern's first new signal boxes was opened at Ilfracombe on 10th April 1924. Plans for this scheme had been prepared by the L. & S.W.R., and the design of the signal box was definitely 'South Western', although a 50-lever Westinghouse frame was installed. At about the same time, the dark and dingy station at Exeter Queen Street was being re-constructed, the track layout being completely revised. A new box with 35 levers, (Exeter Central 'B'), was opened on 13th September 1925, and a new 'A' box with 90 levers on 15th June 1927. It would seem not only were the plans for this work drawn up by the L. & S.W.R., but also much of the equipment ordered by that Company, as both these signal boxes, though constructed by the Southern Railway, were typically 'South Western' in design and were fitted with Stevens lever frames.

These West Country schemes were purely mechanical, and retained semaphore signals, as did the new box at Hastings, opened on 25th May 1930. Containing an 84-lever Westinghouse 'A2' frame, it replaced the old East and West boxes.

The year 1932 marked the beginning of further large re-signalling schemes. The former L.B. & S.C.R. main line to Brighton was still controlled by semaphores, and with the ever-increasing traffic, punctuality suffered badly, particularly during foggy weather. It was therefore decided to completely modernise the line with colour-light signalling. The Westinghouse Company again secured the contract, and the work was carried out in stages between Coulsdon North No. 1 box and the Brighton during that year. The task, as can be imagined, was a large and complex one. Not only was it necessary to provide continuous track circuiting in connection with the colour-lights, but a new power box had to be provided at Brighton–all with the minimum of interruption to traffic. The new box at Brighton, fitted with a 225-lever style 'L' miniature lever frame, was brought into use on 16th October 1932. Several of the intermediate boxes were retained to control the new signalling, and two new mechanical boxes were opened, (Haywards Heath and Keymer Crossing), whilst a new mechanical frame of 130 levers was installed in the existing 'Central' box at Three Bridges. Altogether, twenty-four mechanical boxes, totalling 1,093 levers, were closed completely, and a further nine boxes, accounting for 324 levers were normally switched out of circuit, their signals working as semi-automatics. Indeed, only eight signal boxes controlled the busy line between Coulsdon and Brighton under normal traffic conditions.

Having vastly improved the Brighton line, the Southern took a look at the former L. & S.W.R. approaches to the Metropolis. The line from Waterloo to Hampton Court Junction was quadrupled throughout its length–the lines being paired by direction west of Wimbledon. East of Wimbledon the lines were paired by use, which involved the

Plate 21.
Interior of Portsmouth Harbour Signal Box, shortly after its opening in June 1946, showing the 47 miniature lever power frame and rotary train describer.

Photo Evening News & Hampshire Telegraph, Portsmouth.

construction of a concrete flyover at Durnsford Road to carry the Up Local Line over the Down and Up Through lines. Unlike the Brighton scheme, most of the existing signal boxes were retained, the only closures being Waterloo 'D', Queen's Road East, Clapham Junction 'D', Clapham Cutting and Durnsford Road. The first stage, from Waterloo to New Malden, and down to Clapham over the Windsor Lines, was brought into use on 17th May 1936, and on that day the line from Waterloo to Surbiton was closed to traffic between 1 a.m. and 7 a.m. to assist the engineers introducing the new signalling and opening the Wimbledon flyover. The next stage involved the construction of two new mechanical signal boxes – Surbiton and Hampton Court Junction. Surbiton is noteworthy as being the first box of the design known as 'Glasshouse' or 'Queen Mary', an innovation used in conjunction with the Southern's streamlined image of the time. This design was very much a break with tradition, and as with all new things, had many critics who considered it the height of ugliness! However, it proved to be a very successful style of building for signal boxes, being light, airy, and easy to keep clean, and similar structures continued to appear until well after the Second World War. Surbiton and Hampton Court Junction opened on 28th June 1936. New miniature lever frames were installed in the boxes at West London Junction and Clapham Junction 'A', replacing the L. & S.W.R. electro-pneumatic equipment. Finally, the power box at Waterloo was opened on 18 October 1936. It contains a 309-lever Westinghouse style 'L' frame divided into three sections–Main Local, Main Through, and Windsor Lines. A great deal of preparatory work was done in advance, with the result that the change-over went so smoothly that the 00.35 train to Hampton Court was signalled by the semaphores and the 01.30 West of England newspaper train by the new colour-lights.

Several new features appeared in the Waterloo re-signalling. The colour-lights were fitted with small side aspects, (known to Railwaymen as 'Pig's Ears'), as an aid to Drivers of multiple unit trains, to permit the driving compartment to be drawn up close to the signal. The practice of providing separate signals for each diverging route at a junction, (as in the Brighton scheme), was discontinued in favour of three-light position junction indicators, except for those on the platform ends at Waterloo and at the immediate approach to the station, where 'Theatre' type route indicators were employed.

Victoria was the scene of further major works. This was re-signalled in something of a hurry following an accident caused by the irregular use of the Sykes' release key—(the area was still controlled by 'Lock and Block'). Work started at Battersea Park Junction, where a 31-lever all-electric frame was brought into use on 16th October 1938. The lines into the terminus changed from 'Lock and Block' to Track Circuit Block when the new Victoria Central box, with its 225-lever power frame, was opened on 4th June 1939. On the 'Eastern' side, the change-over from three-position semaphore to colour-light was completed on 25th June 1939, the existing 200-lever frame in Victoria 'A' being adapted.

A number of comparatively minor schemes were executed between 1936 and the outbreak of war in 1939. The line between Woking and Guildford was equipped with colour-lights, the intermediate box at Worplesdon being open only as required to shunt freight traffic to the station sidings, the signals becoming semi-automatic. Haslemere received colour-light signals in the station area, controlled by the existing mechanical signal box, as did Havant. A new box of the 'Glasshouse' type, containing a 131-lever power frame, was opened at Woking to replace the old Yard and Junction boxes. All these improvements were brought into use on 27th June 1937, which must have been a very busy day for the Signal Department.

New signal boxes of the 'Glasshouse' type were opened during 1938 at Horsham on 24th April, Dorking North and Templecombe on 15th May, and Bognor Regis on 29th May. The Horsham and Dorking schemes included the provision of colour-light signals in the station areas, and Templecombe is worthy of note as being the farthest west that this design of signal box penetrated. There were, in fact, very few new boxes constructed west of Templecombe until BR days. The branch terminus at Seaton had received one in 1936, but it was not of the 'Glasshouse', or indeed any other classifiable design. In other areas 'Glasshouses' continued to be opened—Ascot 'B' on 16th October 1938, and Strood Junction and Strood Tunnel on 29th January 1939.

With the declaration of War, the modernisation programme had to be shelved, some items being postponed until the return of peace, and some cancelled permanently. Such new works as did take place were confined to the provision of additional sidings and loops to cater for war-time needs, and the making good of bomb damage, from which the Southern, with a high route mileage in London on viaducts, suffered harshly. Several signal boxes were lost as the result of enemy action, and much damage caused to the signalling system as a whole. An example of trouble heaped upon the S.R. as the result of war conditions is the story of Blackfriars. This signal box was destroyed by a bomb on 19th April 1941, putting the busy City station completely out of action. By 2nd June, a temporary ground-level box, complete with illuminated diagram and power frame, had been opened to control the main line signals only, which were reduced to two aspects – red and yellow. The box was eventually rebuilt as a 'Glasshouse' with a 119-lever Westinghouse 'L' power frame, which opened on 11th August 1946. Portsmouth Harbour was one box well away from London that suffered heavy war damage. Here again, it was re-built to the 'Glasshouse' design and fitted with a 47-lever power frame, opening on 1st June 1946.

The remainder of the story really belongs to British Railways, with whom this book is not directly concerned. However, it is interesting to note that BR continued for a time with the Southern's 'Glasshouse' design. Wimbledon 'A' (1948), and Three Bridges, (April 1952—replacing the old 'Central' box), are examples. The latter has a 150-lever Westinghouse 'A3' frame, and at the time of writing, is the largest mechanical box on the Southern Region. BR also erected a number of new mechanical boxes between Salisbury and Exeter, all with Westinghouse 'A3' frames, but these were to a BR design. The last LARGE mechanical box to be opened by the Southern Region was on 14th April 1957 at Weymouth, which has a 116-lever frame and replaces two elderly G.W.R. boxes.

PART TWO – THE SOUTHERN RAILWAY AND WORLD WAR TWO

The lines of the Southern may well be said to have been in the 'Front Line' as regards wartime operations. Not only did their lines lead to the English Channel ports, but also served areas used intensively for military training, such as Aldershot and Salisbury Plain. It is hardly surprising, then, to note that much new signalling had to be installed to cater for the great rush of wartime traffic. This had been true of the pre-grouping companies, who were forced to construct many a new signal box to serve the needs of an Army camp or supply depot. There was Winchester Loop, on the main Southampton line, opened in 1918 to give access to an additional troop platform. A box at Worgret Siding had been opened the same year to operate a siding into an Australian Army camp, and in 1917 the Amesbury branch had received an additional box at Boscombe Down, where a siding led off to the new airfield. Unfortunately, no photographs of these First World War boxes appear to have survived, if, indeed, any were ever taken.

New signal boxes constructed during the Second War fall into two main categories. Some were entirely new block posts, opened to serve depots and camps where there had been nothing before. Others were to replace smaller boxes at stations where the old layout needed to be enlarged because of increased military activity in the area. An example of the latter is Dinton.

Dinton had, in fact undergone alterations during the First War, when a branch was constructed to Fovant Camp. Traffic to and from this camp had at times been very heavy to the extent that shunting operations at Dinton frequently caused serious delays to the West Country services. The Southern must have borne this in mind, for with the onset of World War Two, it was decided to provide loops and additional siding accommodation in an effort to minimise traffic delays. Fovant Camp was not re-opened, but the stores depots around the station were enlarged. The situation was further aggravated in 1942 by the opening of an R.A.F. supply depot at Chilmark. Although access to this was controlled by a separate box, all the traffic circulated via Dinton, which made this normally peaceful wayside station very busy indeed. The new Dinton Box was opened on 8th November 1942, and was almost double the size of its predecessor.

Traffic on the former South Eastern Line became so heavy, that between Reading Spur and North Camp, practically every block section was divided by an intermediate to keep the traffic flowing.

Any route leading to the port of Southampton came under heavy pressure in time of war. During the 1940s, the G.W.R. had found it necessary to re-signal the otherwise quiet cross-country route from Didcot to Shawford Junction (near Winchester). This involved the construction of new boxes at all the stations, and the lengthening of the crossing loops. Between Salisbury and Southampton, four goods loops were provided at Kimbridge Junction, where a new box was opened on 21st May 1943. On the same date, an entirely new box was opened to control the other end of these loops, known as Awbridge. On this section, other new boxes were opened to serve supply depots at Dean Hill and Lockerley, whilst at Redbridge, where the line from Salisbury joins the main Waterloo-Bournemouth line, the lever frame was extended by four levers in 1942, and a double line, running parallel to the main line, was opened from there into Southampton Western Docks. Prior to this, all docks traffic had to run via Eastleigh, an area which became very congested with additional war-time traffic.

There were many such alterations all over the Southern system. These, plus the task of making good the damage caused by enemy action, kept the Signal Department fully occupied.

The S.R. war-time signal box can hardly be described as handsome, but it must be remembered that they were often erected in rather a hurry and on a restricted budget. Any form of decorative work would have been a gross waste of time and money. However, they were very solidly constructed, so that the blast from a bomb would do little more than blow out the windows. Most of these war-time boxes have now been demolished, but a few still stand to remind us of the importance of rail transport in time of strife.

Plate 22.

Dinton signal box, on the Salisbury-Exeter line, opened on 8th November 1942, replacing the original box when considerable extensions were made to the layout. It contained a 32-lever Westinghouse 'A2' frame, installed 'back to traffic', an idea that the Southern had by then adopted as standard. The design is austere, reminding us of the circumstances that led to its construction. This box closed on 2nd May 1967, when this section of the former West of England Main Line was converted to single track. The connections to the sidings are now operated by two ground frames.

Photo B. L. Jackson

Plate 23.
South London received rather more than its fair share of bomb attacks during the Second World War, and the Southern found it advisable to fortify some signal boxes. This picture of Cambria Junction clearly shows the strong anti-blast brick walls that encased the original structure.

Photo courtesy National Railway Museum, York.

Two further examples of war-time boxes:

Plate 24.

The diminutive box at Froyle, between Alton and Bentley, opened to serve a siding into a Ministry of Food Cold Store. It was closed several years ago, following a long period of virtual disuse.

Photo B. L. Jackson.

Plate 25.

Dean Hill Box, between Dean and Dunbridge, was opened on 3rd May 1940 to serve an admiralty depot. It is still in use, and houses a 16-lever Westinghouse frame and gate wheel. Note the general appearance is less grim than Dinton and Froyle, more windows being provided.

Photo G. F. Gillham

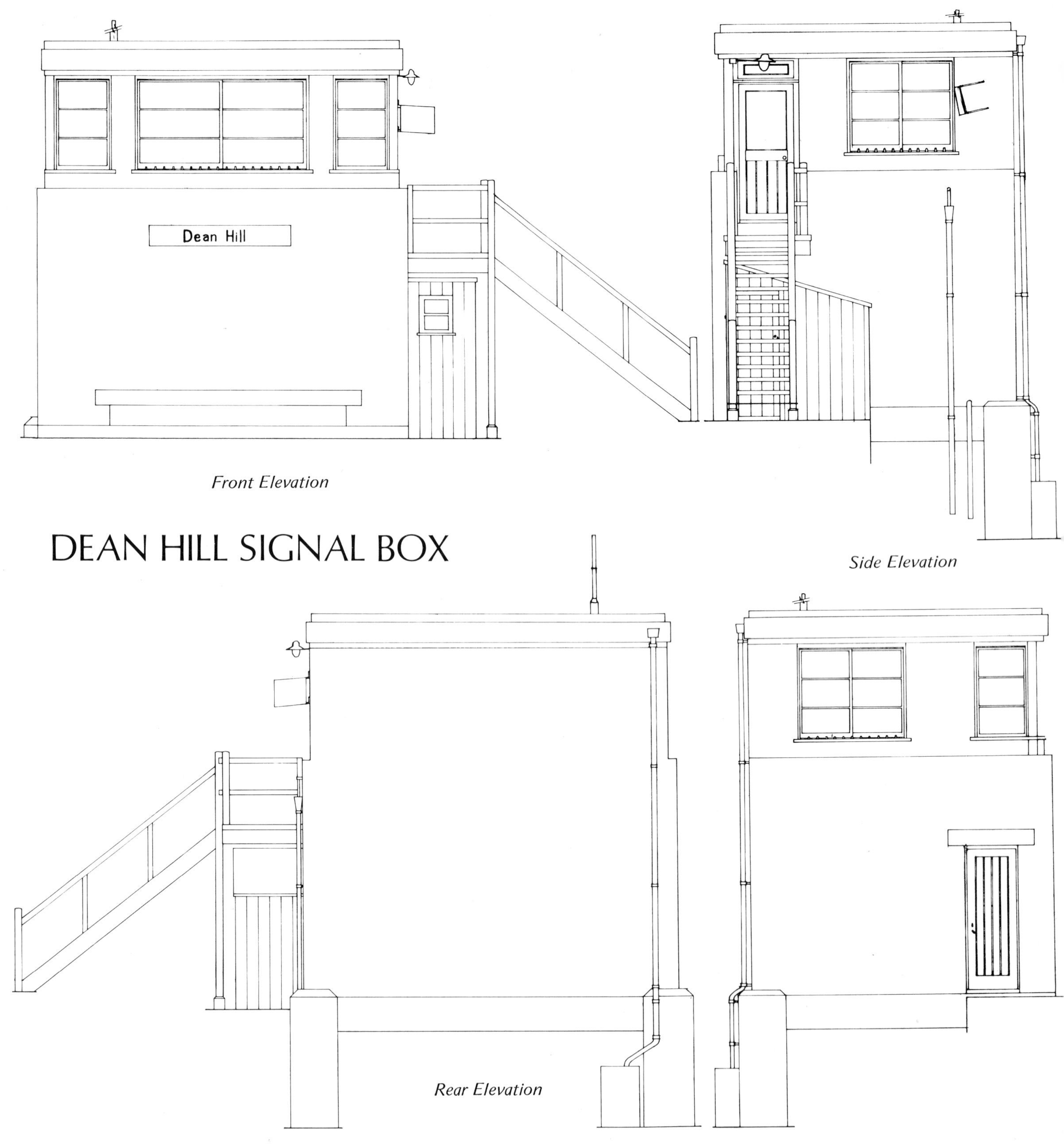

NOTES.
TYPICAL S.RLY. DESIGN OF WARTIME BOMBPROOF BOX.
THE STRUCTURE IS BRICK-BUILT WITH A CONCRETE ROOF.
IT RESTS ON A CONCRETE BASE, AND TWO CONCRETE
PIERS AT THE REAR AS THE GROUND SLOPES DOWN.

DRAWN AS MEASURED AND PHOTOGRAPHED 29·12·75

Fig. 5.
Scale drawing of Dean Hill Signal Box.

Drawing G. J. Bowring

5. Signals, and their Application to Traffic

Everybody, I suppose, knows what a semaphore signal looks like. Until the recent wide-spread introduction of colour-light signalling, they were a part of the scene at every railway station. Regular passengers even obtained a rather rudimentary idea of their purpose, knowing, for instance, that when the signal at the end of the platform moved out of the horizontal position, there was a train about. Every signal on the line has its name and a definite purpose for being there, and although a 'Home', a 'Starter', and an 'Advanced Starter' might be exactly the same in appearance, their functions are different.

The most easily distinguished signal is, of course, the 'Distant'. These days, all Distant arms are painted yellow with a black chevron near the end of the arm, which is itself notched or 'Fish-tailed'. These are the only 'Running' signals that may be passed by trains when the arm is 'ON', as they act purely as caution signals. A driver passing a Distant that has not been pulled, must immediately bring the speed of his train under control, being prepared to find the next 'Stop' signal at danger. The signalman cannot pull his 'Distant' until he has operated all the 'Stop' signals applicable to that particular line of traffic.

Figure 6 shows how a section of main line is broken up into 'Block Sections'. Only one train is permitted to occupy a Block Section on any one track at a time, in fact, modern signalling instruments virtually enforce this, thereby keeping a safe interval of distance between following trains. Other than complex systems of working such as 'Permissive Block', there is an instance where two trains may occupy a Block Section at the same time. This is illustrated in the lower diagram (Figure 7). Here we have an instance where the middle box, 'B', has been abolished and its place taken by Intermediate Block Signals. The absolute Block Section is now between 'A' and 'C', but by use of the intermediates, the Signalman at 'C' can pull off his local signals to admit a train into the advance section provided that the previous train has cleared the overlap track circuit up to his Intermediate. In such instances, it is the Intermediate Block Signal that is released by 'Line Clear' on the instrument from the box in advance, and not the Starting or Advance Starting Signal, as would be the case under ordinary working.

'Intermediates' are of great value where the section has been lengthened by the closure of a signal box, but where a number of boxes have been abolished, the tendency is to track-circuit the whole line and install a series of 'Automatic' signals, which may be two, three, or four aspect according to the density of the traffic. In such cases, Block Instruments are dispensed with, signalmen describing the trains to each other by bell only, or on magazine Train Describers. This is called 'Track Circuit Block', and under this system it is not necessary for the signalmen to send any 'Is Line Clear?', or 'Train out of Section' signals, as he can see the state of the line by looking at his illuminated track diagram. Provided the track circuit between his 'starting' signal and the first automatic signal is showing clear, he simply 'Pulls Off' for the next train, describing it to the box in advance in one of the ways mentioned.

Whether a line is signalled by semaphore or colour-light, there is one type of 'Section' that remains the same. This is the 'Signal Section', and is the distance between two consecutive 'Stop' signals applying to the same line. As with the 'Block Section', only one train is permitted to enter a 'Signal Section' at a time, except where 'Subsidiary' signals are provided to warn the driver of the occupation of the line ahead. Here lies the main difference between a 'Running' signal and other types. When a 'Running' signal is operated, the drivers of the train may assume that the line is clear at least as far as the next 'Running' signal. However, such things as ground disc signals give no such assurance, and authorise a movement only as far as the line is clear, which may be only a matter of feet, to allow vehicles to be attached to the rear of a standing train, or shunting movements where a vehicle or portion of the train may have been left on the main line.

Figure 8 shows the layout of signals at a typical S.R. wayside station, and incorporates many features commonly found at such places.

Several things about this little layout will attract the attention of the enquiring mind. First, no doubt, will be the question 'Why are Ground Signals 10 and 16 fitted with yellow arms, instead of red discs as are the others?' Study the relative positions of discs 7 and 15. It would obviously be unsafe to pass either of these in the 'on' position, as the result would be derailment at the end of the short trap points. However, in the cases of 10 and 16, there is a definite route available other than through the points onto the main line, and shunt movements may pass these signals in the 'ON' position provided they are taking the alternative route. Should a movement require to come through the points, then it cannot do so until the signal is operated.

Another item which is bound to draw attention, is that the Up Starting Signal has TWO arms. These are called 'Co-acting' arms, and work as one at the operation of the lever. In our diagram, the footbridge, and possibly also the station buildings, restrict the visibility of this signal, a difficulty which is overcome by providing a very tall post, with one arm near the top for viewing at a distance above such obstructions, and another arm near the bottom for easy observance by a driver whose train may be brought to a stand at the signal. Co-acting arms are now out of date, although a number still survive. The more modern alternative is demonstrated by the Down Inner Home. Again, visibility is restricted by the adjacent overbridge, but instead of providing a tall signal, a signal of standard height is provided, the position of the arm being electrically repeated by the 'Banner' repeater on the approach side of the bridge.

On the subject of ground discs, the diagram shows the standard Southern arrangement. Thus disc 5 would be pulled for movements through points 6 and 8, and also straight back along the Down Line as far as disc 12. Disc 9 is operative through points 8 and 11, but *not* for a 'straight back' movement, as this would take the shunting outside 'Station Limits'. Disc 18, however, would read in three directions—through points 13, 17, or back along the Up

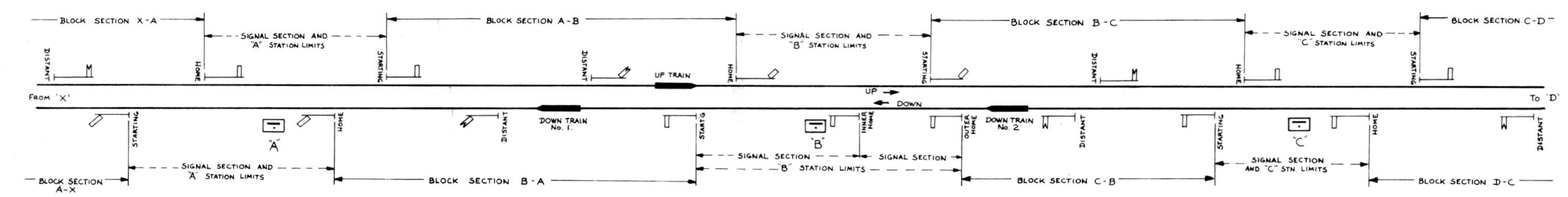

Fig. 6. *(above)*
The diviston of a double line of railway into Block Sections, Signal Sections, and Station Limits, giving the nomenclature of all running signals.

Fig. 7. *(below)*
Illustration of the way in which Block working is modified by the introduction of Intermediate Block Signals.

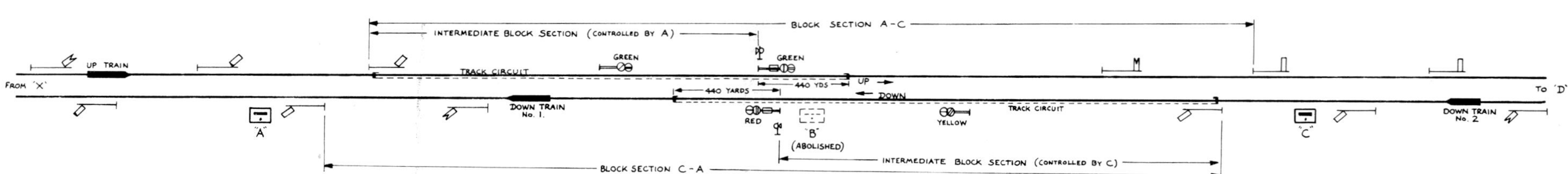

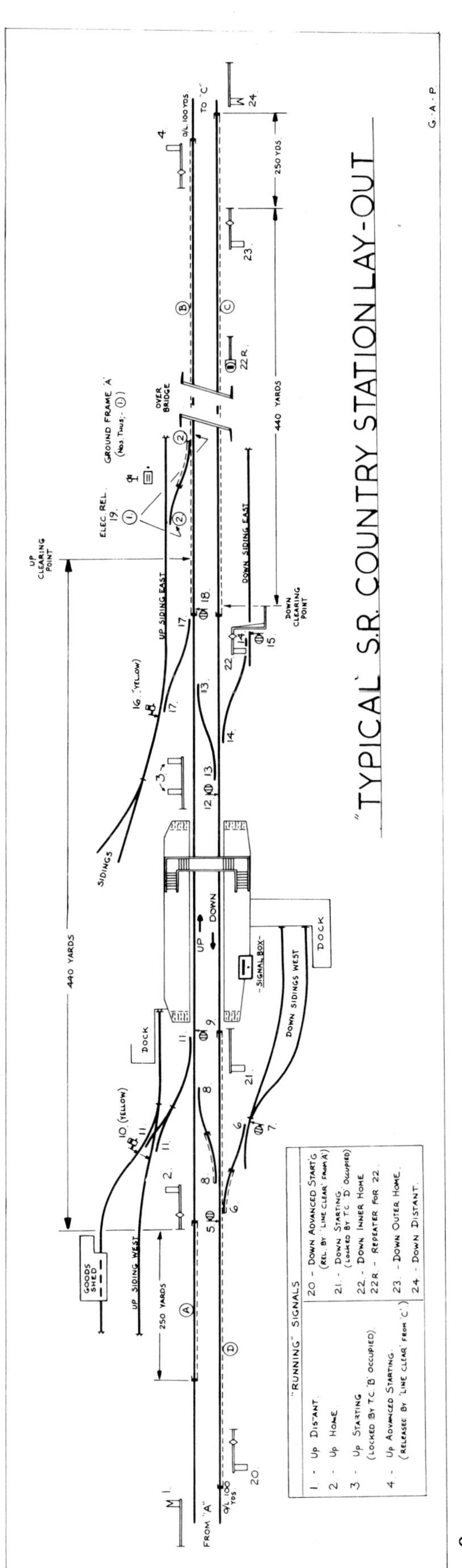

Fig. 8.
Signalling diagram of a 'Typical' small SR country station. The running signals are named, and the position of the Up and Down Clearing Points indicated. The functions of the Ground Disc signals are explained in the text.
NOTE: This layout is not meant to represent any actual location on the Southern Railway, but is intended solely to demonstrate the layout and function of signals.

Line to disc 9. Disc 12, like No. 9 would apply through points 13 and 14 only, as although an 'Outer Home' is provided, and a 'straight back' movement would not necessarily pass beyond station limits, unless a 'Limit of Shunt' indicator is provided, there is nothing to prevent a driver proceeding towards the box in rear on the wrong line. As already mentioned, discs 7, 10, 15, and 16 apply to one movement only—from the siding to the Main Line.

What are the operational snags of such a lay-out? On the Down Line, there are none, as with an Outer Home situated 440 yards on the approach side of the Inner Home, the signalman is free to shunt through any of his connections or obstruct the Down platform, and still accept a Down Train from the box in rear. The same would apply if only one Home Signal were provided, on condition that it was sited not less than 440 yards from the fouling point of the first set of points. However, on the Up line, the Signalman is rather more restricted in his movements. His Up 'Clearing Point' falls about half-way between the two connections to the Up Sidings East, and therefore once an Up Train has been accepted, the only points on the Up Side that he can use are those operated from Ground Frame 'A'. Furthermore, all shunt movements, or standing engines or vehicles, must be removed from the Up Line, or moved beyond the clearing point, before an Up Train can be accepted. In cases such as this, any shunting being carried out on the Up Line should be protected by the signalman sending the 'Blocking Back Inside Home Signal' bell code, (2 pause 4), to the box in rear, and placing his Block Instrument for the Up Line to the 'Train On Line' position.

The diagram also illustrates the Southern standard arrangement of Track Circuits. 'Approach Tracks', (those leading up to a Home or Outer Home signal), usually extend for a distance of 250 yards on the approach side of such signal, whilst Track Circuits leading up to an Advanced Starting Signal often have an overlap of 100 yards beyond that signal.

The subject of signal configuration is also worthy of study. Where there are diverging lines, a separate arm is provided for each route, leaving the driver in no doubt as to which way he is going. Many years ago, the arms for diverging lines were often mounted one above the other on a common post, the reading of them being 'Top to bottom—Left to right'. However, this method has long been illegal, (although the Up Platform Starting Signals at Exeter Central 'A' retained this form until recent years), and the arms are now mounted on separate 'Dolls' of varying height, the highest one applying to the route with the least restriction of speed. There are also some fanciful signals with only one arm. The reason for some of these creations is usually siting difficulty, or occasionally, cramped location. It is this great variety in configuration which gives railway signalling such interest.

Now we have looked at the reasons and functions of signals, we can look through the pages that follow with a greater understanding. Some of the points already mentioned will be amplified in the captions to the photographs.

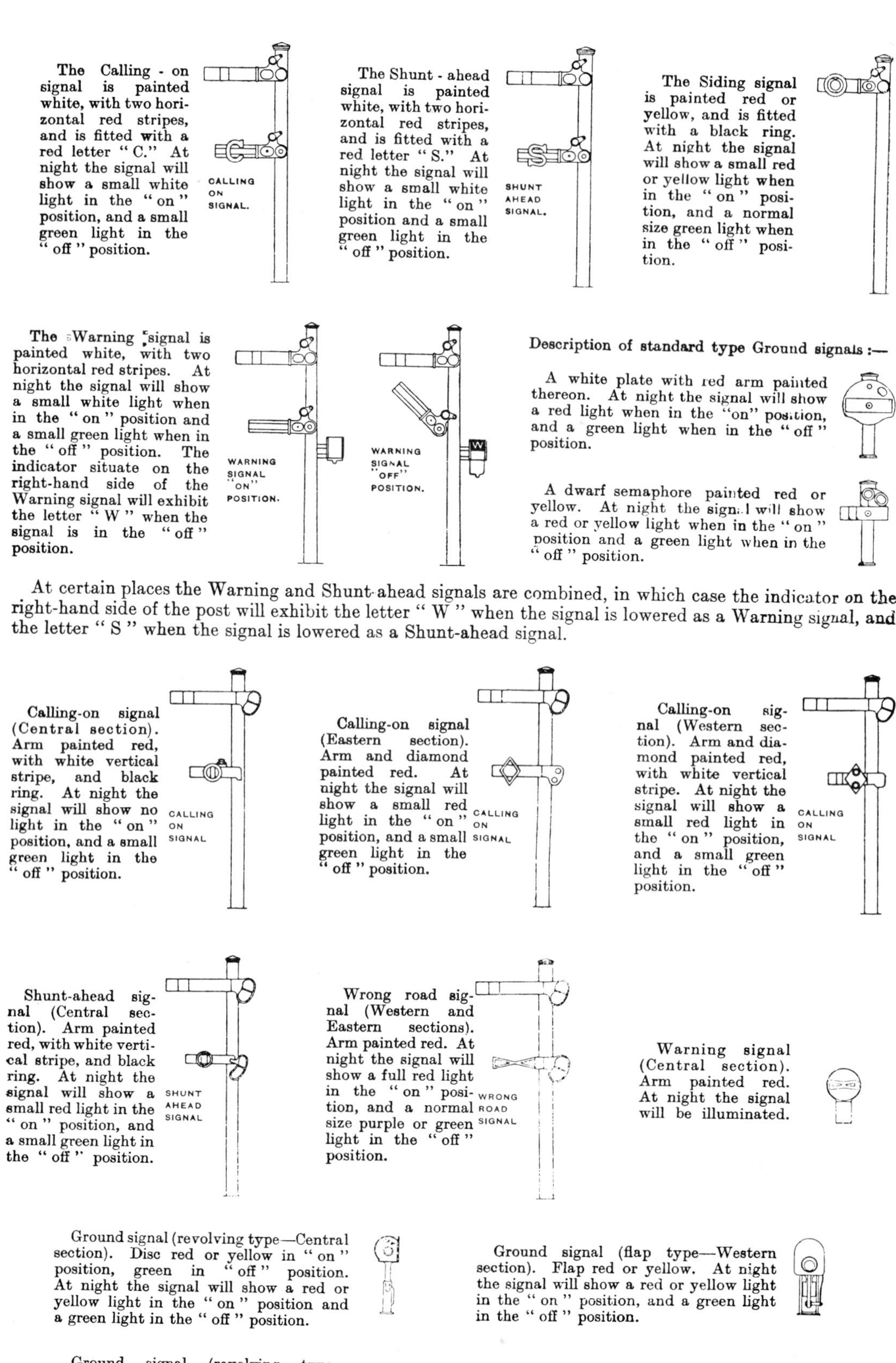

The Calling-on signal is painted white, with two horizontal red stripes, and is fitted with a red letter "C." At night the signal will show a small white light in the "on" position, and a small green light in the "off" position.

CALLING ON SIGNAL.

The Shunt-ahead signal is painted white, with two horizontal red stripes, and is fitted with a red letter "S." At night the signal will show a small white light in the "on" position and a small green light in the "off" position.

SHUNT AHEAD SIGNAL.

The Siding signal is painted red or yellow, and is fitted with a black ring. At night the signal will show a small red or yellow light when in the "on" position, and a normal size green light when in the "off" position.

The Warning signal is painted white, with two horizontal red stripes. At night the signal will show a small white light when in the "on" position and a small green light when in the "off" position. The indicator situate on the right-hand side of the Warning signal will exhibit the letter "W" when the signal is in the "off" position.

WARNING SIGNAL "ON" POSITION.

WARNING SIGNAL "OFF" POSITION.

Description of standard type Ground signals :—

A white plate with red arm painted thereon. At night the signal will show a red light when in the "on" position, and a green light when in the "off" position.

A dwarf semaphore painted red or yellow. At night the signal will show a red or yellow light when in the "on" position and a green light when in the "off" position.

At certain places the Warning and Shunt-ahead signals are combined, in which case the indicator on the right-hand side of the post will exhibit the letter "W" when the signal is lowered as a Warning signal, and the letter "S" when the signal is lowered as a Shunt-ahead signal.

Calling-on signal (Central section). Arm painted red, with white vertical stripe, and black ring. At night the signal will show no light in the "on" position, and a small green light in the "off" position.

CALLING ON SIGNAL

Calling-on signal (Eastern section). Arm and diamond painted red. At night the signal will show a small red light in the "on" position, and a small green light in the "off" position.

CALLING ON SIGNAL

Calling-on signal (Western section). Arm and diamond painted red, with white vertical stripe. At night the signal will show a small red light in the "on" position, and a small green light in the "off" position.

CALLING ON SIGNAL

Shunt-ahead signal (Central section). Arm painted red, with white vertical stripe, and black ring. At night the signal will show a small red light in the "on" position, and a small green light in the "off" position.

SHUNT AHEAD SIGNAL

Wrong road signal (Western and Eastern sections). Arm painted red. At night the signal will show a full red light in the "on" position, and a normal size purple or green light in the "off" position.

WRONG ROAD SIGNAL

Warning signal (Central section). Arm painted red. At night the signal will be illuminated.

Ground signal (revolving type—Central section). Disc red or yellow in "on" position, green in "off" position. At night the signal will show a red or yellow light in the "on" position and a green light in the "off" position.

Ground signal (flap type—Western section). Flap red or yellow. At night the signal will show a red or yellow light in the "on" position, and a green light in the "off" position.

Ground signal (revolving type—Eastern section). Dwarf semaphore, red or yellow with white ball in "on" position and green in "off" position. At night the signal will show a red or yellow light in the "on" position and a green light in the "off" position.

Wrong road shunt signal (Western and Eastern sections). Dwarf semaphore arm white with red cross. At night the signal will show a red light in the "on" position and a green light in the "off" position.

Fig. 9.
Types of signal in general use on the Southern Railway. *(Taken from official Publication)*

SIGNAL POST SIGNS

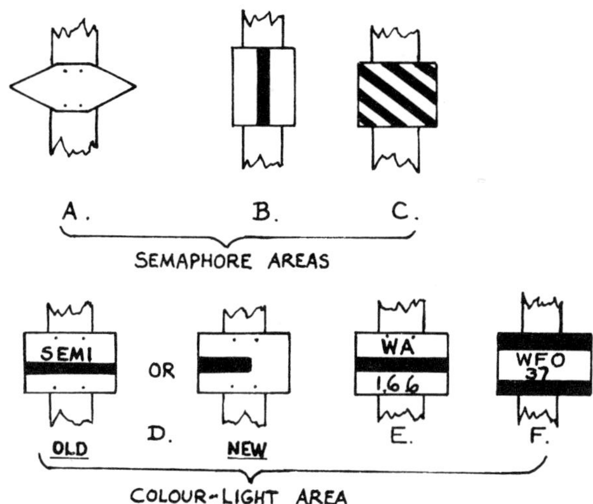

Many signals have plates attached to them, each of a distinctive design and conveying additional instructions to the drivers. These plates are illustrated above, and their meanings are as follows:-

Plate 'A'. Signal exempt from 'Rule 55'. (With the issue of the new BR rule book, the number of this rule had been changed.) It denotes that a track-circuit, treadle, or other reminder appliance is provided, and that the signalman is therefore aware of the presence of the train at the signal. It is not necessary for the driver to contact the signalman by 'phone, or go to the signal box, unless his train is detained for an unusually long time.

Plate 'B'. Denotes an 'Intermediate Block Home Signal'.

Plate 'C'. Telephone, communicating directly with Signalman, provided at base of signal. Driver to contact Signalman immediately if his train brought to a stand at such signal.

Plate 'D'. Old and new pattern plates to denote a 'semi-automatic' signal.

Plate 'E'. An automatic signal, showing the serial number. Drivers must quote this number when telephoning the signalman. The prefix 'WA' means 'Western Automatic', and shows that the signal is situated in the Southern's South Western section. In the Central section the prefix 'CA' is used, whilst the South Eastern section use the letter 'A' only.

Plate 'F'. Colour-light signal controlled from a signal box, bearing the prefix letters of the controlling box and the lever number. 'WFO' is a prefix which has been used by two boxes, Southampton Tunnel Junction being the first. This box was closed before the introduction of colour lights at Andover, and the same prefix was later used for Andover 'B' box.

POSITIONS OF DIAMOND SIGNS
(Rule 55(a))

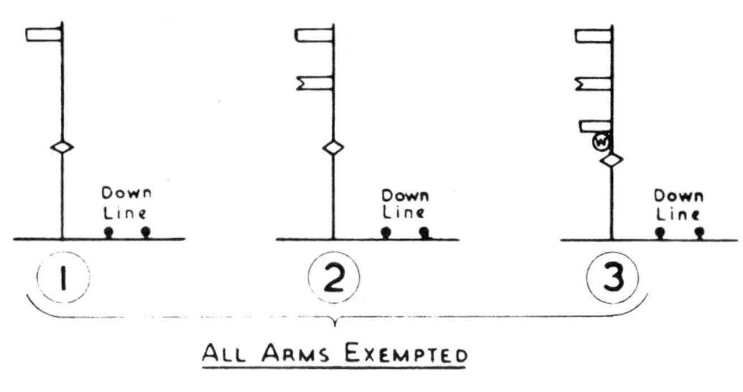

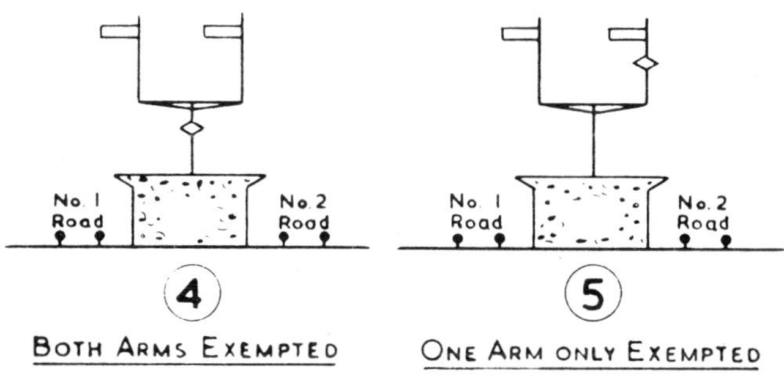

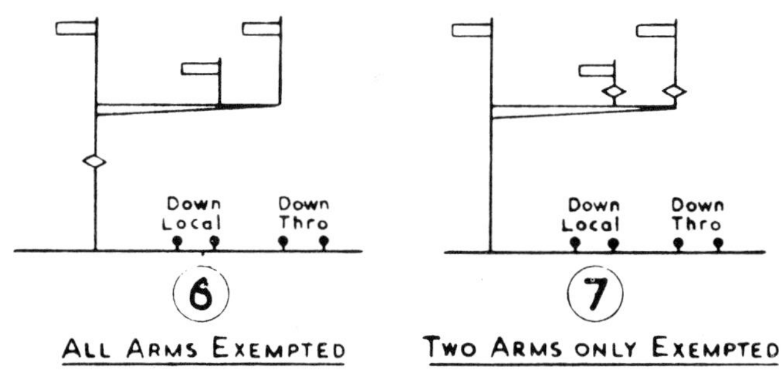

Fig. 10.
Sketches showing standard S.R. positioning for 'Rule 55' exemption diamonds.

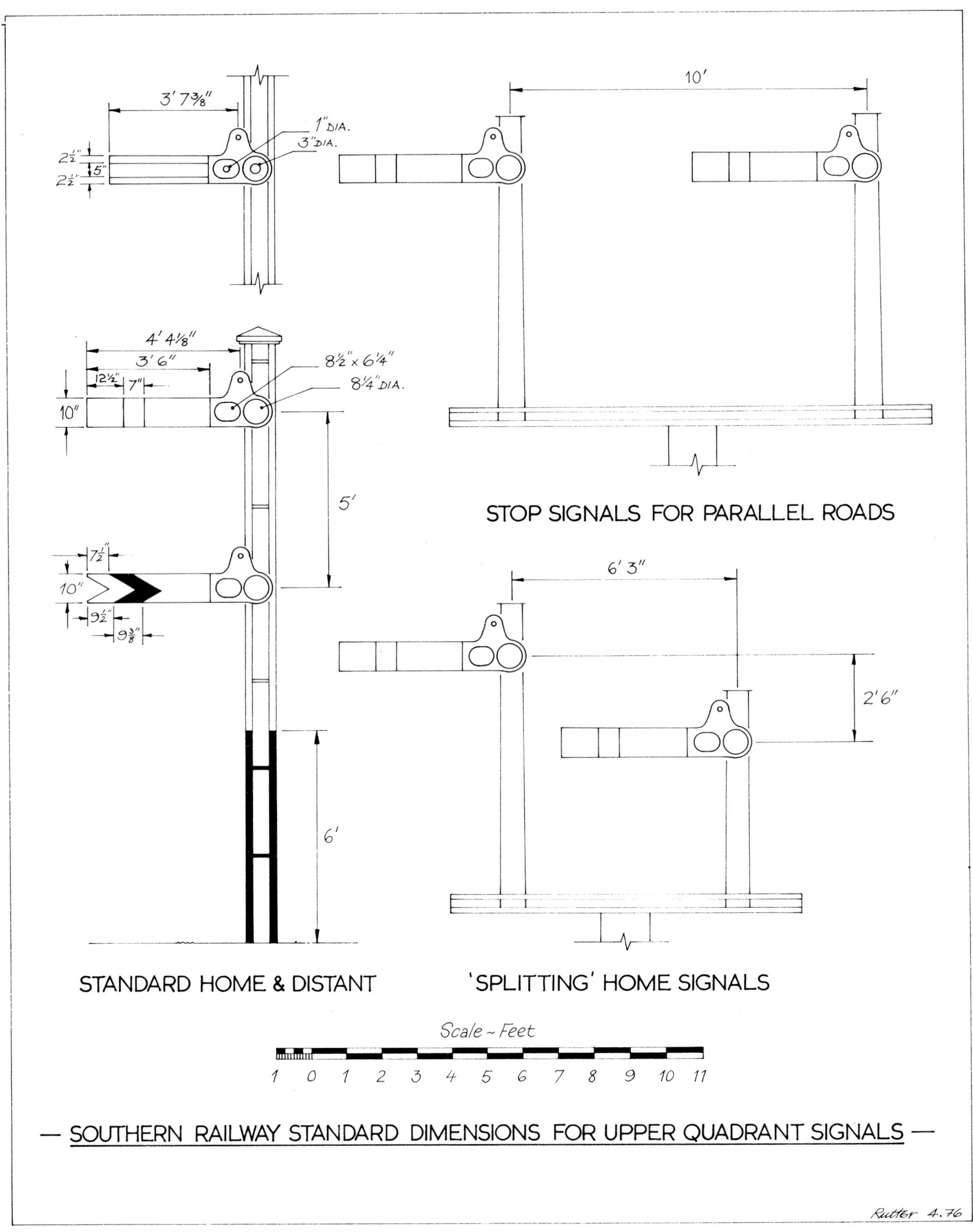

Fig. 11. *Scale dimensions for S.R. upper quadrant signals.* *Drawing P. D. Rutter*

Fig. 12.

Dimensions of arms on shunt signals, and 'Banner' repeater signals, and measurements of illuminated 'Limit of Shunt' indicators.

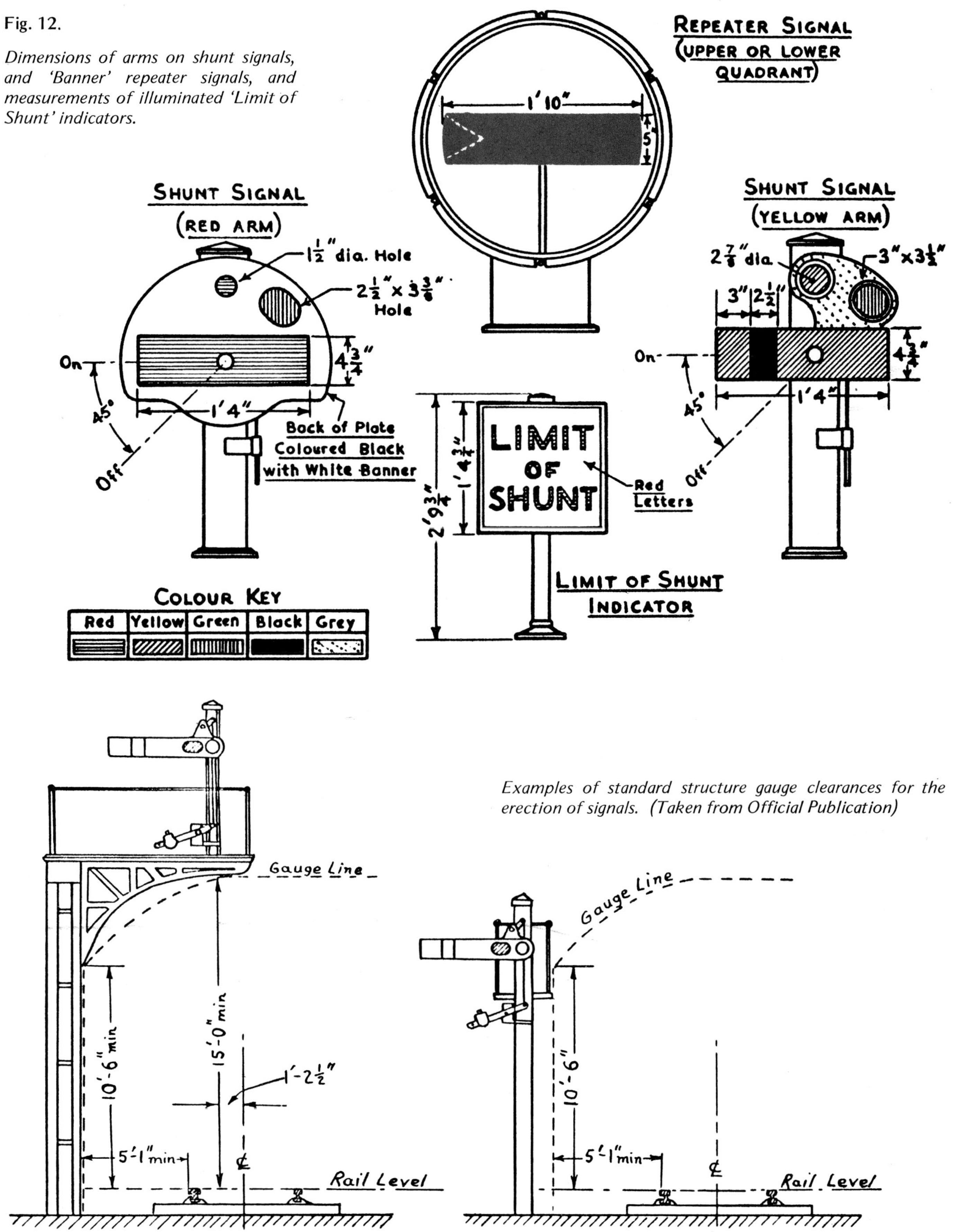

Examples of standard structure gauge clearances for the erection of signals. (Taken from Official Publication)

Two fine examples of ex-S.E. & C.R. wooden-post signals.
Plate 26 *(left).*
Shows the Up Distant Signal at Godstone, photographed in April 1950. The fitting for the Coligny-Welch lamp can be seen on the right-hand side of the lamp case, dating back to the days when the arms and lamps of Distant Signals were red. This particular signal has now been restored to pre-grouping condition, and is on display at the National Railway Museum, York.

Photo D. J. W. Brough

Plate 27 *(right).*
The Up Starting Signal at Cranbrook, taken in September 1950. Note the large finial, of McKenzie and Holland type.

Photo D. J. W. Brough

Plate 28.

Detail of a S.E. & C.R. wooden gantry at Redhill. Note the absence of ornamental finials, the tops of the dolls being capped with a rectangular metal fitting. This was a common feature on the 'South Eastern', and similar caps were later adopted by the Southern Railway for use in connection with 'Rail-built' signals.

Photo D. B. Clayton.

Plate 29.
S.E. & C.R. 'Stop' Arm, with elevated shunting signal below, at Betteshanger. The main arm is of steel, and the post of concrete, the signals themselves being operated by rods instead of the more usual wire. Note the chain linking the arm of the shunt signal to its operating rod. A close-up of this pattern of S.E. & C.R. shunt signal can be found on page 41 (Plate 36).

Photo P. Ransome Wallis

Plate 30.
London, Chatham & Dover Railway signal, designated 'Starting Back from Down Slow', at Shortlands. Note the distinctive finials used by that Company. Photograph taken 14th May, 1949.

Photo D. Cullum

Plate 31.
The interesting Down Platform Starting Signals at Bromley North in May 1949. The post and dolls are of L.C. & D.R. origin, but the two main arms are replacements of very early Southern Railway days. The one remaining L.C. & D.R. arm is the lower one, mounted on the main post, applying to trains crossing from the Down Fast to the Down Slow.

Photo D. Cullum.

Plate 32.
The Up Home Signal at Cranbrook, on the now closed Hawkhurst branch, photographed in May 1961. This rather charming S.E. & C.R. signal has a wooden post and doll, but the arm is of pressed steel. The Westinghouse-type shunt signal mounted on the gallery is of the standard SR design, and obviously a replacement for an older signal. Because of the curvature of the line at this point, the structure has been erected on the 'wrong', (i.e. right-hand), side of the line to aid drivers of approaching trains.

Photo J. Scrace

Plate 33.
The Up Starting Signal at Clock House, with lower Distant arm for New Beckenham. 'Stevens' signals, like this one, were widely used on the L. & S.W.R., but only made the occasional appearance on S.E. & C. territory. In this case, the post is much shorter than usual to allow for viewing under the station canopy. A detonator-placing machine was located at this signal for use in foggy weather, when an audible warning, in the form of a small explosion, was given to Drivers when passing the signal with the Distant arm 'on'. The single lever operating this machine can be seen immediately inside the railing.

Photo J. Scrace.

Plate 34.
An unusual adaptation of the standard Westinghouse ground signal at Plumstead. The arm is of slightly greater length than the usual 'miniature arms' that were attached to these signals, and is 'ringed' as in the older pattern of siding signals. Although installed in British Railways days, it is tempting to suggest that it is an exact replica of an older signal that once stood on the site.

Photo J. Scrace.

Plate 35.
S.E. & C.R. lattice signal gantry at Tunbridge Wells West 'B'. This has wooden arms of less than standard length, kept low on the structure for easier viewing from a train emerging from the nearby Grove Tunnel.

Photo J. Scrace.

Plate 36.
S.E. & C.R. Ground Signal, still carrying the initials of that Company on top of the lamp case, preserved at Haven Street, Isle of Wight. The mechanics of these signals were extremely simple. To lower the arm, the signal lever would pull on the chain attached to the left-hand end. When the tension was released by the replacement of the lever, the heavy counterweight, itself built into the arm at the opposite end, would pull the arm back to normal, and take up any slack in the wire.

Photo B. L. Jackson.

Plate 37.
S.E. & C.R. ringed arm shunting signal, controlling movements from the goods sidings to the single line at Westerham, Kent. Signals of this type were once common on most railways for controlling traffic entering or leaving sidings, but the ringed arm has been declared obsolete for many years, (although one or two still survive), its functions being taken over by ground disc signals.

Photo J. H. Aston.

Plate 38.
Detail of the S.E. & C.R. counterweight and fittings at the base of the signal in plate. The controlling signal wire, connected to the lever in the signal box, is spliced to a short length of chain which runs round the vertical wheel and connects with the counterweight arm. The drive between there and the signal arm is of steel rodding. It was a favourite practice on many railways to use short sections of chain round both flat and vertical wheels, as these sections of the wire run were the most subject to wear.

Photo J. H. Aston.

Plates 39 and 40.
S.E. & C.R. concrete post junction signal at Woodside. The arms on the left-hand doll, (lowered in the second plate), apply to the Selsdon line, and those on the right-hand doll to the Addiscombe line. 'South Eastern' and 'Brighton' concrete posts, though never very numerous, were mostly of the design depicted here, the post being pierced at regular intervals. The L. & S.W.R. however, used posts of solid concrete.

Photos D. Cullum.

SIGNALS CONTROLLED FROM INTERMEDIATE GROUND FRAME

On the South Eastern, ground frames were often given two running signals, (Distant and Home), to protect shunting movements. Special short arms were used in these instances, as illustrated by the two plates on this page.

Plate 41 *(left).*
Shows the Up Distant for Crowhurst Siding Ground Frame.

Plate 42 *(below).*
Shows the Up Home for Williams' Siding, both on the line between Redhill and Tonbridge. The train in the lower photograph is the 2.12 p.m. from Tonbridge to Redhill, hauled by locomotive No. 31193, on 10th November, 1951.
Photos D. Cullum.

Plate 43.
The Down Branch Distant for Peasmarsh Junction photographed in October 1923, when it still had a red arm and Coligny-Welch reflector. This device, (clearly displayed to the right of the main signal spectacle), showed an illuminated chevron at night, and had a visibility of about two hundred yards in clear weather. When the lamps of all running signals exhibited red lights, they must have been a great boon to drivers in picking out, and correctly obeying, the signals along their route.

Photo The late E. Wallis.

Plate 44.
'Up Guildford' Starting Signal at Christ's Hospital North — a good example of a 'Brighton' concrete post signal. The lower arm is a 'Shunt Ahead' Signal, for authorising movements beyond the signal as far as necessary to clear a set of points for shunting purposes.

Photo The late E. Wallis.

Plate 45.

Standard L.B. & S.C.R. 'Stop' signal, with 'Brighton' pattern disc signal to right of the post, at Sheffield Park, on the Bluebell Railway. It illustrates a variation in 'Brighton' practice—the use of a disc signal instead of the 'Shunt Ahead' arm as shown in Plate 47. If a movement was required to pass the signal and enter the single line for shunting purposes the disc signal only would be operated.

Photo A. Vaughan.

Plate 46.

Eastbourne in L.B. & S.C.R. days, showing a variety of that Company's signals. Three of the Platform Starters, (facing the camera), have small 'Shunt Ahead' arms. The lower Distant arms on the Home Signal gantry are lowered to indicate that the line is clear to the buffer stops—an idea introduced by Saxby in 1878.

Photo Lens of Sutton.

Plate 47.

Another view of the signal illustrated in Plate 45, at Sheffield Park, before being restored to its original condition. The small 'Shunt Ahead' arm has the same application as the disc (see caption to Plate 45).

Photo B. L. Jackson.

Plates 48 and 49.
The old L.B. & S.C.R. 'Blind arm' Home Signal at Faygate. Although similar to the standard co-acting arm signal, it will be noted that the upper arm has no lamp or spectacles, night indications being given by the lower arm only. Plate 48 shows a front view of the signal with arm at 'Danger', and Plate 49 shows the rear view, with arms 'Off'.

Photos D. B. Clayton.

Plate 50.
A fine example of a wooden junction signal with lower co-acting arms at Groombridge. It illustrates several ways of overcoming siting difficulties. On the approach side of this signal, the line is on a left-hand curve, and a road overbridge adds to the problem. The signal is therefore erected on the right-hand side of the line, so that it can be seen more easily by the Driver as his train rounds the curve, and the upper arms give him a long range view of the indication of the signal over the bridge, whilst the lower ones can be viewed through the arch of the bridge for short-range observation.

Photo Lens of Sutton.

Plates 51 and 52.

Front and rear views of an L.B. & S.C.R. junction signal with arms of equal height. This structure formed the 'From Forest Row Home Signals' at Ashurst Junction. The lower picture shows class 'C2X' 0-6-0 No. 32546 at the head of the 2.39 p.m. train from Three Bridges to Tunbridge Wells West, on 13th September, 1950.

Photos D. J. W. Brough

Plate 53.
L.B. & S.C.R. signals suspended under the station canopy at East Croydon. These were removed when the area was provided with colour-light signalling in 1954.

Plate 54.
The unusual Up Branch Starting signal gantry at Sutton. Although the arms are of 'Brighton' pattern, they are stamped 'S.R.' In fact, this gantry was erected by the Southern Railway shortly after the grouping. The arms have now been re-fitted as upper quadrants.

Photos D. B. Clayton.

Plate 56 *(above).*
The old 'Brighton' slotted post signal at Beddington Lane Halt. The post carries the Home and Starting signals (applicable to opposite directions), and Distant for Mitcham Junction.

Photo D. B. Clayton.

Plate 55 *(below).*
The tall Home Signal at Grange Road—a typical L.B. & S.C.R. structure with square-section wooden post. Note the position of the ladder, which runs up the front of the signal, and extends right to the top of the post.

Photo D. B. Clayton.

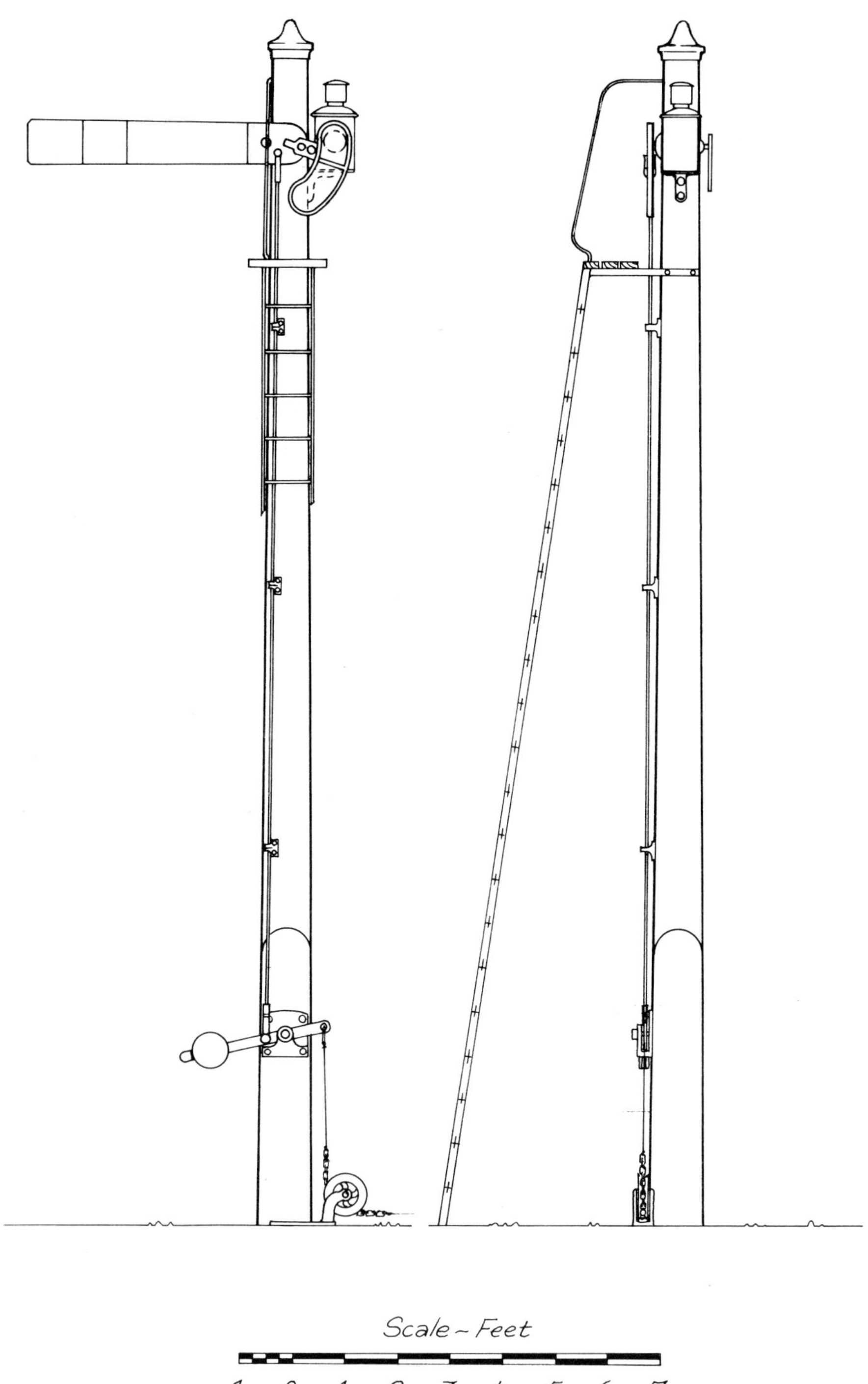

Fig. 13.
Scale drawings, (front and side elevations), of standard L.B. & S.C.R. wooden-post 'Stop' signal. A section of the ladder has been omitted from the front elevation drawing in order to show detail of counterweight etc.

Drawing by P. D. Rutter.

Plate 57.
The Down Home Signal at Pulborough, with banner-type repeater for Hardham Junction Down Distant on post. Note the large letter 'R' on the face of the repeater—a feature long since discontinued. Photograph taken in May 1923.
Photo The late E. Wallis.

Plate 58.
The 'Brighton' never used lattice-post signals on a big scale, so this Up Starting Signal at Banstead merits attention if only for that reason. However, it has other features of interest. Because of its confined location, wedged in by the station buildings on one side and a bridge on the other, an ordinary straight-post signal would be very difficult to observe from the cab of an approaching engine. The main arm is therefore bracketed out, and elevated well above the station roof. This gives an excellent 'long-range' view, but would again be difficult to see from an engine standing in the platform. A miniature repeater arm is provided to overcome this, mounted on the lower part of the post virtually at Drivers' eye level. The spectacle plate beneath the main arm is in fact the Distant Signal for 'A' Intermediate Signal Box, which was only opened occasionally for race traffic, the arms of its signals being removed at other times.
Photo D. B. Clayton.

Plate 59.
A fine gantry of L.B. & S.C.R. signals, photographed at Epsom Downs in April 1952. The arms facing the camera are Inner Home Signals for platforms 2 and 3, (note numbers on arms), with a lower 'Calling-on' signal for platform 3 for bringing a train into the platform when already partly occupied. The other two arms are the platform Starting signals.

Photo D. B. Clayton.

Plate 59a.
Another view of these fine signals.

Photo D. J. W. Brough

Plate 60.
'Brighton' version of the ringed-arm siding signal, with wooden post and arm. This one, the 'From Up Siding' signal at Pulborough, was photographed in May 1923.
Photo The late E. Wallis.

Plate 61.
Bricklayers Arms Junction—the Up Home Signal Bridge, carrying also the Down Distant Signals for New Cross Yard. The route to which each signal applies is painted on a board at the base of the appropriate doll. The lower Distant arms were still red, and exhibited a red light at night when in the 'on' position, so Coligny-Welch reflectors were provided, the diamond shapes of which can clearly be seen to the right of the Distant Signal lamp.
Photo The late E. Wallis.

Plate 62.
Wooden-post 'Gallows' type signal, with three L.B. & S.C.R. pattern discs, (immediately above the station name-board), forming the 'From Brighton Loop' Starting signal at Lewes. View taken in July 1923.

Photo The late E. Wallis

Plate 63.
Ringed-arm siding signals at East London Up Junction, (New Cross), photographed in 1926. This signal controlled movements from a siding to three separate routes, the application of the arm being 'top-to-bottom—left-to-right'. Note the use of a standard L.B. & S.C. 9-inch finial on a cut-down post.

Photo The late E. Wallis.

Plates 64 and 65.

Detail studies of a 'Brighton' ground signal, now in the care of the 'Bluebell Railway' at Sheffield Park Station. These signals are of the revolving type, and when at 'Danger', exhibit a red target, (with a white hand pointing towards the line to which it applies), in the direction of an approaching movement. When pulled to clear, the targets turn through a quarter circle, and the green face, with a white cross painted thereon, is shown towards the shunt movement.

Photos B. L. Jackson

Plate 66.

'Limit of Shunt' signals are not usually workable, and in modern signalling, are nothing more than an illuminated board with 'Limit of Shunt' painted thereon. However, one of the more unusual features of L.B. & S.C.R. signalling was the provision of Workable 'Limit of Shunt' signals, as pictured above at Horsham in 1925. They were distinguished by the large 'L' on the face of the disc. Behind the signal is the slotting gear, (as the signal was operated by more than one signal box), of the 'Drop-Off' type.

The application of working 'Limit of Shunt' signals calls for some explanation. They were only to be found at locations where there were either two signal boxes, or a ground frame as well as a signal box. When one of the boxes or the ground frame was not manned, the limit of shunting movements was in the spot marked by such a signal. However, during the time the other box or ground frame was open, the limit could be extended under certain conditions as laid down in the special instructions for the place concerned. The disc signal could then be operated, the red face bearing the letter 'L' being turned parallel to the track, and no longer visible to drivers.

Photo. The late E. Wallis.

Plate 67.
'Brighton' mechanical repeater under the station canopy at East Grinstead (High Level). Note the full-size lamp spectacles.

Photo J. Scrace.

Plate 68.
Most railway signals are purely visual, but occasionally they take an audible form, such as with this L.B. & S.C.R. mechanical gong at Sheffield Park (Bluebell Railway). Gongs such as this are operated by a lever (painted green) in the signal box, and rung whenever it is necessary according to the local instructions. Often they are used to warn shunters of the approach of trains, or to advise them to clear the main line of standing vehicles in order that another train can pass.

Photo B. L. Jackson

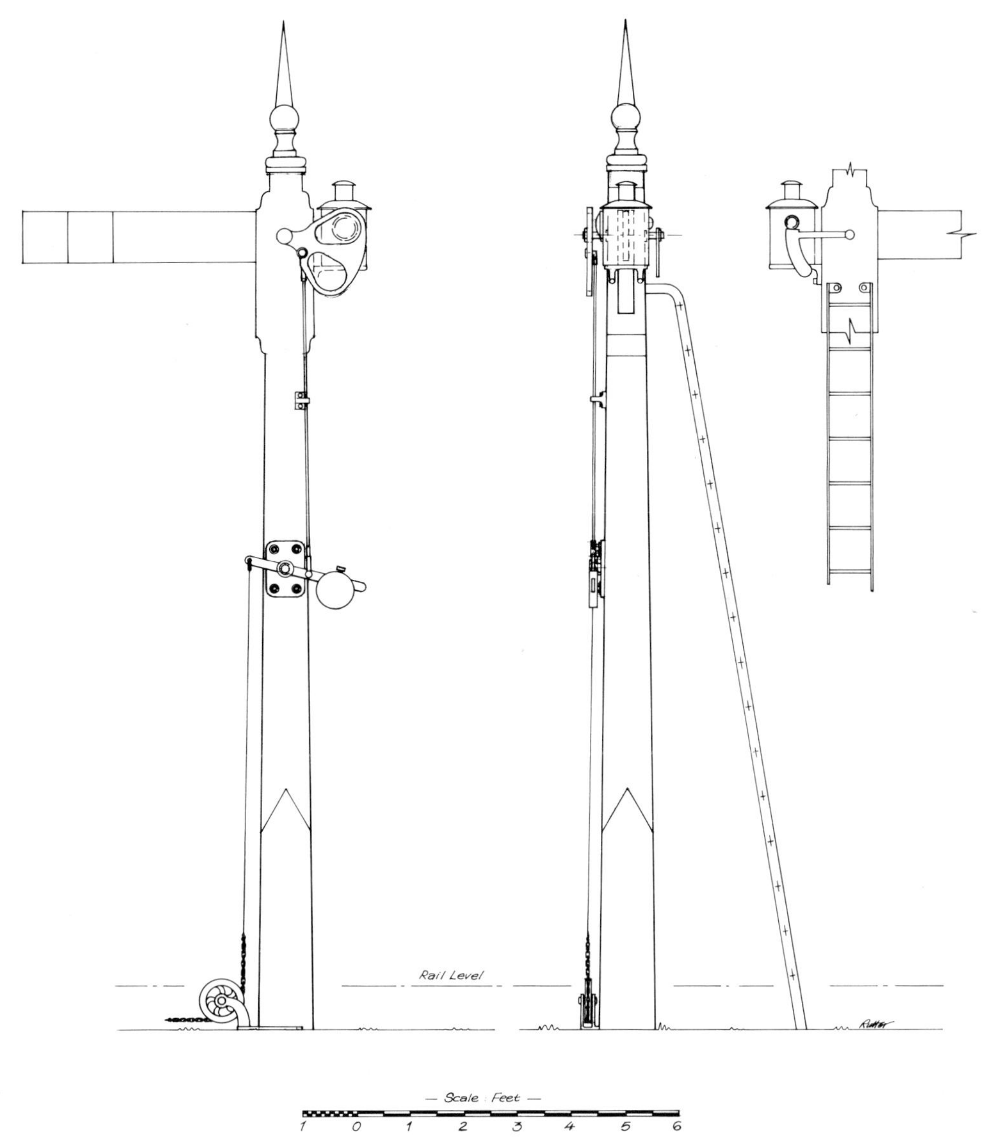

Fig. 14.

Front and side elevations of a McKenzie & Holland pattern 'Stop' signal, including small 'detail' drawing, (on right), showing rear fixing of ladder, and arrangement of lamp back-blinder. Signals of this type were used to a limited extent by all the Companies in the South of England, although none of them adopted them as standard.

Drawing P. D. Rutter.

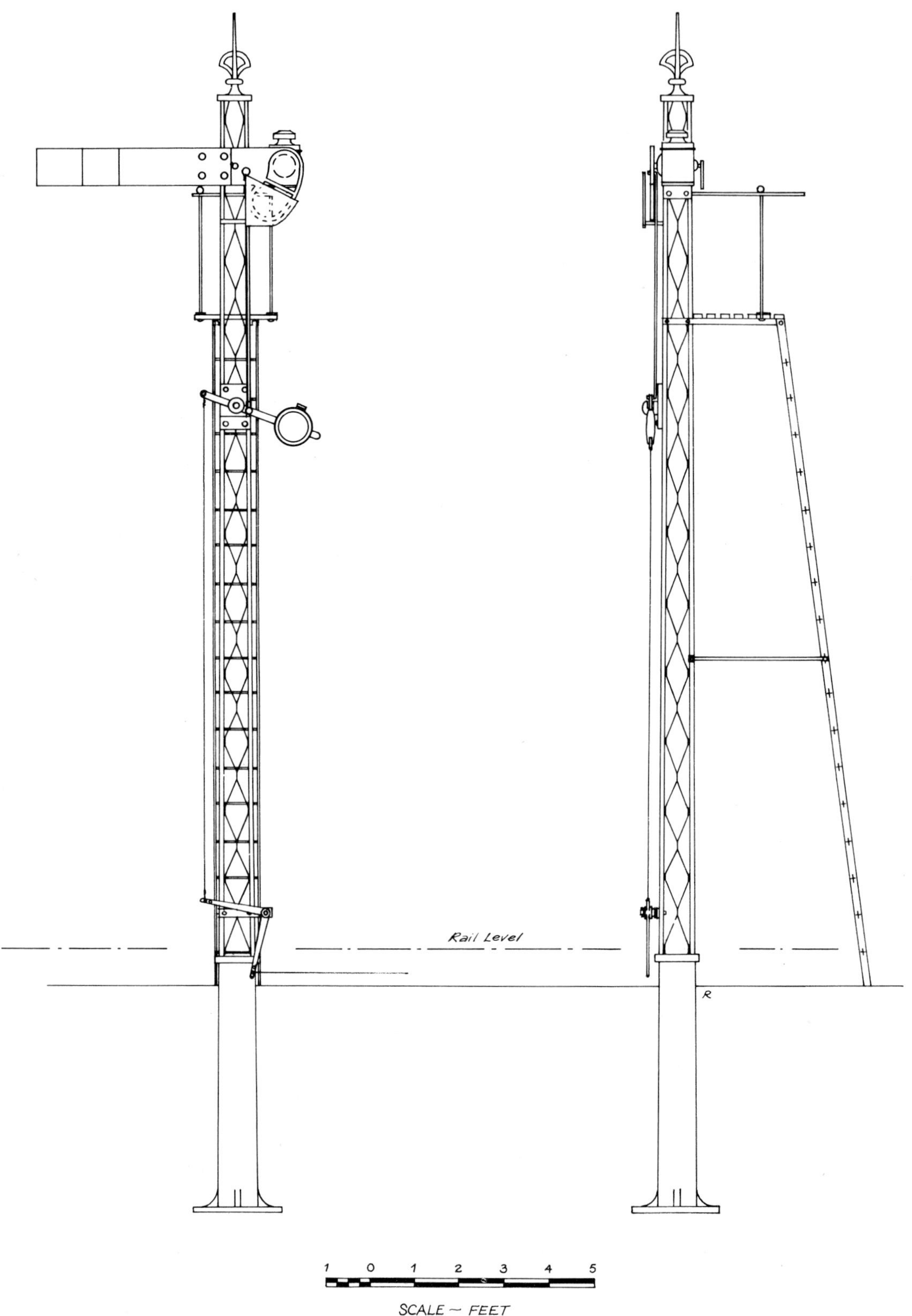

Fig. 15.
Scale drawing of a standard L. & S.W.R. lattice-post 'Stop' signal.
Drawing P. D. Rutter

Plate 69.
A survivor of the three-phase time interval days—the Up Distant for Mottisfont, on the now-closed line from Andover Junction to Romsey. In its original form, the arm would have been mounted in the slot to give three indications, the 'Clear' signal being given by the arm dropping out of sight within the slot. When this type of signalling was abandoned, the arm was re-mounted on the front of the post.

Photo G. Kinsey

Plate 70.
Platform starting signals of the McKenzie & Holland pattern at Portsmouth Harbour. The arms are pivoted, and work through, a slot in the posts. The two miniature-arm shunting signals are not of McKenzie & Holland design, and are a later addition.

Photo Lens of Sutton.

Plate 71.
Once the era of slotted posts was over, the South Western mainly used steel lattice posts in signal construction. However, wood was used occasionally, as pictured here in the Down Starting signal at Stockbridge.

Photo G. Kinsey.

Plate 72.
Another example of an L. & S.W.R. wooden-post signal, the Up Distant at Mortehoe and Woolacombe, on the steeply-graded line from Barnstaple to Ilfracombe. This signal has a pressed steel arm.

Photo J. Scrace

Plate 73.
L. & S.W.R. concrete-post signal, forming the Down Advanced starter at Mortehoe & Woolacombe. As on the other 'Southern' lines, concrete was never greatly used for signal posts by the 'South Western'. Their design differed from that found on other lines in that the post was solid and not pierced at intervals to reduce weight.

Photo J. Scrace

Plate 74.

L. & S.W.R. wooden recessed bracket signal at Cosham. The Distant arm on the bracket doll is the original, pivoted in a slot in the post, whilst the two main arms show the more modern method of 'outside' mounting.

The 'Stop' signal is worked by Cosham Station Box as an Advanced 'Starting' signal, the distant arms being controlled by Cosham Junction. Note the slotting counterweights on the main post, which prevent either of the distant signals operating until the 'Stop' signal is pulled. The distant on the bracket applies to the spur to Farlington Junction, (avoiding Portsmouth), whilst the distant beneath the 'Stop' arm applies to the Portsmouth line.

Photo Lens of Sutton.

Plate 75.

Lattice signals were the type most favoured by the L. & S.W.R. This example—the Up Main Home Signals at Eastleigh West—is complete with L. & S.W.R. arms, and demonstrates that Company's love of lofty signals with lower co-acting arms. The signals at 'Clear' are for the Up Through line, with Eastleigh East Up Through Distant. Next to them comes Eastleigh East Up Distant for trains taking the Romsey line, then, nearest to the camera, two arms of equal height, one reading to the Up Local line, and the other to the Salisbury Loop Platform. Small lower co-acting arms are provided to repeat all the 'Stop' signals, though the distant arms are not reproduced. The arm with the letter 'S' attached applies to the Salisbury loop, and is used to signal a train into that line when it is already partially occupied.

Photo J. H. Aston.

Plate 76.
A favourite form of signal on the L. & S.W.R. was the lofty lower quadrant with co-acting arm. This photograph shows such an arrangement in use as a platform starter.
Photo courtesy National Railway Museum.

Plate 77.
Close-up study of a L. & S.W.R. concrete post signal at Surbiton. Note the 'Rule 55' sign attached to the post just beneath the arm.
Photo courtesy National Railway Museum.

Plate 78 *(above).*
L. & S.W.R. platform Starting Signals at Exmouth. The arms read, (left to right), Platform 1 to Exeter, Platform 1 to Littleham, Platform 2 to Exeter, and Platform 2 to Littleham. Over in the goods yard can be seen the Up Goods Starting Signal, fitted with a 3 foot upper quadrant arm, with a disc on the post reading to the shunting spur.
Photo Lens of Sutton.

Plate 79 *(left).*
Stevens' 'Pillar' or 'Flap' shunting signal, once a common sight on the L. & S.W.R. The flap was painted red, and dropped forward when pulled to show a green face. This specimen was photographed at Sunbury in 1952, and must have been one of the last survivors.
Photo D. B. Clayton.

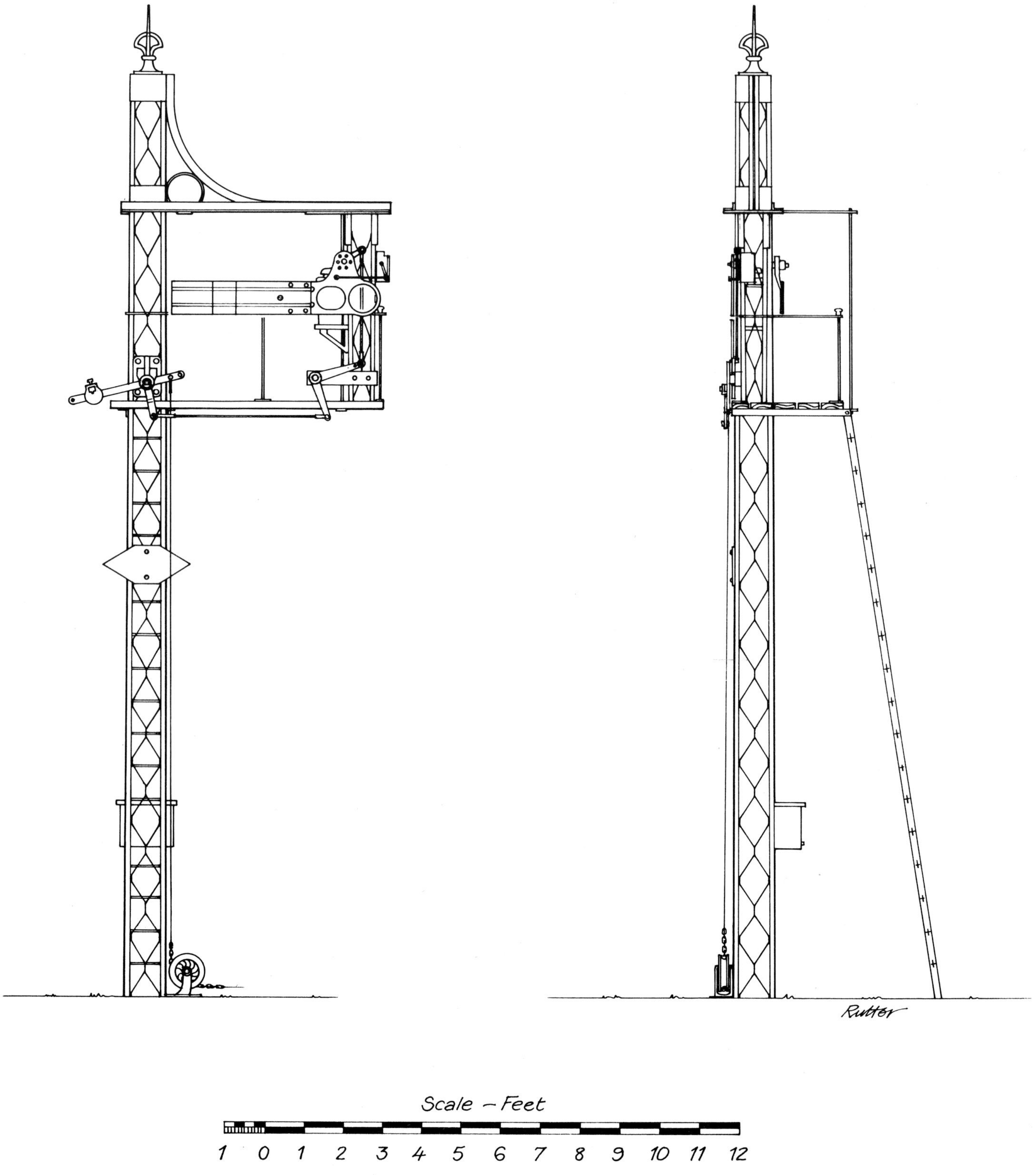

Rutter

Fig. 16.
Scale drawing of L. & S.W.R. lattice 'Suspended Doll' type signal, fitted with S.R. upper quadrant arms and 'Rule 55' diamond. Drawing based on the Home Signal at Swanwick, on the Southampton to Portsmouth line.

Drawing P. D. Rutter.

Plate 80 *(right).*
One of the pair of lattice-post 'gallows' type junction signals that once graced the platform ends at Broadstone, Dorset. This one is the Up Main, (from Hamworthy Junction) Starting, the higher arm routing trains to the main line to Brockenhurst, (via Wimborne), and the lower arm, to the former 'Somerset & Dorset'.

Photo G. Kinsey

Plate 81 *(left).*
The Up Home Signals at Evercreech Junction North, an example of signal construction using a single bull-head rail as the main post. The arms applied as follows:
Top Left—To Highbridge Line.
Top Right—To Bath, (Main), line.
Ringed Arm—To Shunt Ahead onto Highbridge Line.
The ground disc to the right of the signal applies to movements from the marshalling sidings.

Photo A. Vaughan

Plate 82.
Elevated ground signal, Westinghouse pattern, mounted on a short lattice post, on the Up platform at Andover. The white diamond painted on the red bar has the same application as the enamel diamond signs on running signals. Following S.R. practice, this single disc once operated for five routes.

Photo J. P. Morris.

Plate 83.
Stevens' 'Bow-tie' wrong-road signal at Evercreech Junction North. Although this is situated on the Somerset & Dorset line the L. & S.W.R. carried out much of the signalling on it, and many signals of this type were once in use throughout the 'South Western' system. The post of this signal consists of a single bull-head rail—a form of construction confined to the S. & D. line, as the S.R. rail-built signals of later years always consisted of two such rails, or four in the case of brackets and gantries. This signal was used to control movements backing from the Down Line to the Up Line.

Photo A. Vaughan.

Investment statement

Value of your investments at 31 December 2021

Name of fund	Number of shares/units	Share/unit price (p)	Value £
OEIC/Unit Trust			
Janus Henderson Global Equity Income Fund E Inc (OEIC)	1,192.42	67.12	800.35
	OEIC/UT Total		**800.35**

Record of income

Name of fund	Pay date	Type of income/ investment	Payment method	Amount £
OEIC/Unit Trust				
Janus Henderson Global Equity Income Fund E Inc (OEIC)				
	30 Jul 21	Distribution	BACS	10.23
	29 Oct 21	Distribution	BACS	5.50

A quick guide to your statement

Acc: Shown in brackets after the name of your fund and stands for accumulation. This tells you that the type of shares/units that you own do not pay out income distributions, any income remains within the fund and is reflected in the share/unit price.

Inc: Shown in brackets after the name of your fund and stands for income. This tells you that the type of shares/units that you own can pay out income distributions to you or have income reinvested.

Sale: Shares/units that you have bought from us.

Repurchase: Shares/units that you have sold back to us.

RSF contribution: Shares/units that you have bought from us via a regular savings plan.

Stock transfer in/out: Shares/units that have been moved between investors into or out of your account.

Summary of investment statement

Account name:	Mr Rodney J White
Account number:	0000775856
Statement for the period:	31 December 2021

Total value of investments at 31 December 2021	**£800.35**
Total value of investments at 30 June 2021	£764.70
Investments made in the period (less withdrawals)	£0.00
Total income generated in the period	£15.73

What's included in this statement?

- Information on the value of your investments
- A record of income/interest distributions generated by your investments during the statement period
- Contact information

Please note:
The value of your investments has been calculated at the last working day within the statement period. Your investments are valued at the price at which your investments could have been sold at that time. All performance and share/unit price information on the fund commentary pages is based on and in reference to the retail share/unit class of the fund in UK sterling.

All performance data includes both income and capital gains or losses and reflects the deduction of any ongoing charges or other fund expenses. There may be differences among portfolio securities, share class currencies and your home currency that will expose you to currency risk. The value of an investment and the income from it can fall as well as rise and you may not get back the amount originally invested. If you have any doubts over the suitability of an investment please contact a financial adviser. Nothing in this document is intended to or should be construed as advice.

Plate 84 *(left).*
Fast disappearing from the world of signalling is the 'Splitting Distant', provided to give advance warning of a diverging route ahead. In modern practice, only one arm is provided, being worked for the route with the least speed restriction through the junction. Trains passing onto the more restricted route treat it as a 'Fixed' distant. This signal, Romsey Up Distants, indicates that the line is clear towards Redbridge, the other arm applying to the Eastleigh line.
Photo J. P. Morris.

Plate 85 *(right).*
The tall Up Starting Signal at Totton, with lower Distant arm for Redbridge. Like the 'Splitting Distant' in the previous plate, the main structure is of L. & S.W.R. vintage, fitted with S.R. upper quadrant arms and fittings. Note the short co-acting arm bracketed out from the main post, the arm being reduced in length to avoid fouling the brickwork of the adjacent footbridge. The Distant for Redbridge is worked electrically, hence the absence of mechanical slotting.

Photo J. P. Morris.

Plate 86 *(right).*
Another example of an old L. & S.W.R. gantry fitted with upper quadrant arms—the Down Home Signals at Totton. The highest arm, ('off'), is for the line to Bournemouth, next to which is the signal controlling access to the Fawley Branch. The short, (3-foot), arm signals trains into the goods yard, and is slotted by a ground lever worked by the shunter to prevent a train being sent into the sidings when a conflicting shunt move is taking place.

Photo J. P. Morris.

Plate 87 *(left).*
Early Southern Railway ground signal of the miniature-arm type. A product of the Westinghouse Brake & Signal Co., they were readily convertible to the familiar disc signals which have long been standard on the S.R. However, signals of this type were still being used in the late 1950s for yellow shunting signals only, although even these have now mostly been replaced by discs.

Photo B. L. Jackson

Plate 88.

Close-up study of the Up starting signals at Christchurch, a further example of an L. & S.W.R. structure fitted with S.R. upper quadrants. Note that the ringed arm (leading to the goods yard), is corrugated, and the main arm flat, a feature that appears in several photographs. The corrugation was intended to give strength and rigidity to the arm, but this was later achieved by turning back the edges of the arm, giving the front a flat appearance.

Photo E. J. White.

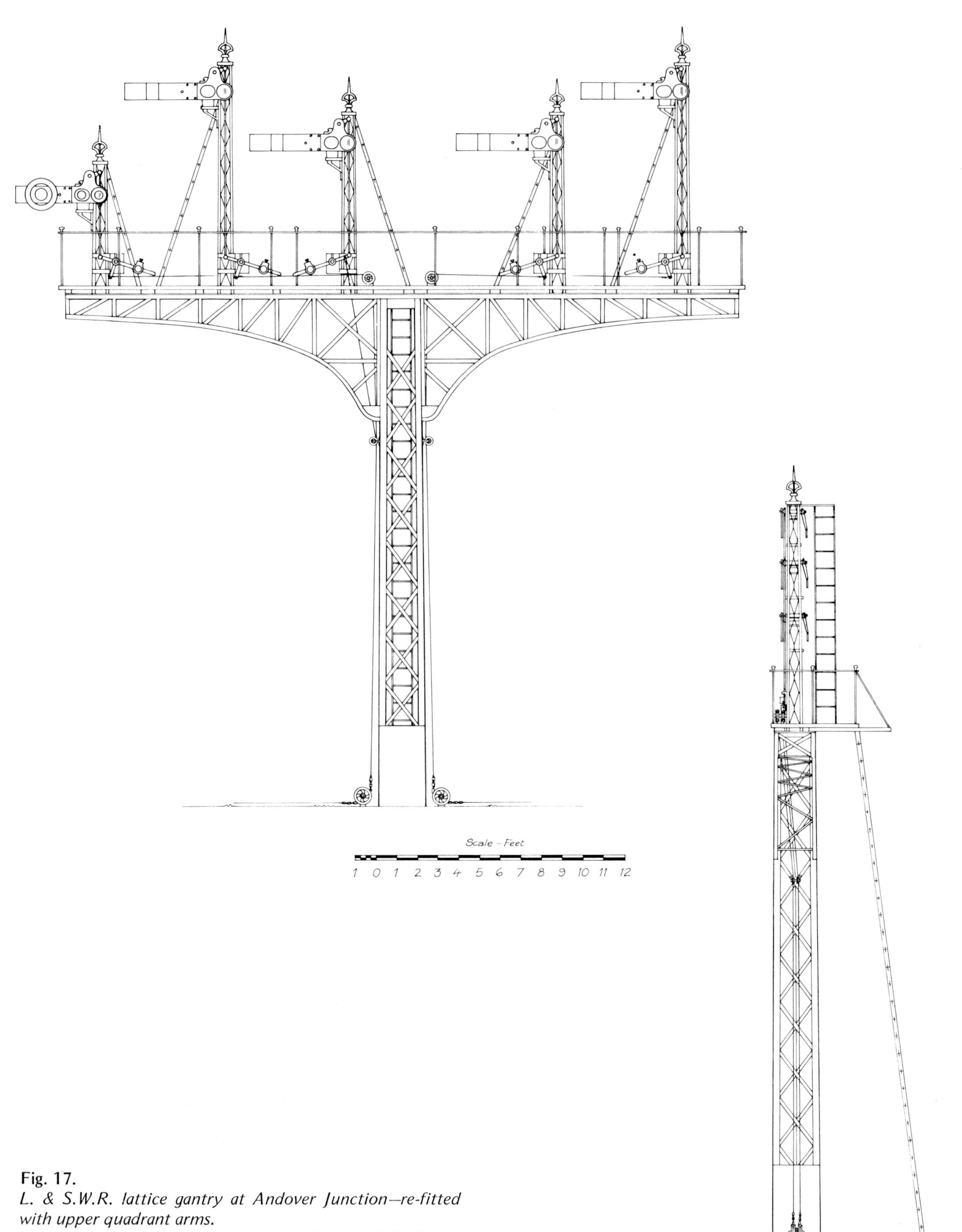

Fig. 17.
L. & S.W.R. lattice gantry at Andover Junction—re-fitted with upper quadrant arms.

Drawing P. D. Rutter

Plate 89 *(left).*
Lattice right-hand bracket gantry, forming the Down Main Inner Home Signals at Barnstaple Junction 'A'. The arm on the right applies to the Down Main, and that on the left to the loop platform. This configuration is slightly unusual for an ex-L. & S.W.R. signal, as that Company generally either bracketed out both dolls, or positioned them on either side of the main post.
Photo A. Vaughan.

Plate 90 *(right).*
The Up Starting Signals at Plymstock were of very unusual construction. The main post was made up of two sections of channel-iron bolted together, the inner one being curved out at the top to form a support for the bracket. The dolls, of equal height, are the usual lattice type.
Photo Lens of Sutton.

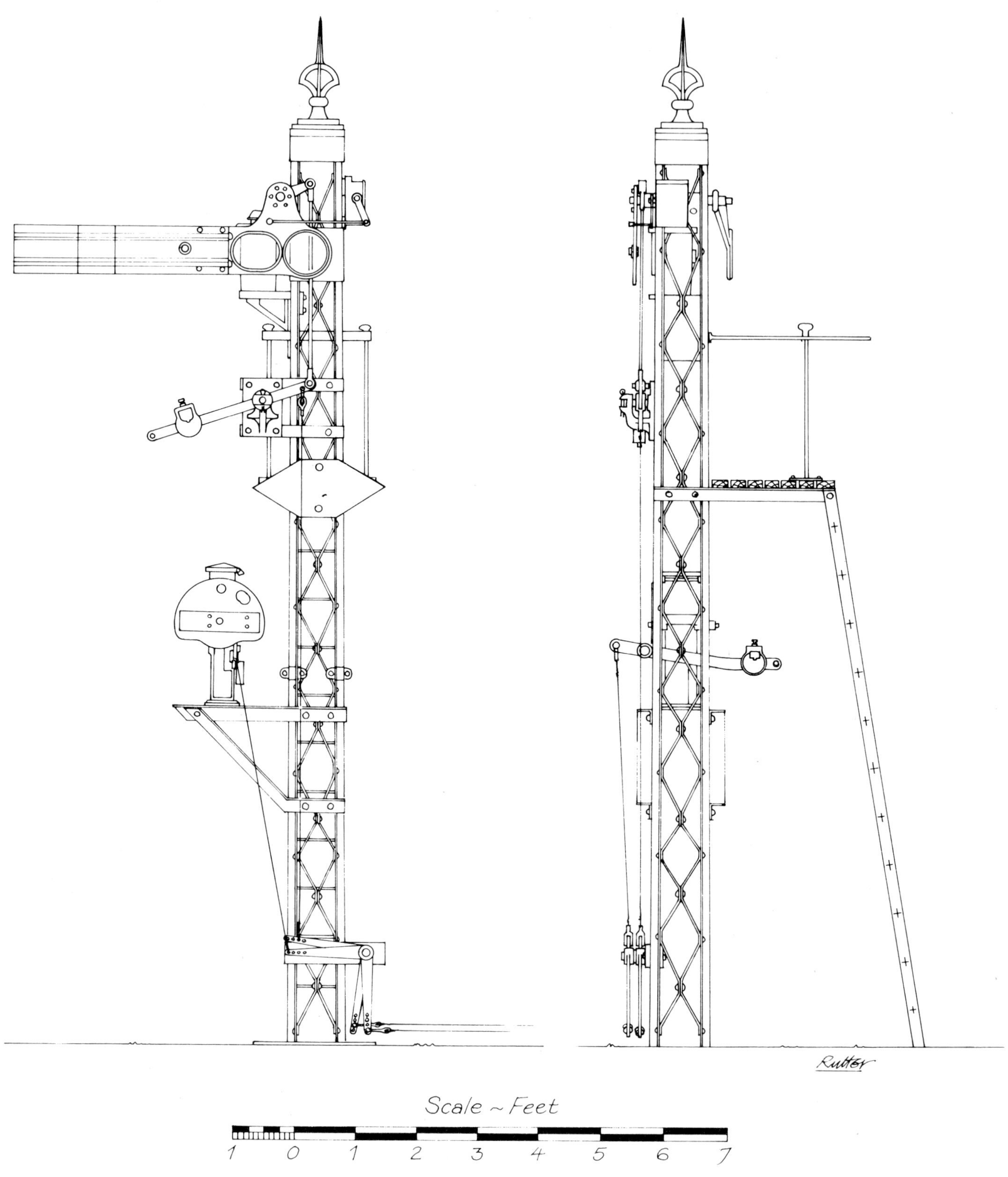

Fig. 18.
Scale drawing of ex L. & S.W.R. lattice signal fitted with S.R. corrugated upper quadrant arm. A Westinghouse shunt disc is attached to the post.

Drawing P. D. Rutter.

Plate 91.

An exercise in signal economy widely used on the L. & S.W.R. is illustrated by this view of Boscarne Junction, showing the Up Home and Down Starting Signals mounted on the same post. In the foreground is a typical 'South Western' ground frame building of the 'lean-to' type.

Photo C. L. Caddy

Plate 92.

Some signal arms were located in pretty cramped places like this one, suspended from the canopy of Redhill Station. When pulled to the 'off' position, the arm almost strikes the roof!

Photo B. L. Jackson.

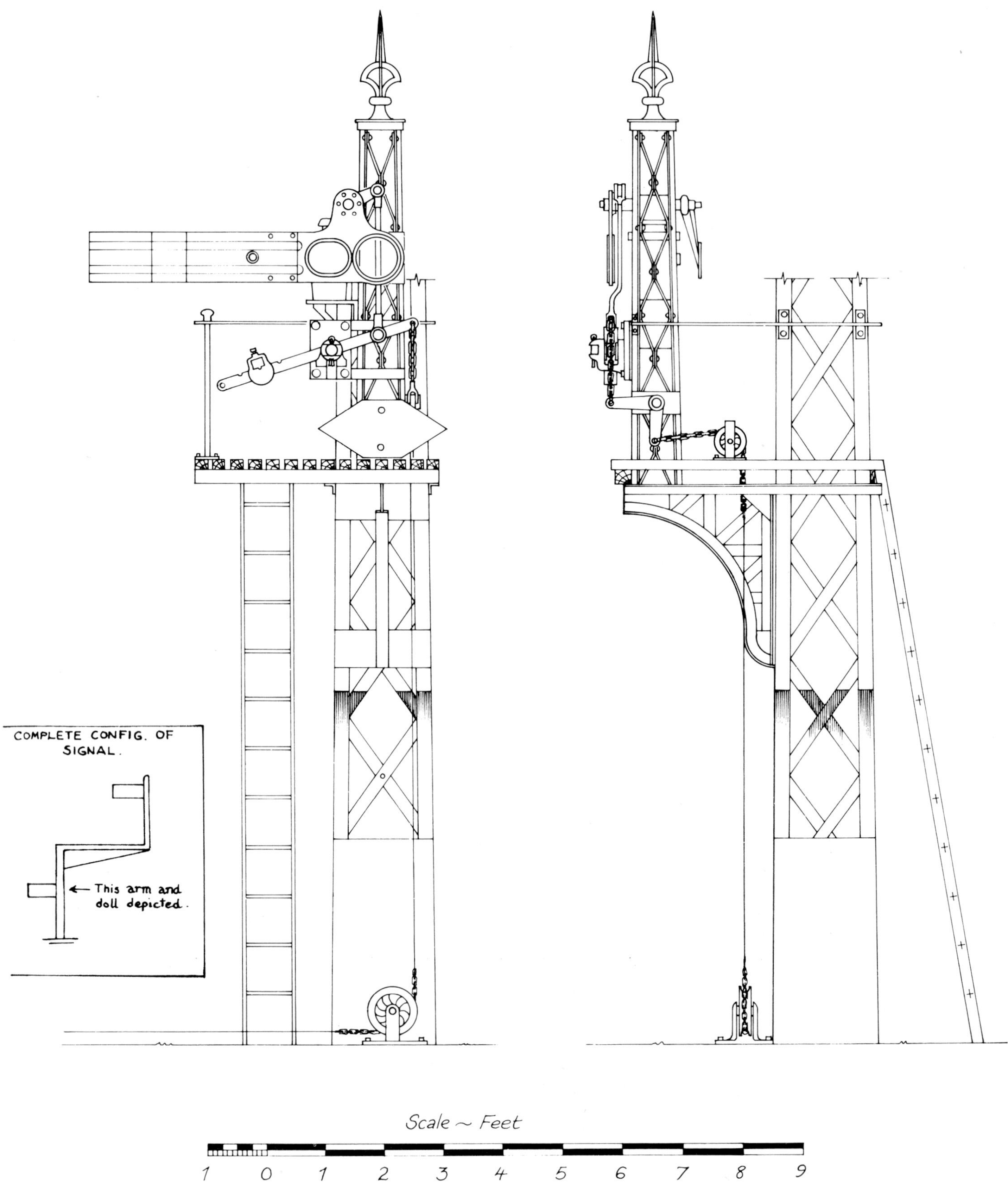

Fig. 19.
Andover Junction 'A' Up Local Home—an example of a lattice forward mounted doll.
Drawing P. D. Rutter

Plate 93 *(right.)*
Once a common sight at the end of many an L. & S.W.R. platform were these tall lattice signals with lower co-acting arms. This one, the Up Starting Signal at Bookham, has been fitted with S.R. upper quadrant arms, but still remains an attractive structure. The Down Home Signal can be seen in the background, and demonstrates the opposite extreme in L. & S.W.R. signals — the very short variety. See plate 76 for these signals in their original form.

Photo J. Scrace.

Plate 94.
It was not always possible to use tall signals with co-acting arms as a means of overcoming siting difficulties. Another way of repeating the position of the main signal was the use of miniature arms, worked mechanically from the signal lever. This view shows a mechanical repeater of L. & S.W.R. pattern, suspended from the station canopy at Southfields. Because of the small size of these repeating arms, they were mounted against a large white board to increase visibility. This type has now vanished from the scene, generally being replaced by Sykes electrical 'Banner' repeaters or illuminated 'Off' indicators.

Photo J. Scrace.

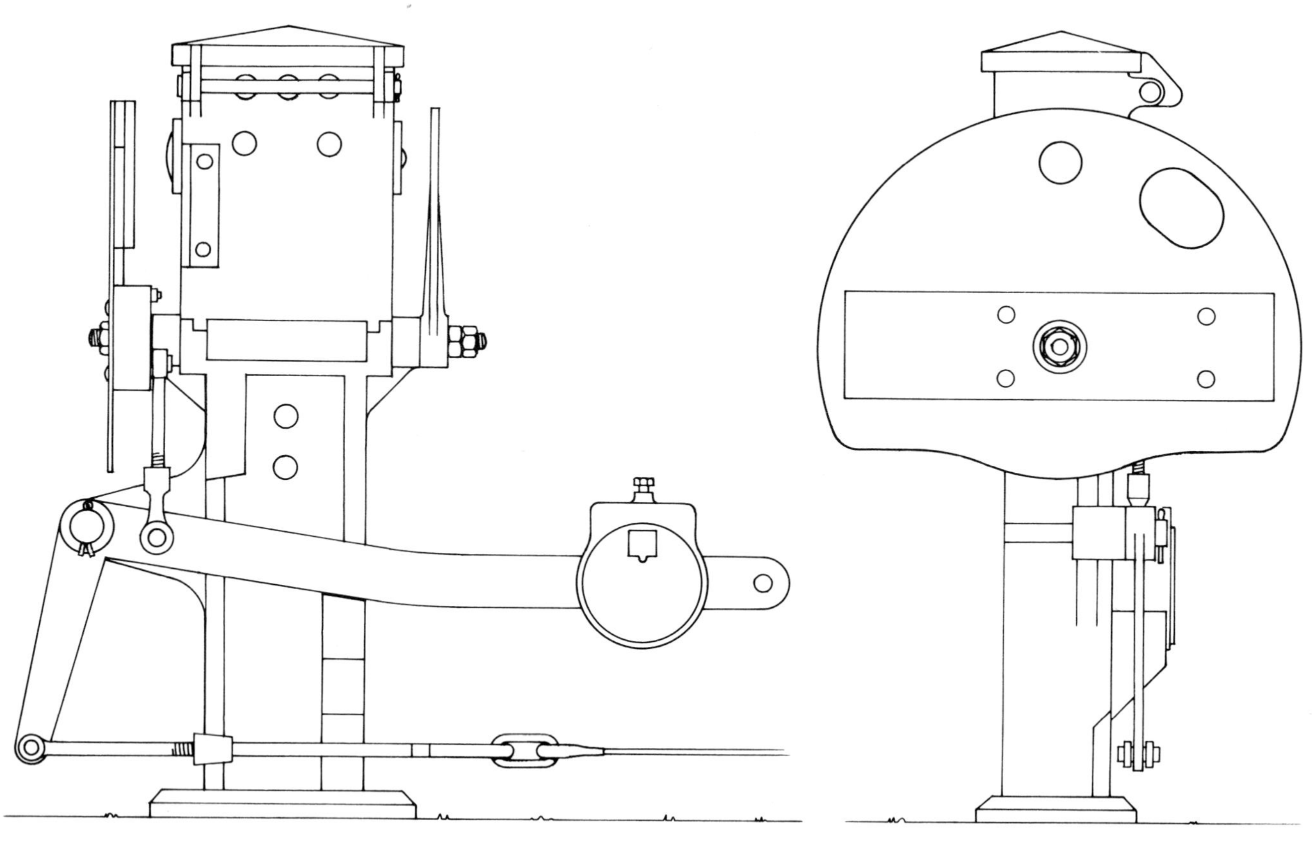

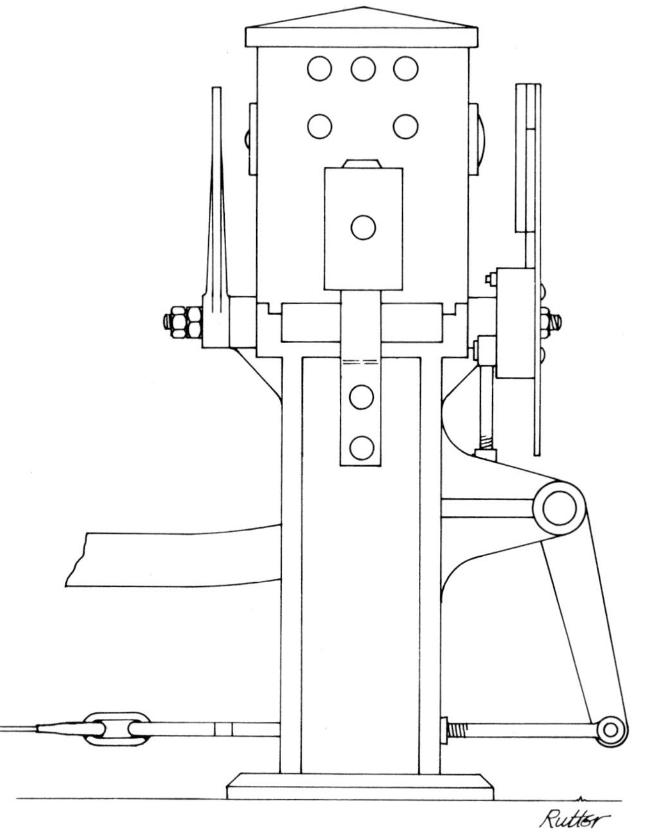

Fig. 20.
Scale drawing of the Westinghouse Brake & Signal Co's ground disc signal, the type which became standard on the Southern Railway. The main 'body' is the same as with the miniature arm pattern, (illustrated in plate 88), but with the target attached in place of the arm.
Drawings by P. D. Rutter.

SOUTHERN RAILWAY 'RAIL-BUILT' SIGNALS

By the early 1930s, the railways of Britain were feeling the need for economy as the result of increased competition from road transport. Some companies sought to achieve this simply by reducing train services, but this could not readily be done on the Southern, a large part of whose system served the thickly-populated 'Commuter Belt', where a frequent service was always in demand. The Southern therefore had to explore other means of saving money, and this they achieved in three ways. First, and most important, was the decision to extend third-rail electrification, this form of traction being very economic where an intensive service was needed. Another saving was made by the extensive use of concrete, a large concrete works being established at Exmouth Junction, (Exeter), to supply everything from fence posts to sectional station footbridges and line-side Permanent Way Department mess and tool huts. Concrete was never used to a great extent for signal posts on the Southern.

The Company hit upon a rather novel idea for the cheap construction of signals—the use of scrap bull-head rail. This has always been the subject of ridicule from lovers of other railways, and to be fair to them, signals made of scrap rail do sound hideous! However, in practice the results were quite attractive, as the following illustrations will show. Whatever one's feelings about such seemingly penny-pinching methods of construction, it must be said that signals of this type were cheap to construct, and very durable, as rails long worn out for their original purpose could give many years of service as signal posts. The idea was so successful, that the Southern Region of British Railways perpetuated it until very recent times when the tubular steel post, as used on the Western and Midland Regions, was adopted as standard for the few semaphore signals still being erected.

Plate 95.
A typical SR short-post 'rail-built' signal, at Brading, Isle of Wight. The vintage train is the 12.05 from Ryde Pier Head to Ventnor, hauled by locomotive No. 24 Calbourne.

Photo C. L. Caddy

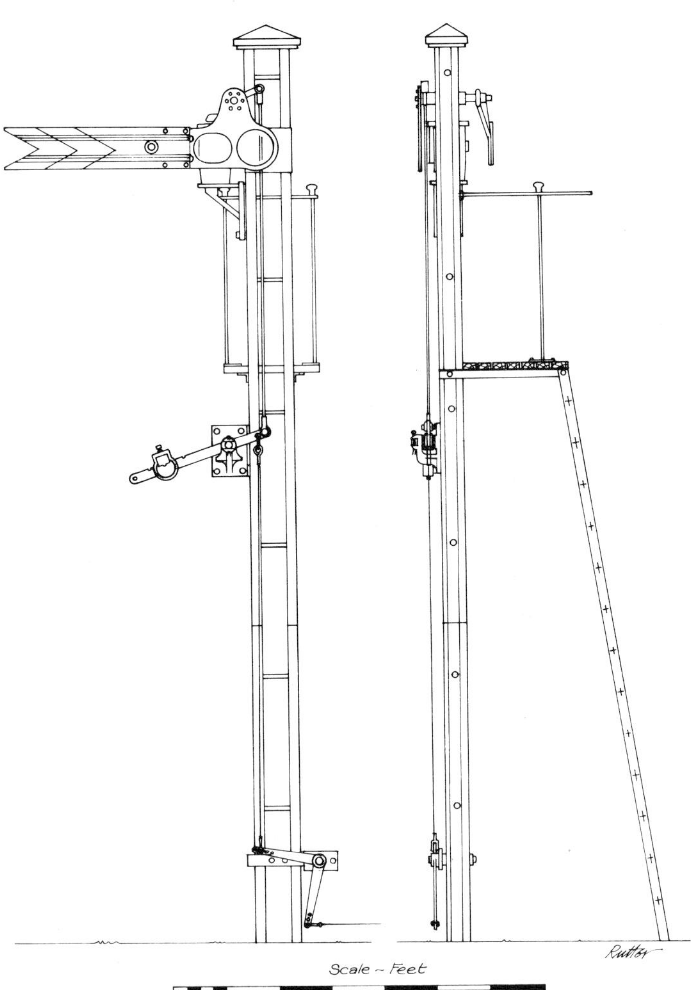

Fig. 21 *(left).*
Scale drawing of standard Southern Railway two-rail signal, with corrugated Distant arm. Straight-post signals such as this were always made of two bull-head rails bolted together, whilst gantries, brackets, and junction signals used four rails to carry the additional weight.

Drawing P. D. Rutter.

Plate 96.
Southern Railway version of the 'Gallows', or suspended doll type bracket signal, on the through line at Exeter Central. The main post is made up of four bull-head rails bolted together, but the doll is of steel lattice construction. Immediately beneath the arm is a 'Rule 55' diamond sign, indicating to the Driver that this section of line is track-circuited and the presence of his train is therefore indicated in the signal box.

Photo B. L. Jackson.

Plate 97.
Southern Railway left-hand bracket signal at Peckham Rye 'A', showing Home Signal, and Distant for 'B' box in 'Off' position. Below is a 'Shunt-ahead' arm, (bearing the letter 'S'), for authorising a movement to pass this signal in order to clear a set of points ahead for shunting purposes only. A typical S.R. Westinghouse pattern ground disc signal can be seen at the foot of the post. Behind the signal is the old 'Brighton' Signal Box, not unlike the one at Bedhampton, scale drawings of which appear on page 115.
Photo D. B. Clayton.

Plate 98.
Rail-built right-hand bracket signal forming the Up Advanced Starter at Weymouth. Although erected by the Southern Region as recently as 1958, the design is identical in every detail to that used by the Southern Railway. Note that, although the main post is made of rails, the doll is of lattice—a standard feature of these signals—as the use of rails on bracket signals would increase the weight and require too much support. In the foreground is an elevated ground signal, mounted on a post of standard two-rail construction.
Photo B. L. Jackson.

Plate 99 *(above).*
Rail-built gantry, forming the Starting Signals from platforms 5, (left-hand arm), and 6, (right-hand arm), at Weymouth. The discs apply to shunting movements out of these platforms. As with the previous photograph, these signals were erected as recently as 1957, but closely follow Southern Railway practice. In this case also, the signal dolls are of lattice construction.
Photo J. P. Morris

Plate 100 *(right).*
Straight post rail-built signal, medium height, with 'Approach Lights' for entering an area signalled by colour lights. This is the Salisbury West Down Advanced Starter, (note the low pressure air cylinder on post), the Approach Lights applying to the new signalling at Wilton. Aspects displayed by such signals are as follows.
Semaphore arm at Danger, (as in picture)—no light displayed in lower colour-light signals, but red light in semaphore arm exhibited.
Semaphore arm 'Off'—Green light in arm blanked out. Lower colour-light signals will show Yellow if next signal is at Red, or Green if signal ahead is at yellow or green.
Photo G. F. Gillham.

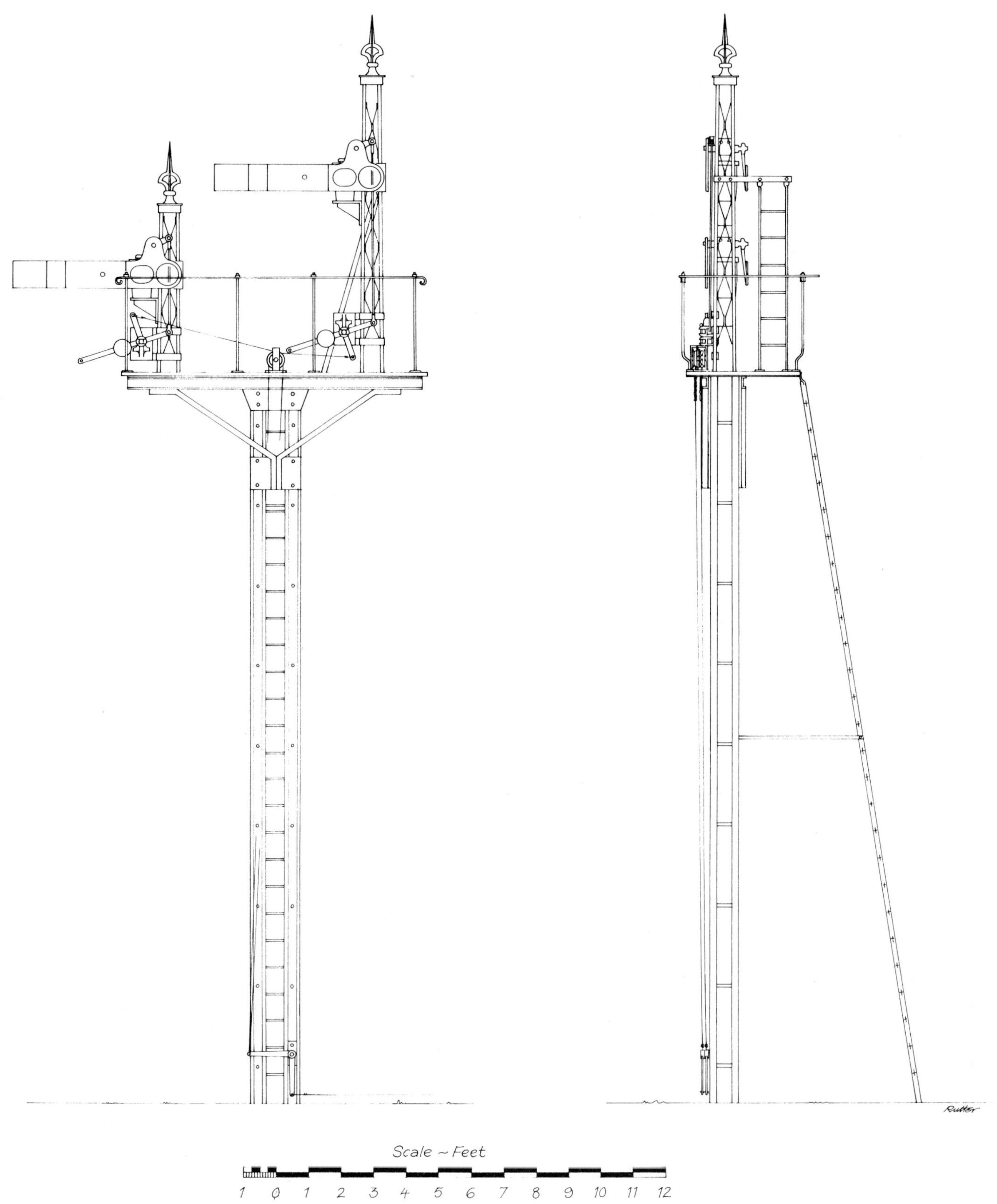

Fig. 22.
Scale drawing of Southern Railway 'rail-built' junction signal with post made of four bull-head rails. Modelled on Down Home Signal, Worgret Junction.

Drawing P. D. Rutter

Plate 101.
'All clear up the through line' at Redhill 'A' box, with distant for Holmthorpe also in the 'Clear' position. Two good examples of rail-built right and left-hand brackets, with the usual lattice dolls. The signals read (left to right), From Up Loop Starting, From Up Local Starting, and Up Through Starting and Distant for Holmthorpe.

Photo B. L. Jackson.

Plate 102.
Signals are sometimes erected several weeks before actually coming into use, and to denote the fact that they are not to be obeyed, a wooden 'X' is fixed to the arm. This view shows the new Down Outer Home at Weymouth in 1956, in position for the opening of the new signal box the following year.

Photo J. D. Blackburn.

Plate 103.
Rail-built left-hand bracket gantry at Waddon Marsh. The centre arm applies to the main (single) line, and the two 3-foot arms control access to sidings on each side of it. The use of four bull-head rails for the main supporting post makes the structure extremely strong and rigid.

Photo E. J. White.

ROUTE INDICATORS

Plate 104.

Shows the mechanical route indicators as used by most of the Companies that made up the S.R. This view is of the Platform Starters at Redhill 'B', showing one signal 'On', with a blank indicator, and the other 'Off', exhibiting the letter 'T', for the line to Tonbridge. Route indicators may only be used at locations where the speed of trains is always low, such as at the entrance to goods yards, and at the end of terminal station platforms, as their visibility from a fast train would be very poor. Where they are used, however, they bring about a great economy in the number of signal arms required, as one arm linked with a route indicator can often do the work of six or more arms without one.

Photo B. L. Jackson

Plate 105.
S.R. electrical route indicator, working in conjunction with an elevated ground signal, at Weymouth. The signal is 'Off', and the route set to number 3 platform. When the signal is 'On', a black ball is displayed in the window of the indicator. With this pattern, the route proving is carried out electrically, a short-handled lever being provided for each indication, one of which must be reversed before the signal can be operated. In the event of the signal clearing, but no route appearing in the indicator, the repeater in the signal box will show 'wrong'.

Photo B. L. Jackson.

Plate 106.
'Theatre' type illuminated route indicator, showing 'T' for Through Line, at Brighton. The three-aspect colour-light signals are of the Southern Railway pattern, with small side aspects, known to railwaymen as 'pigs' ears'. These are very useful when multiple unit trains are operated, as the driving cab can be pulled up very close to the signal, its indications being observed through the side aspects.

Photo B. L. Jackson.

'BANNER REPEATERS'

As already stated, obstructions frequently restrict the visibility of signals to such an extent that it becomes necessary to repeat the arms. On the SR, the Sykes' electrical 'Banner' signal was adopted as standard for this purpose. These consist of a glass-fronted case, inside which a black arm, pivoted in the centre, turns against a white background. At night the signals are illuminated from behind, so that the arms are shown in silhouette. Where a 'Distant' arm is repeated, the repeater arm is fishtailed in the same way as the signal.

Plate 107.
Shows a pair of Banner repeaters at Millbrook. The signal itself is on the 'blind side' of the concrete footbridge, hence the need to reproduce its indications.

Photo E. J. White.

Plate 108.
Shows the smaller pattern for repeating the platform starting signal at Eastbourne. As this is a terminal station, and all trains therefore have a standing start from the platforms, speed is always low, rendering the use of full-size 'banners' unnecessary. In this case, the lamp standards, name-board, and other impedimenta on the platform, coupled with the curvature of the line, make viewing of the signals difficult.

Photo B. L. Jackson.

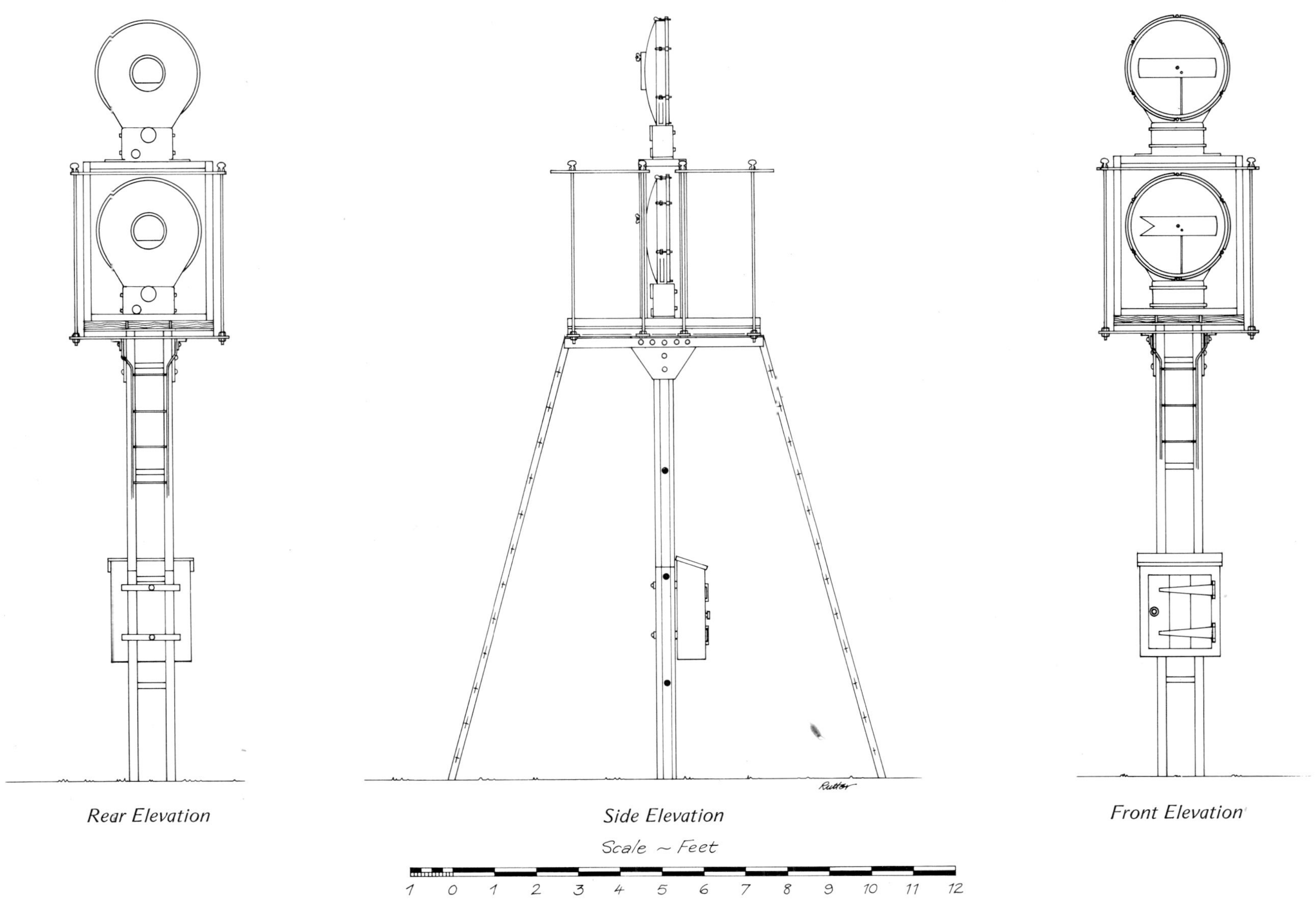

Fig. 23.
Scale drawing of a pair of 'Sykes' electrically operated 'Banner Repeater' signals, mounted on twin bull-head rails. These signals give the same indication by day and night, being illuminated from behind by electric lamps to show the black arms in silhouette. This one has repeater arms for a stop signal with lower distant arm, and is modelled on the 'Up Starting Signal' repeater at Redbridge.

Drawing P. D. Rutter

6. Signal Boxes

The lines of Southern England possess a greater variety of signal box design than any other area, and it is therefore impossible in a book of this size to illustrate more than a few examples. Some of the 'standard' designs of each company are shown, as well as some of the more unusual, but to really do the subject justice, it would be necessary to cover practically every box individually.

Why, one might ask, is there such a variety in the South, when large concerns such as the L.M.S. and G.W.R. managed on a handful of basic designs? There are a number of reasons for this. First, it must be remembered that the area was originally operated by four separate companies, each with their own ideas on signal box architecture. Their designs were modified with the passing of the years, so that each Company had at least three designs which could virtually be described as 'standard'.

A secondary reason stems from the love of economy—a passion shared by all the lines in the South. From this sprang unusual boxes like that at Dunbridge, (see plate 114), which was not constructed as a signal box at all, but converted into one from a crossing-keeper's cottage. It also gave rise to boxes being extended rather than re-built when alterations were made to a track layout. These extensions, though often quite small, had the effect of turning a perfectly 'standard' box into something quite unique in many cases.

Add to all this the various designs introduced by the Southern Railway, which ranged from those based on pre-grouping practice, to the 'Streamlined', and it is obvious that the variety is tremendous!

In the pages that follow, I have tried to give a fair sample of the boxes to be found throughout the Southern system. The 'South Western' has perhaps more than its fair share of the available space, but then that Company possessed a greater variety of designs than any other. Like the other Railways, they had 'standards', but they succeeded in playing an almost endless set of variations on their main theme.

Plate 109.
Bournemouth West Junction box, unfortunately minus its nameboard. This box was opened in March 1888, as part of the large scheme which opened up the Bournemouth Direct line, (via Sway), and the link line between Bournemouth East and Bournemouth West. The design, with wooden roof vent and railed cat-walk around the outside of the windows, (the panes of which are the small square shape associated with early L. & S.W.R. boxes), is typical of 'South Western' structures of the period.

Photo G. Kinsey.

Plate 110.
The very Victorian design of Milford Goods, Salisbury. The date of construction is unknown, but it was almost certainly the oldest South Western box to survive into recent years. It was originally called Milford Junction and obviously goes back to the time when Milford was the passenger terminus in the city. It contained a 28-lever Stevens frame, much of which was spare in latter years. The box was closed in December 1969.
Photo G. F. Gillham.

Plate 111.
Another early pattern of L. & S.W.R. box, although not so antique as that at Milford. Again, the date of building is unknown. This box was fitted with a 15-lever Stevens frame, and lasted until 22nd May, 1969.
Photo G. F. Gillham.

Plate 112.
The lofty L. & S.W.R. box at Yeoford, Devon. The timber upper storey is of the standard design used by the Company pre-1880, but it is elevated to a considerable height on a tower-like base of local stone, in order to furnish the Signalman with a reasonable view of the track layout under his control. The line at this point is on a long right-hand curve, and is crossed at a point near the signal box by a road over-bridge, and a structure of the usual height would have had a very restricted outlook. This box was abolished on 18th August, 1968, and demolished soon afterwards.
Photo D. J. W. Brough.

Plate 113.
'South Western' signal box in brick and timber at Liphook. It contained a 20-lever frame, and was taken out of use on 16th February, 1975, when this section of the Portsmouth Direct line was re-signalled with colour lights. A scale drawing of this box appears in Fig. 24, opposite.
Photo G. Bowring.

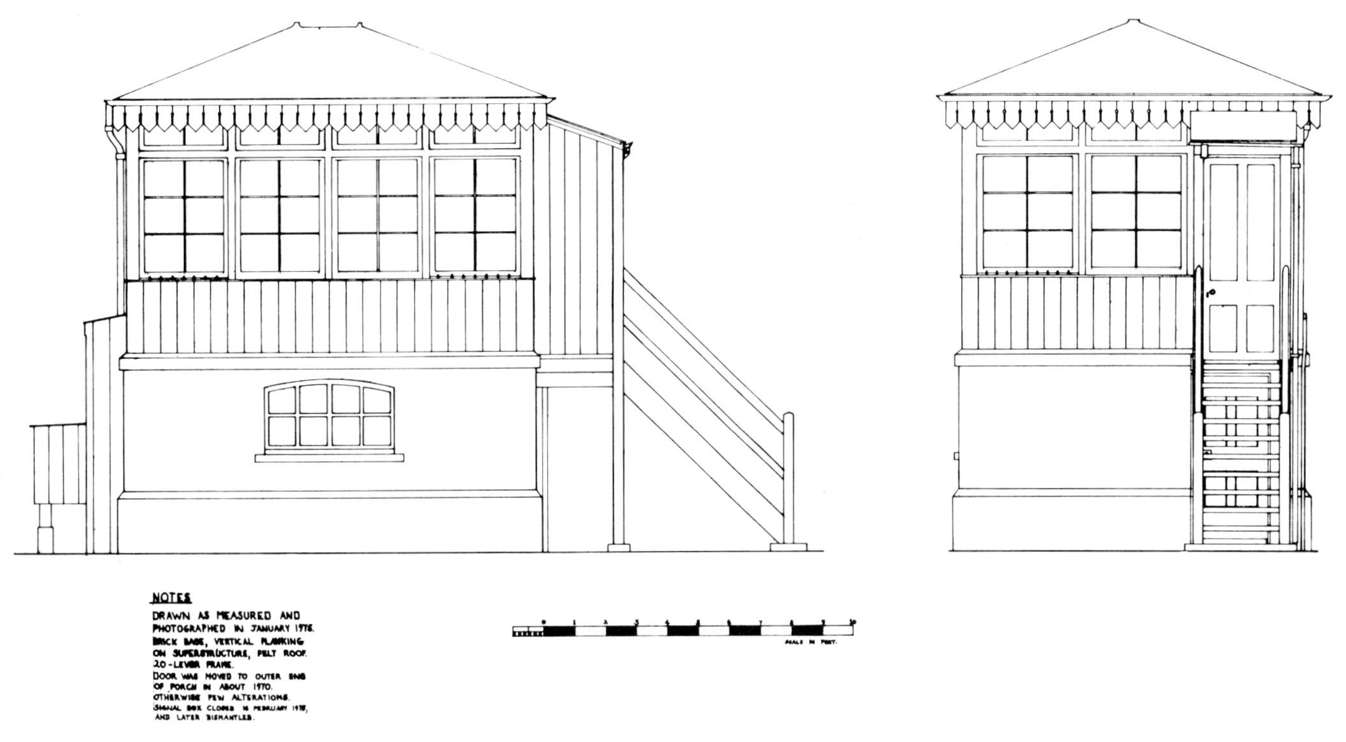

Front Elevation

End Elevation

LIPHOOK SIGNAL BOX

End Elevation

Rear Elevation

Fig. 24.
Scale drawing of the L. & S.W.R. signal box at Liphook, a photograph of which appears in Plate 113.
Drawing G. Bowring

Plate 114.
Dunbridge is not so much a signal box—more a converted cottage. The original cottage building still stands under, and all around, the box, with locking where the sitting room used to be. Date of conversion not known, but the 'superstructure' is very like the standard 1880s.

Plate 115.
The completely non-standard box at Wimborne, closed on 30th October, 1966. The lofty all-brick design is found nowhere else on the Southern, so to date it is impossible. This box contained a 29-lever Stevens frame.
Photos G. F. Gillham.

Plate 116 *(right).*
Another completely non-standard and undatable design—the cramped Salisbury Tunnel Junction. The interior of this box is so small, that the 21-lever Stevens frame and the booking desk take up most of the space. For this reason, the sink and signalmen's lockers are housed in the porch.

Plate 117 *(below).*
If there was a design anything like Wimborne, it was surely this brick box at Broadstone. In its original form, it was a short, square, structure. The newer brickwork of the extension stands out quite clearly in this view. It was closed on 18th October, 1970.
Photos G. F. Gillham.

Plate 118 .
Typical L. & S.W.R. box at Netley, on the Southampton to Fareham line. Scale drawings of this structure appear on the opposite page.

From a colour slide by D. M. Lee.

Plate 119.
The most unusual signal box at Buriton Siding, on the Portsmouth direct line. It has about it something of the air of a country cottage, and is quite unlike any other L. & S.W.R. signal box.

Photo G. Kinsey

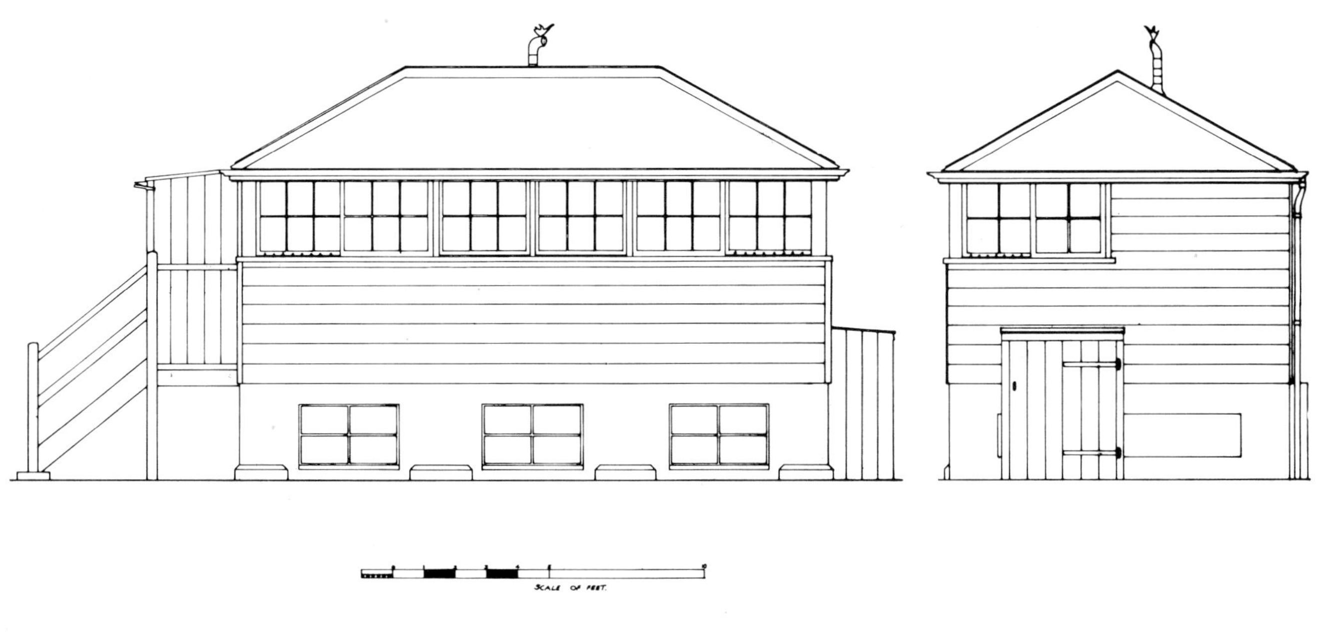

Front Elevation *End Elevation*

NETLEY SIGNAL BOX

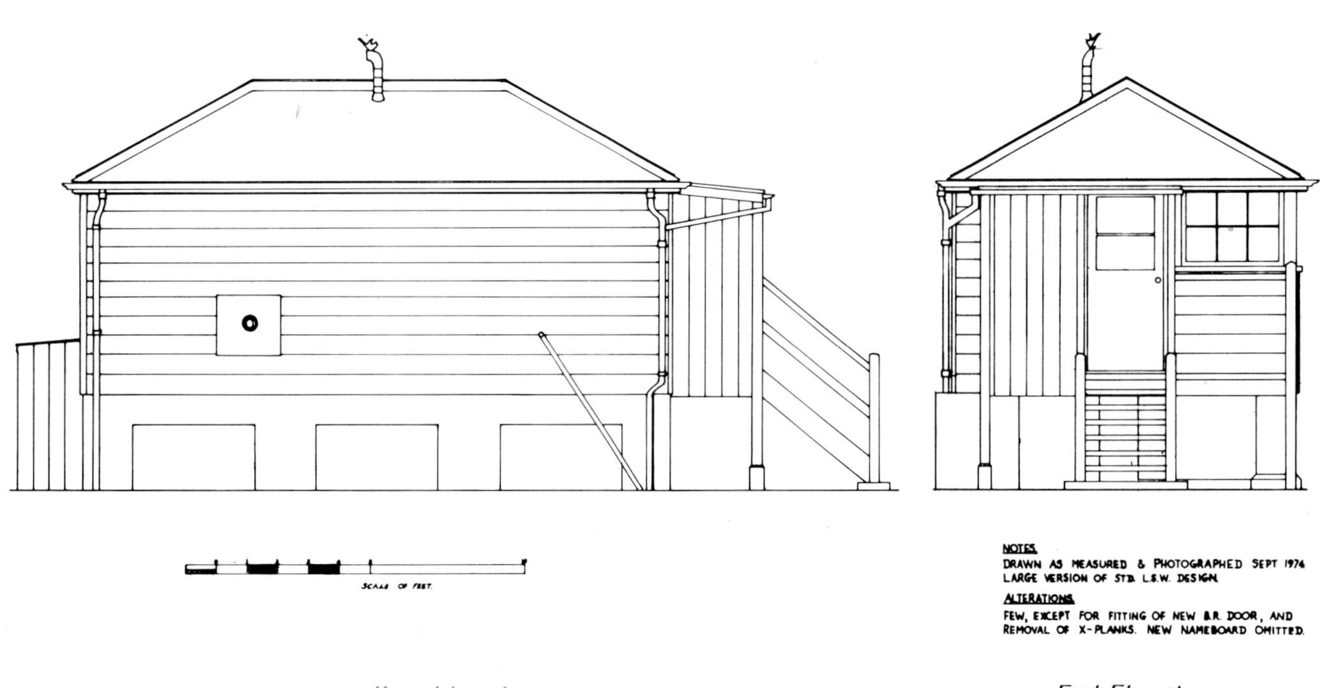

Rear Elevation *End Elevation*

Fig. 25.
Scale drawings of Netley signal box, a large version of the standard L. & S.W.R. timber box on a brick base. This structure is situated on the platform, hence the short steps up to the door.

Drawings Graham Bowring.

Plate 120.
Worgret Junction signal box, opened 20th May, 1885 with the opening of the line to Swanage. Note the typical 'South Western' features of the period, including large roof vent and railed cat-walk around windows. This box was abolished on 23rd May, 1976, on which date control of the points was transferred to a five-lever ground frame.

Photo J. P. Morris.

Plate 121.
A larger L. & S.W.R. box at Weybridge. Compare this with Worgret Junction (above), and it will be seen to have a number of similar features. The roof vent is absent, but the design of the windows, including the railed cat-walk, is identical. This box survived until 22nd March, 1970, when the area was taken over by Surbiton panel.

Photo Lens of Sutton.

Two boxes from the early part of this century.

Plate 122.

Shows the box at Barnstaple Town, erected in 1910. This design with the central brick pillar, was used by the 'South Western' from about 1890 onwards.

Photo G. F. Gillham.

Plate 123.

Shows the large brick box at Grateley, built in 1901 to house the experimental 'Low-Pressure' pneumatic frame of 70 levers. It reverted to mechanical working in 1915, when a 66-lever Westinghouse frame was installed. The basic design is very similar to the 'standard', (illustrated in the plate above), but with the unusual addition of a projecting look-out window at the end furthest from the camera.

Photo C. L. Caddy.

Fig. 26.

Scale drawings of Farncombe East signal box, on the Portsmouth direct line, a typical example of the L. & S.W.R. brick-built structure with central pillar between the windows. It was constructed about 1896, and contained a McKenzie & Holland lever frame.

Drawing G. Bowring

NOTES

DRAWN AS SURVEYED SEPT. 1975.
BASICALLY IN ORIGINAL CONDITION.
NO NAMEBOARD IS FITTED.
BUILT BY THE I.W.R.

NOTE THAT THERE ARE THREE STOREYS:
THE COAL-BUNKER IS ENTERED VIA THE DOOR AT THE REAR;
THE LOCKING-ROOM VIA THE DOOR UNDER THE PORCH;
AND THE WORKING PLATFORM VIA THE STAIRCASE.

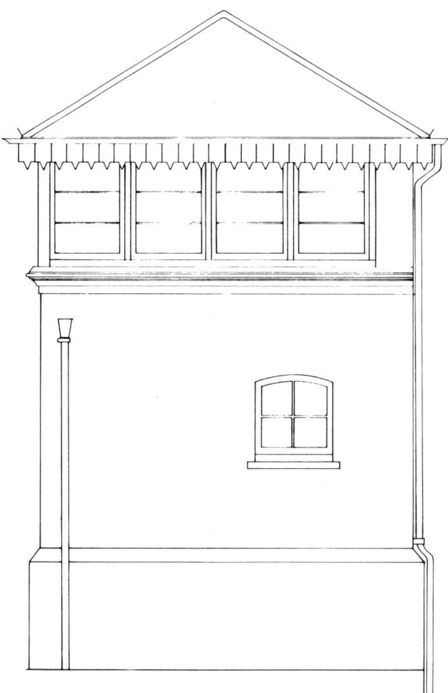

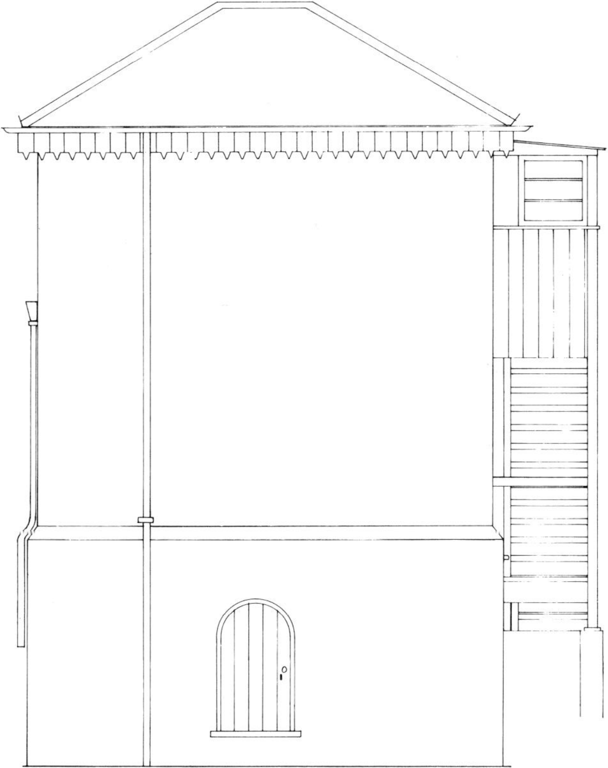

BRADING SIGNAL BOX

SCALE OF FEET

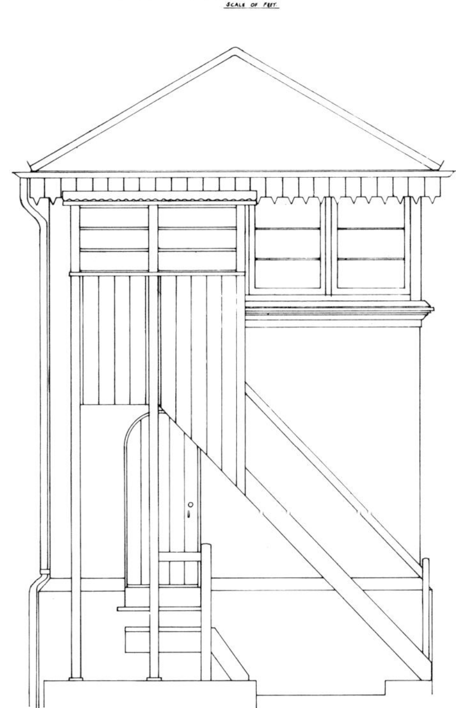

Fig. 27.
Scale drawings of former Isle of Wight railway signal box at Brading.

Drawing G. Bowring.

Plate 124 *(above).*
The unusual box at Launceston contained two lever frames, one of 18 levers for the 'South Western', and another to control the G.W.R. station behind it. This gives rise to its spacious appearance.

Photo C. L. Caddy.

Plate 125 *(left).*
Torrington box was yet another non-standard type. The windows, each with four large panes, are definitely not 'South Western' standard. Note also how the roof is extended at one end to form a 'lean-to' porch. Local stone forms the basic structure.

Photo G. F. Gillham.

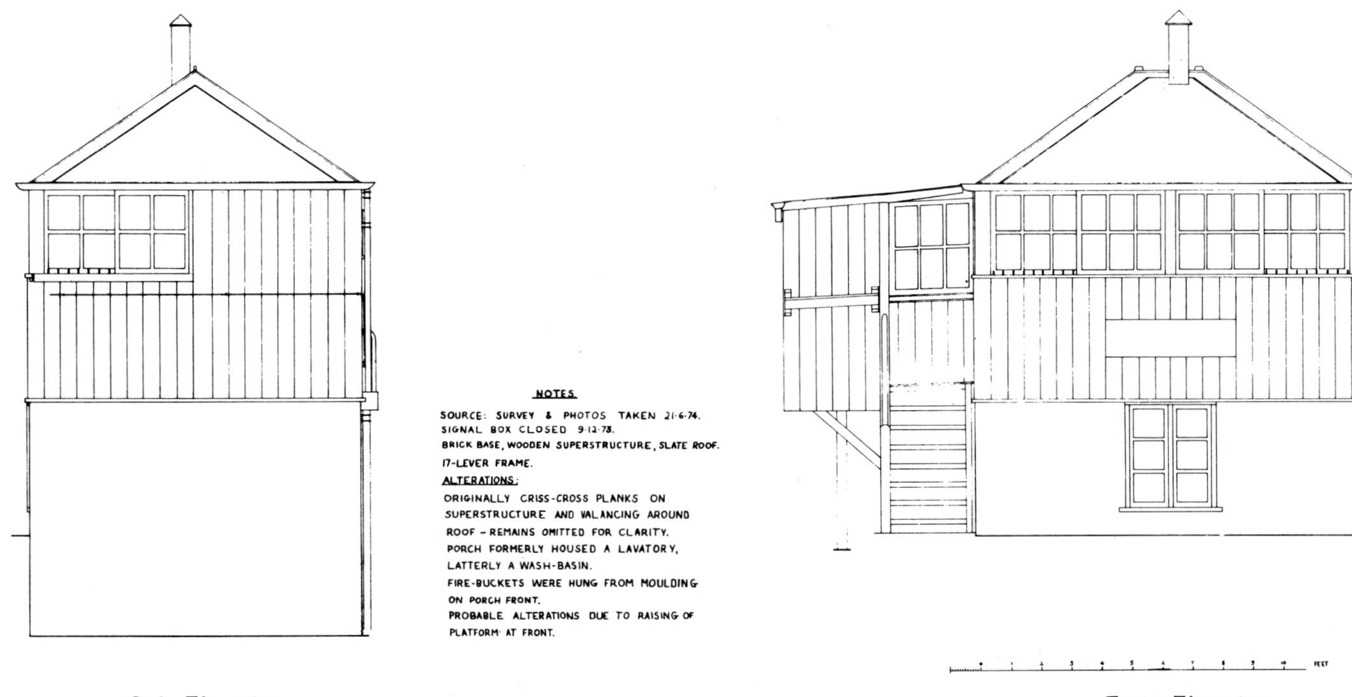

Side Elevation

Front Elevation

WITLEY SIGNAL BOX

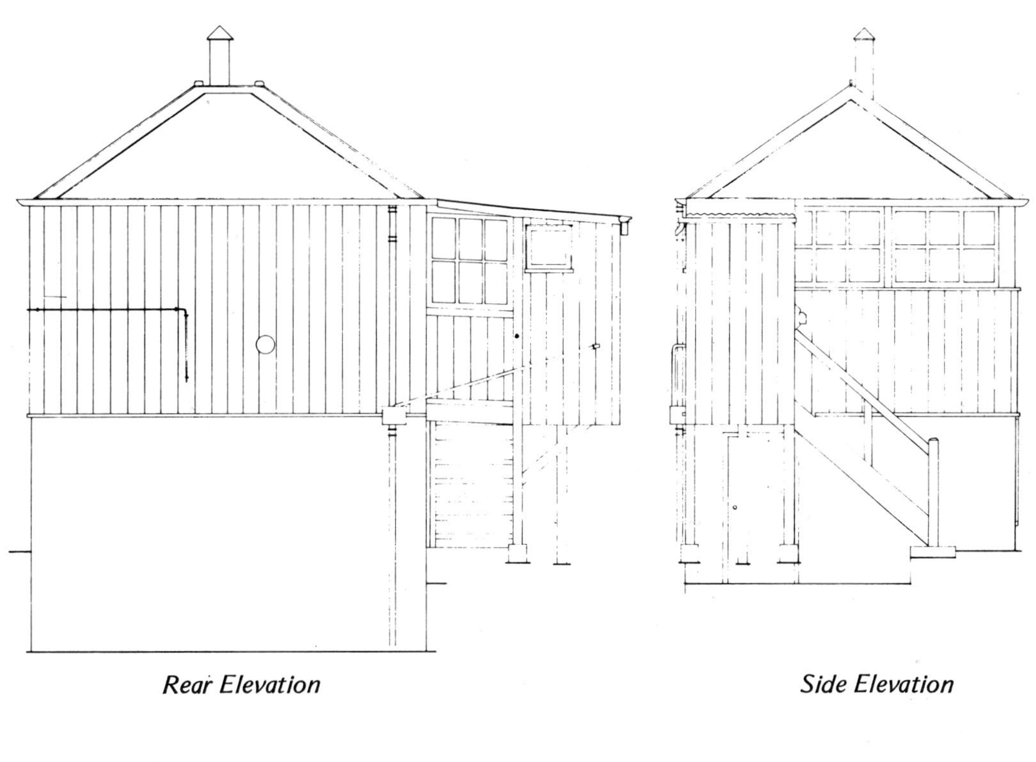

Rear Elevation

Side Elevation

Fig. 28.
Scale drawings of L. & S.W.R. signal box at Witley.
Drawing by G. Bowring

Plate 126.

Typical ground-level signal box as found throughout the L. & S.W.R. system. This one, Woodfidley Crossing, was in a very isolated situation in the heart of the New Forest, hence the churns of drinking water, (half obscuring the name-plate), which were replenished daily by the pick-up goods train. Boxes such as this contained Stevens 'Knee' lever frames, with levers at $4\frac{5}{8}$ inch centres, the locking being encased above floor level. Note the iron roof vent.

Photo G. Kinsey.

L.B. & S.C.R. BOXES

Two very different L.B. & S.C.R. boxes.

Plate 127 *(left).*
Uckfield, opened in 1882 with a 23-lever 'Rocker' frame, re-locked with tappets in 1910. This box is still in use.

Plate 128 *(below).*
Also of 1882 vintage is this large box at Eastbourne. As originally opened, it contained a 108-lever Saxby & Farmer 'Rocker and Grid Iron' frame, replaced with a 72-lever frame on 14th November, 1934. This box is also still in use, and this view may be compared with the earlier one in plate 46.
Photos E. J. White.

Plate 129.
The small L.B. & S.C.R. box at Hurst Green Junction, photographed in June 1923. The small "top-light" windows were a feature much used by the company, the design being an adaptation of the Saxby and Farmer standard box.
Photo The late E. Wallis.

Plate 130.
Horsham West Box, photographed in 1925. This is one of the original "boxes on stilts", and by the time this view was taken, it was obviously in a shaky condition. (Note the shoring timbers.)
Photo The late E. Wallis

Plate 131.
Last survivor of the Brighton Railway 'box on stilts' design. Compare this with the box depicted in Plate 4, and it will be seen to be virtually the same, except for the absence of signals sticking through the roof. This box, Hardham Junction, between Pulborough and Amberley, is now removed.

Photo D. J. W. Brough

Plate 132.
Race traffic has always been a feature of the lines of Southern England, and in the pre-motor age, reached large proportions, requiring the provision of many additional trains. To keep the traffic flowing, several minute signal boxes were erected to shorten the Block Sections, and were manned only as required in conjunction with special race trains. Such a box was the one illustrated here, known as 'B' Intermediate, on the L.B. & S.C.R. Epsom Downs line between Belmont and Banstead. Latterly, the box was only opened on two days each year—Derby Day and Oaks Day. For the rest of the year the signal arms were removed and stored in the signal box. The signals, (extreme left of the picture), are the Down ('On'), and the Up ('Off') Inner Homes. Note the absence of spectacle glasses and lamps, as the box was never open during the hours of darkness.

Photo D. J. W. Brough.

Plate 133.
Three Bridges Central box—one of the 'piano' type design that originated in 1875. *Photo The late E. Wallis*

Plate 134.
Lofty all-timber box, erected about 1910, at Horsham Junction.
Photo H. Farr.
Produced by courtesy of the E. Wallis collection.

Plate 135.
A more typical L.B. & S.C.R. design, based on the Saxby and Farmer type, only of all-brick construction. This one, at Petworth, contained a frame of 18-levers. It was closed on 22nd December, 1957.
Photo J. H. Aston

Plate 136.
Brick-and-timber box at Horsted Keynes South (re-named Horsted Keynes when the North box was closed in 1932). It contains a 40-lever frame, and is now the property of the Bluebell Railway.
Photo Lens of Sutton.

Plate 137.
Small "Brighton" box of all-timber construction at Knights Hill Sidings. Note the ornamental metal ventilator-cum-finial on the roof. A scale drawing of this type of box appears on *page 115.*

Plate 138.
At quiet country stations and on branch lines, economy of working was often obtained by combining the duties of signalman and porter. To facilitate this, the block instruments were installed in the ticket office, and the lever frame positioned on the platform and fenced in by iron railings to discourage unauthorised persons from operating the levers. This view shows such an arrangement at Mayfield.

Photos courtesy National Railway Museum.

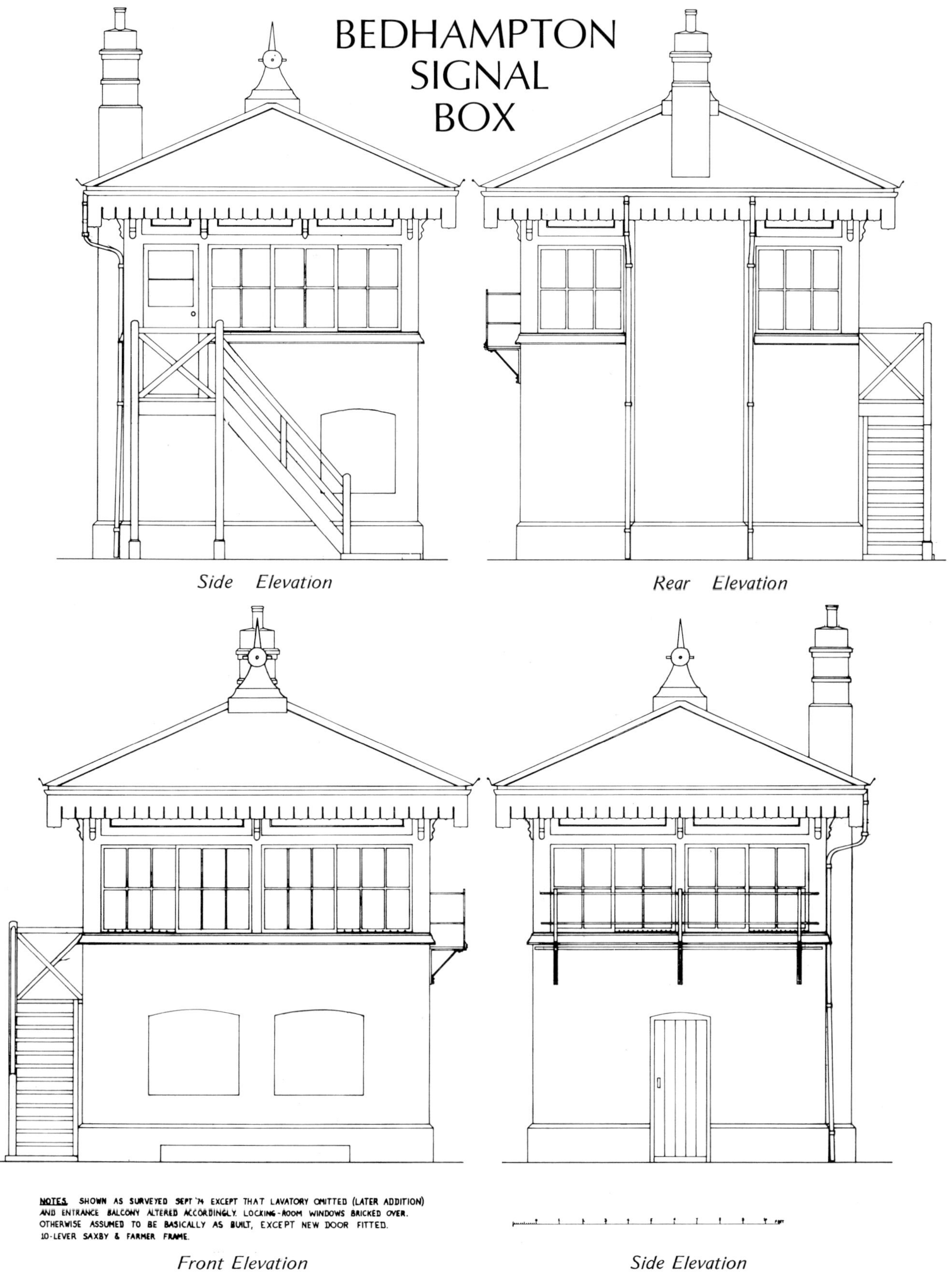

Fig. 29.
Bedhampton signal box, an ornate 'Brighton' design in brick, with wood around the windows. Note the ornamental roof vent.
Drawings G. Bowring.

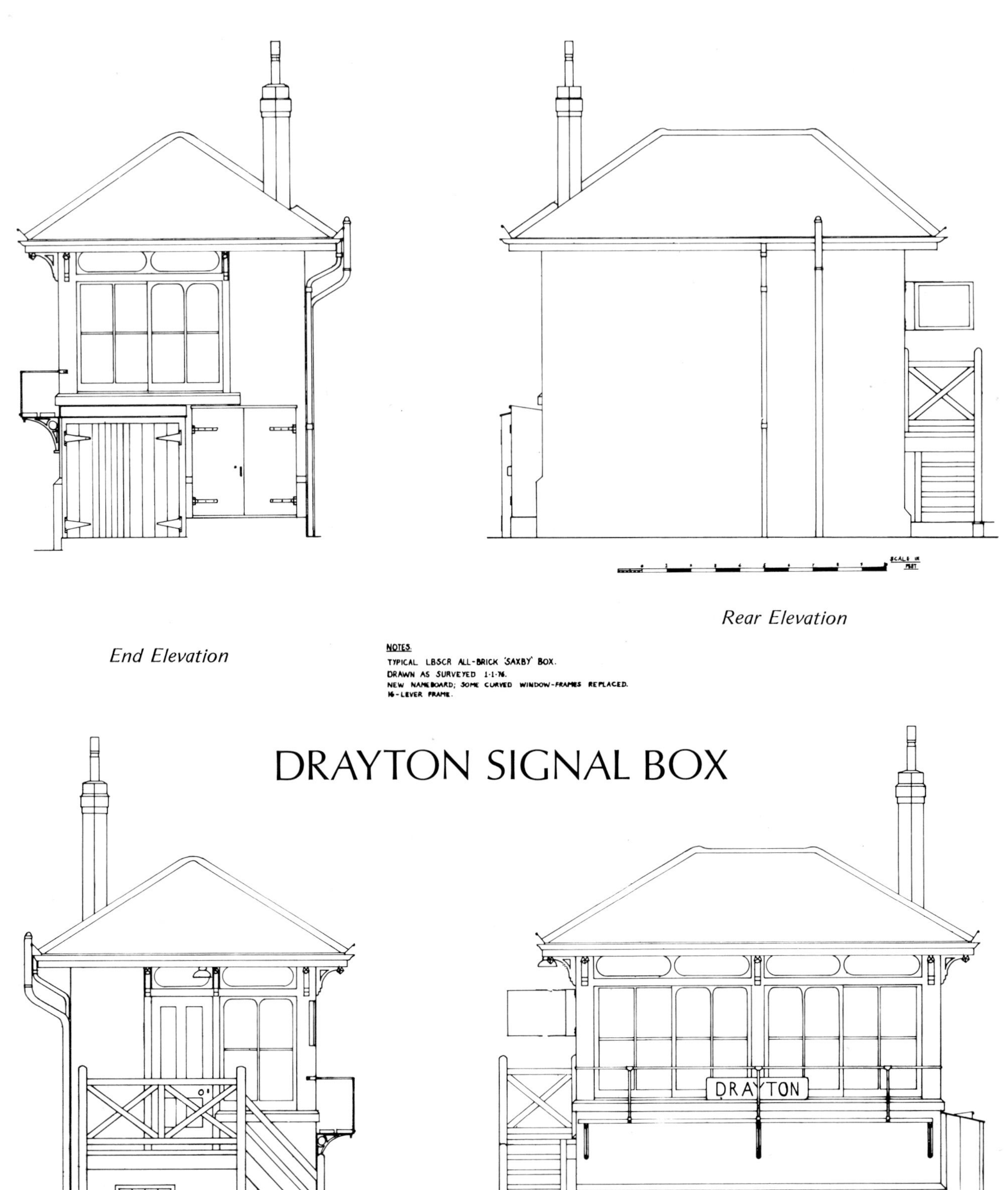

Fig. 30.
Scale drawings of L.B. & S.C.R. 'Saxby' style brick box at Drayton.
Drawing G. Bowring.

Plate 139 *(above).*
The old 'Brighton' box at Pouparts' Junction, near Clapham, photographed during an industrial dispute in the early years of the century. This box, opened in 1895, is not typical of L.B. & S.C.R. design. Note the walkway around the windows, and the large roof vent. It contained a frame re-locked in 1907, and was closed on 12th October, 1952.
Photo Lens of Sutton.

Plate 140 *(right).*
The neat structure of Mitcham box, again, not typical of L.B. & S.C.R. design. Note the Saxby & Farmer signal with lower 'Shunt' arm. Signals of similar appearance were to be seen throughout the 'Brighton' system, but this one is slightly unusual in having a lattice post.
Photo Lens of Sutton.

Plate 141.
Brapool Cutting box, one of the L.B. & S.C.R. section-splitting boxes closed under the Brighton line re-signalling scheme on 6th October, 1933.

Photo J. H. Aston.

Plate 142.
An early L.B. & S.C.R. signal box at Hailsham. Boxes of this type were once a common sight on L.B. & S.C.R. branch lines, but have now almost completely vanished.

Photo B. L. Jackson.

Plate 143.
An example of a 'Brighton' ground level signal box at Adversane Crossing (between Billingshurst and Pulborough). Note the unusual style of nameboard lettering, using large serif letters. The box has now been demolished, the crossing gates being replaced by automatic half-barriers.

Photo D. J. W. Brough.

Plate 144.
A Saxby & Farmer all-timber signal box at Northwood, (on the L.B. & S.C.R. between Ockley and Capel and Warnham). The maker's plate can be seen immediately beneath the nameboard. This box, now demolished, was on the Down side of the line, and stood on the boundary between Surrey and Sussex.

Photo D. J. W. Brough

Plate 145.
The 'South Eastern' was unusual in its choice of sash-cord windows for boxes. The neat and well-kept box at Edenbridge typifies the small box of this type.
Plate 146.
Shows another example of this design at Snodland. Here the neatness is marred by an extension, built to house the gate wheel.
Photos B. L. Jackson.

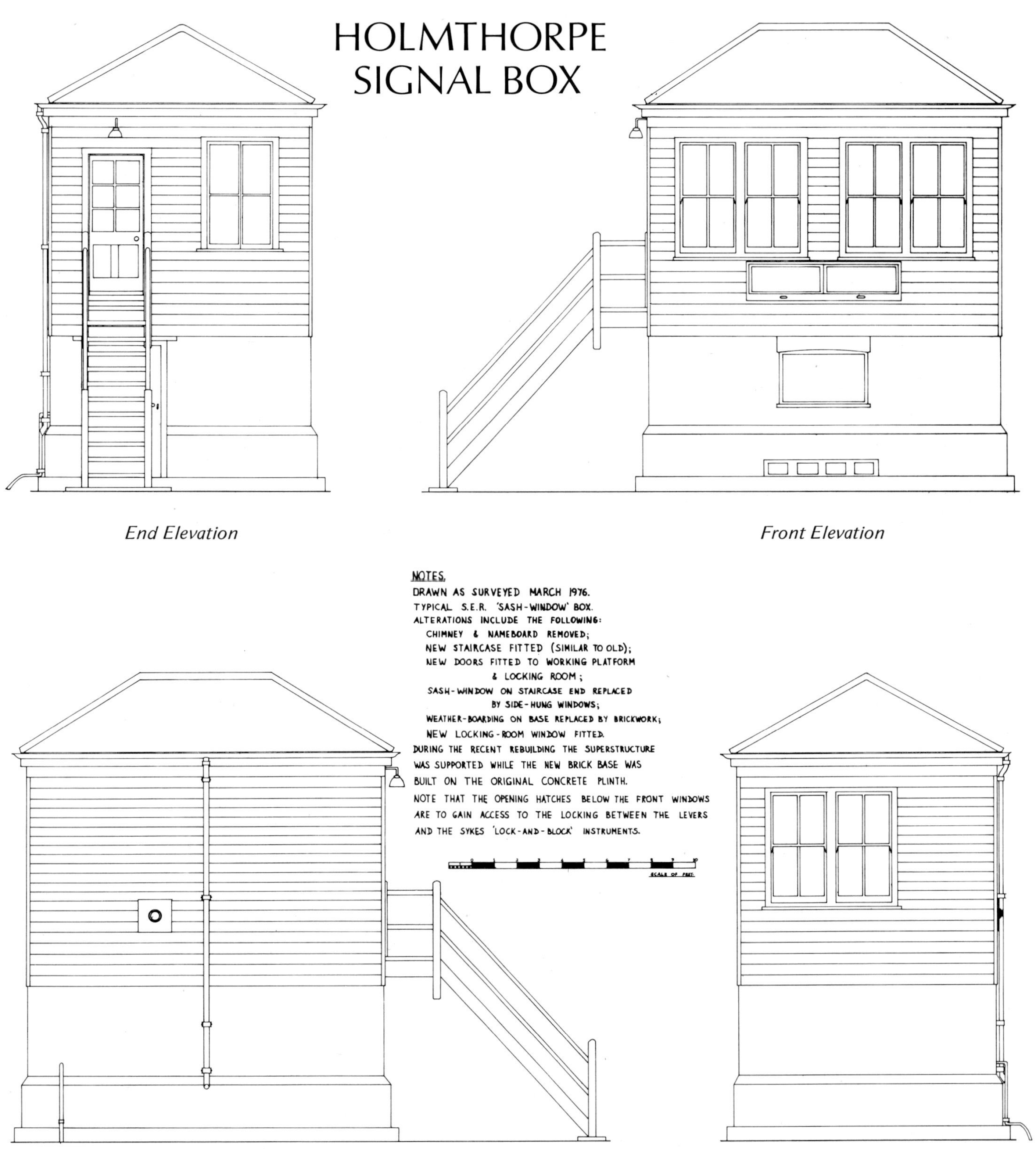

Fig. 31.

Scale drawings of 'South Eastern' signal box with sash windows, at Holmthorpe, near Redhill. Details of the structural alterations are given on the drawing, but in spite of these, it remains a good example of this design. Note the little trap doors immediately beneath the windows, provided to give easy access to the locking between the lever frame and the Sykes' 'Lock and Block' instruments.

Drawing G. Bowring

Plate 147.
Canterbury has two boxes elevated on ironwork, this one at Canterbury East, and the other at the West Station. Here, however, the reason for this type of box is not at all apparent, as there would seem to be ample space to construct a conventional box. This 'South Eastern' box had sliding windows, and railed cat-walk after the manner of the L. & S.W.R.

Plate 148.
Detail of the supporting structure of Canterbury East box. Note the signal wires and point rodding coming down from the floor above. A number of steel battery cupboards are also in evidence.

Photos B. L. Jackson.

Plate 149.
Canterbury West box, a good example of a 'South Eastern' box spanning the tracks. Such boxes are spacious, and give a good view of the layout, but are generally inclined to be draughty.
Photo B. L. Jackson.

Plate 150.
A 'South Eastern' crossing cabin with original nameplate 'Tangley Crossing Signals'. The S.E.R. never used the words 'Box' or 'Cabin' on nameboards, or even just the plain name, as on the L. & S.W.R. 'Signals' was the title given to anywhere that worked one, even if only a ground frame.
Photo Lens of Sutton.

Plate 151.

On the G.W.R. and some other lines, it was quite a common occurrence for signal boxes of all-timber construction to be moved about as a box became surplus to requirements at one location, and it was found necessary to open one at another. The box building would be dismantled, and conveyed to the new site in sections. Sometimes a new locking frame would be provided, but often the original frame, suitably re-locked for the new track layout, would follow it. This kind of thing was, however, rare on the Southern. One instance occurred in 1926, when the old 'South Eastern' box at Waterloo Junction was moved to Ryde St. John's Road, on the Isle of Wight. Plate 151, (above), shows it at its Isle of Wight location.

Photo B. L. Jackson.

Plate 152.
The Southern Railway signal box at Hastings opened on 25th May, 1930 to replace the old East and West boxes. It contains a Westinghouse 'A2' frame of 84 levers. This design was used by the SR immediately prior to the 'glasshouse' era.

Photo E. J. White.

Plate 153.
A slightly earlier S.R. box, at Reigate, opened on 10th March, 1929. It contains a 24-lever frame, and is still open. There seems to be a slight 'Brighton' influence about the design, the small top-light windows being a particular favourite with that Company.

Photo Lens of Sutton.

Plate 154.
The Southern Railway were obliged to erect this new box at Tulse Hill in 1945, its predecessor having been bombed. The design is 'wartime austerity', of the type built during the war to deal with increased military traffic. (See pp. 24-28).
Plate 155.
Several boxes of the 'glass-house' type housed power frames, like this one at Woking, opened on 27th June, 1937.
Photos courtesy National Railway Museum, York.

Plate 156.

Southern Railway 'Glass-house' box at Bognor Regis, shortly after opening in May, 1938. This became virtually the standard S.R. box for many years. Note the old L.B. & S.C.R. signals.

Photo R. H. Clark

Plate 157.

Even Southern 'Glass-houses', although alike in general appearance, had a few minor differences of detail. Here, at Templecombe, the windows are very different to those at Bognor. This box was opened on 15th May, 1938, and contained a 60-lever Westinghouse frame, now greatly shortened.

Photo C. L. Caddy.

GROUND FRAMES

Many people are somewhat confused by the term 'Ground Frame', being uncertain as to the difference between that and a small signal box. Indeed, the matter is a little confusing, as from the outside, there is no way of telling a covered ground frame from a signal box. In fact, some 'Ground Frames' were once signal boxes, and possess elevated lever frames, which further adds to the confusion. However, there are several things that distinguish between the two. First and foremost, a ground frame is not fitted with Block Instruments, and has no authority over the running of traffic. Secondly, any points operated from a ground frame must be released by the supervising signal box. The person operating the ground frame cannot work points to admit any movement onto the running line until his levers are released by the Signalman. The Southern Railway standardised on the electrical release lever, but there are also mechanical releases, such as 'Midway Locks', and such methods as Sykes' Cabin Door Control. On single lines, ground frames are released by inserting the tablet or token for the section in which the frame is situated into a lock on the leading lever, which is usually that operating the Facing Point Lock. The tablet or token cannot be withdrawn until all levers are restored to the normal position.

Plate 158.
L.B. & S.C.R. Ground Frame, Christ's Hospital, photographed on 4th October, 1933. Note the mechanical indicators showing that both the Up and Down Facing points are 'Free'. The levers, (left to right) are as follows:

No.	Description	Painted
1	*'Down & Up Points Locked/Free'*	*Blue*
2	*'Up Branch/Down Branch to Down Branch Points'*	*Black*
3	*'Disc in North Box—Want Bolt Lock'*	*Yellow*

Photo the late E. Wallis.

GROUND FRAMES

Plate 159.
Ground frames, as a rule, offer little scope for architects. However, this unique structure at Daggons Road, on the now-closed line from Salisbury to West Moors, with its 'pagoda' roof, shows originality! The small window panes are a familiar L. & S.W.R. feature, but otherwise there is nothing 'standard' about it at all.
Photo C. L. Caddy.

Plate 160.
This more grandiose edifice at Tisbury Gates has more of the appearance of a ground-level signal box. Indeed, many years ago, it was one. The windows have much larger panes than was usual on the L. & S.W.R., and the position of the nameboard, completely detached from the building and resembling a station nameboard, is most unusual.
Photo B. L. Jackson.

Plate 161.
The most common design for Southern ground frames is the 'lean-to' type. This one at Roundstone Crossing is slightly elevated on a brick base, presumably to give the crossing-keeper a better view of road traffic. Most ground frames of this type, however, had the door at ground level.
Photo C. L. Caddy.

Plate 162.
Yet another variation in L. & S.W.R. ground frame design, showing that Company's favourite method of nameing. The words "East Sidings Points" give no clue to its actual location—Chertsey.

Photo G. Kinsey.

Plate 163.
Railway Signal Company 'knee' frame in the gate box at East Burton Crossing, near Wool. Frames such as these were specially made to be installed at ground level, the lever tails being dispensed with, and the locking encased above floor level. The levers are therefore considerably shorter than those found in an 'elevated' signal box.

Photo B. L. Jackson.

Plate 164.
The Engine Line Ground Frame at Redbridge, a standard Southern 2-lever open ground frame, controlled by Electrical Release levers in the Signal Box and at Ground Frame. The numbering, (1 for the Release and 2 for the Points), is common to all such frames. Note the long metal casing containing the mechanical locking, and the telephone, housed in the box marked 'X'.

Photo G. Kinsey.

7. Signal Box Equipment and its Operation

The exteriors of signal boxes, as illustrated in Chapter Six, are all that most non-railwaymen see of the world of the signalmen. The interiors are strictly private, and therefore not accessible to the general public, and present a complicated appearance to those not versed in the art of signalling. Over the years, equipment has become increasingly complex, and even the fittings in a small country box are capable of bewildering those who have never entered a signal box before.

Of course, the largest item of equipment is always the lever frame, which occupies the full length of the structure along either the front or the back wall. In pre-grouping boxes, it is usually installed at the front of the box, but the Southern Railway preferred to keep the window-space free of obstruction, and installed their frames at the back. There were a few places where the lever frame was 'end-on' to the running line, (such as in the old L. & S.W.R. Box at Dorchester), but these were never very common. Above the levers is the 'Block Shelf', on which are fixed the various bells and instruments. Small items, such as signal and lamp repeaters, release keys, bell plungers, etc., are fastened to the front of this shelf, where they can be easily reached or observed by the Signalman. In most boxes, the block instruments and bells are placed at each end of the shelf, the intervening space being reasonably clear of fittings. On the Southern, it is standard practice to provide a plunger and a tapper for each block bell, the plunger being at one end, immediately beneath the 'accepting' block instrument, and the tapper at the far end. This saves the Signalman a lot of walking, as on other railways it is often necessary for him to walk the full length of the frame in order to ring a bell.

Fixed above the block shelf, at a point about half-way along the frame, is the track diagram—a drawing of the layout controlled by the box on which are shown the various lever numbers and their functions. The standard Southern diagram of today is the 'illuminated' variety, on which the track circuits are picked out in four colours—orange, green, blue, and yellow. When a train occupies a track circuit, a red lamp on the diagram becomes illuminated. Each track circuit indication actually has two miniature light bulbs, so that should a filament 'blow', the light will still be shown by the remaining bulb. In boxes with large frames, (sixty levers and over), two such diagrams are provided, one at each end of the frame.

The remainder of the box contains a booking desk, upon which the Signalman keeps his 'Train register' book or pad, a small table where he can sit for his meals, a chair or two, a cooker and heating stove, and a sink. There are also usually a set of lockers—one for each man employed at the box—for the Signalmen's personal effects. On a convenient wall, as close to the booking desk as possible, a notice board is provided, upon which are posted details of train alterations, and other important notices. There will also be at least one glass-fronted frame, containing the 'special instructions' for the box concerned.

The only signalling instruments NOT placed on the block shelf are those connected with the operation of single lines, such as tablet or staff instruments. These are much too large and heavy, and are therefore placed on stoutly-built tables of their own at the ends of the signal box. Yet another vital item of equipment is the clock. On the Southern, these come in all shapes and sizes, there being no 'standard issue' as on the G.W.R. The clock is usually fixed on an end wall, where the Signalman can see it wherever he is working.

No two signal boxes are alike—even if the track layout and size of the frame is identical. Each box has its own atmosphere. Some are kept thoroughly clean and tidy, with every brass fitting highly polished and the brown lino on the floor like a mirror. A few discarded rugs from the Signalmen's homes will often add a homely touch. In others, the men may be kept too busy to bother about cleaning, and the floor will be dull, the brass tarnished, and the lever-tops finger marked. The view from the windows also contributes to the 'atmosphere', a quiet country box often gaining in the pleasantness of its outlook anything it loses in operational interest. 'Big Town' signal boxes often have bleak surroundings, but are more interesting to work, by virtue of the additional traffic found in such locations.

Having briefly described what one might expect to find on entering a signal box, let us take a look at the wide variety of equipment installed in them. Like every other aspect of Southern signalling, it is not possible to illustrate everything found on the system. However, I hope that the illustrations which follow will stimulate interest in these fast-vanishing structures.

PART ONE — LEVER FRAMES

Stevens' frames were greatly favoured by the L. & S.W.R., and although they were used occasionally by the other pre-grouping companies that formed in Southern, it is with the 'South Western' that they are always associated. Many of the original ones incorporated 'Push and Pull' levers, a system that operated two signals by one lever. These stood 'half-way' in the frame when 'Normal', and were pushed forward to work one signal, and pulled back to work the other. By this means, the size of the lever frame could be greatly reduced, but they had the effect of making the frame look very untidy. Another snag with them was that the wire adjustment was very delicate, and extremes of temperature often affected the working of the signals badly. These two considerations probably out-weighed any advantage that was gained by a reduction in overall length of the frame, but despite this, 'Push and Pull' levers still remain at a few boxes today. (See fig. 34, page 133 for drawings.)

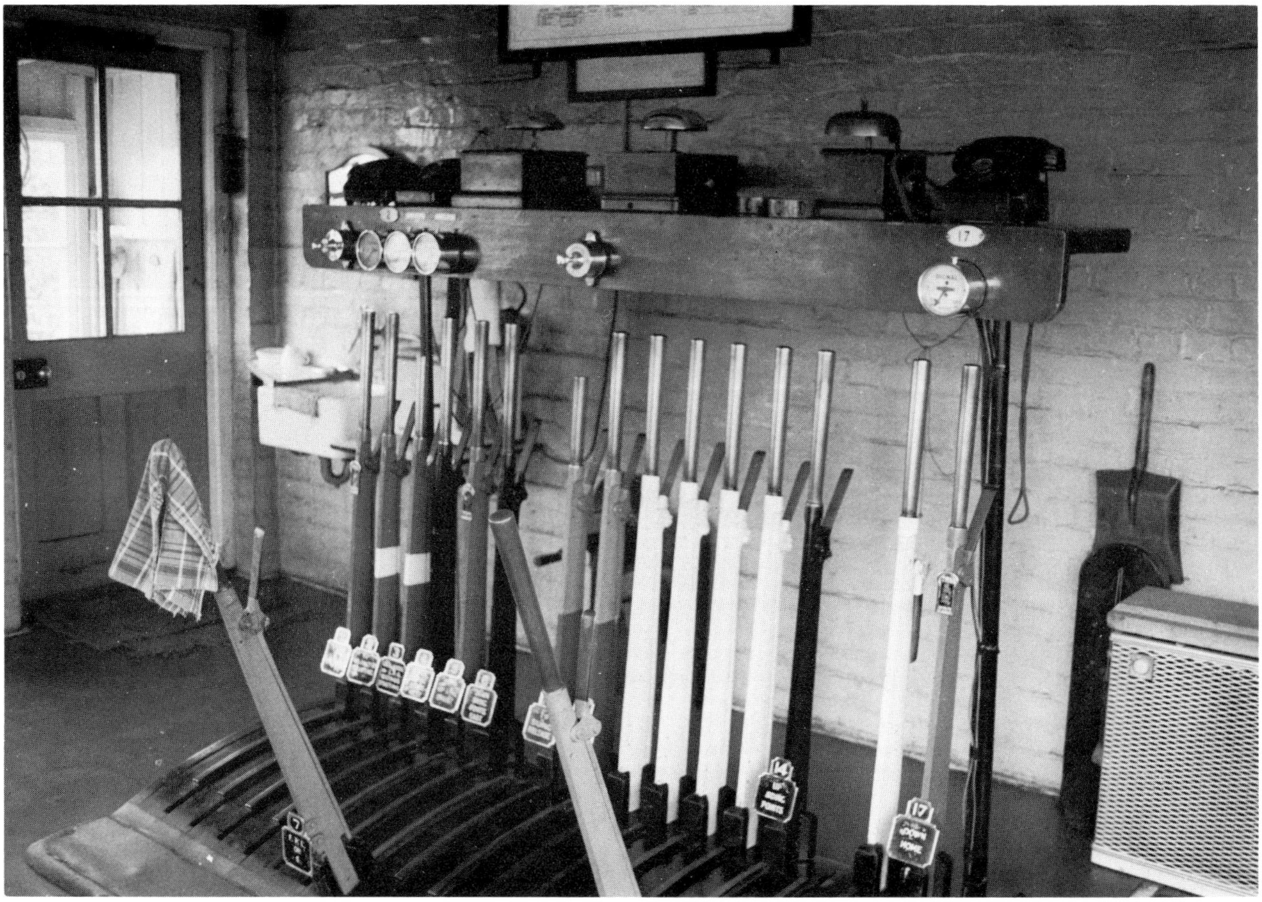

Plate 165.

The 17-lever Stevens' Frame at Fawley, terminus of the single-track branch from Totton, now open for oil trains only. The levers are at $4\frac{1}{8}$ inch centres, and stand almost vertical when 'Normal'. This frame still has the old Stevens' description plates, cast in brass to the very distinctive shape. Because the line is single, and the only instrument is a Key Token, the Block Shelf looks rather empty. Note the duster over the top of lever 7. Most Signalmen use these when working levers, as it prevents the polished tops of the levers from becoming finger-marked.

Photo B. L. Jackson.

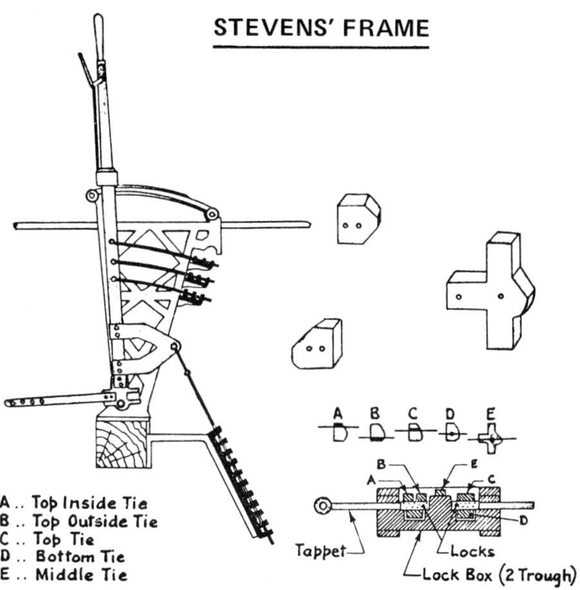

STEVENS' GROUND FRAME

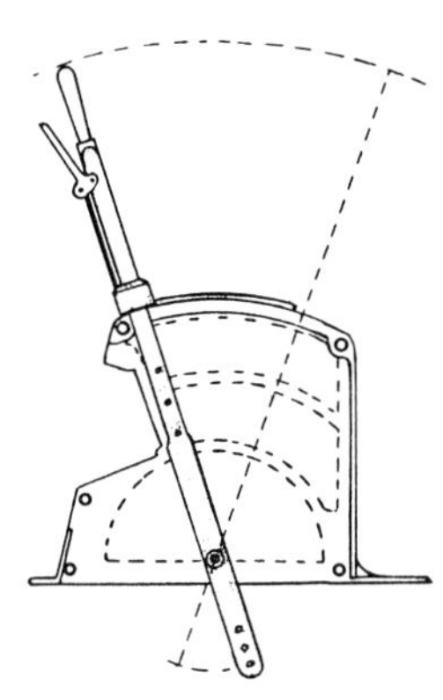

Fig. 32 *(left).*

Official instructional sketch of Stevens $4\frac{1}{8}$ inch centre elevated lever frame, showing locking components.

Fig. 33 *(above).*

Stevens' ground-level lever frame, with levers at $4\frac{5}{8}$ inch centres.

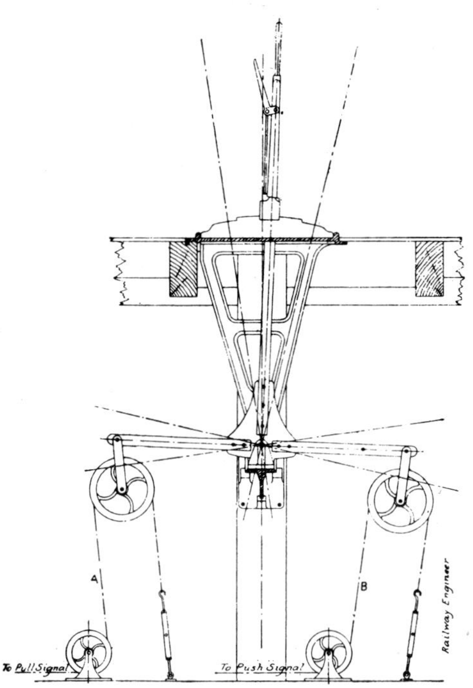

Fig. 34 *(left).*
Mention has already been made of 'Push-and-Pull' levers; an arrangement often employed by the L. & S.W.R. to avoid extending a locking frame when it was found necessary to provide additional ground signals. This drawing illustrates the connections required to work two signals by this method.

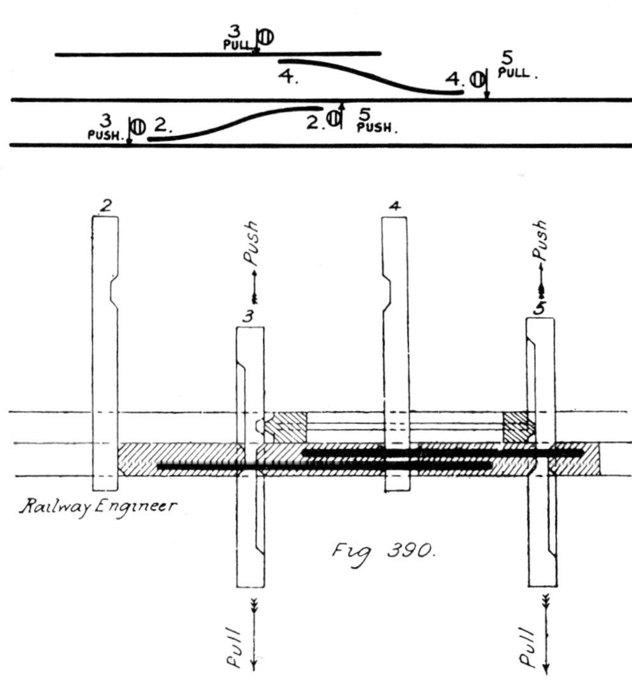

Fig. 35 *(right).*
Diagram showing typical signalling layout employing a 'Push-and-Pull' lever, and the special tappet locking required.

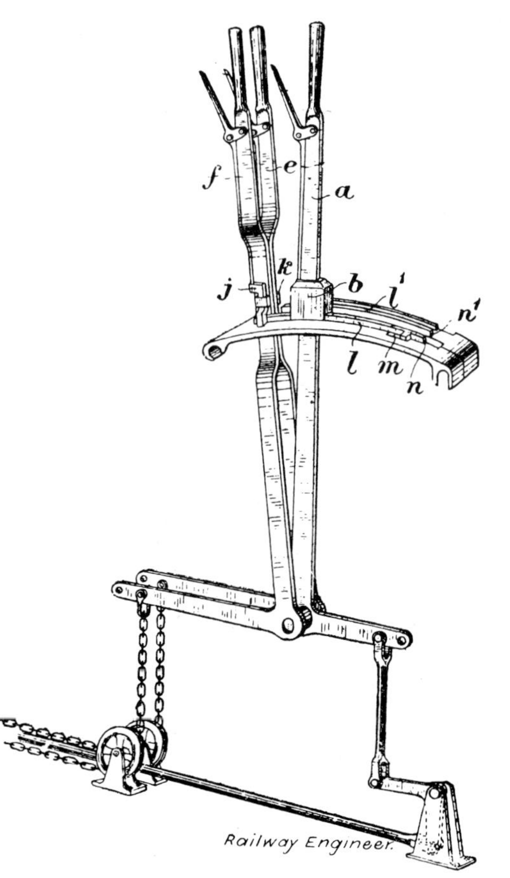

Fig. 36 *(left).*
The L. & S.W.R.'s Signal superintendent at Exeter in the 90s' was E. Russell, a man who seems to have possessed quite an inventive turn of mind. Perhaps his best known invention was the self-rising gate stop for level crossings, but he also designed an alternative method of lever economy to the "push-and-pull" lever. As with his other inventions, Russell's levers were manufactured under licence by Stevens and Sons. The numbering of a frame containing "Russell" levers was, of necessity, rather odd. Say, for example, the lever working the points was No. 6, the corresponding Russell levers for the ground signals would be 6A to the signalman's left, and 6B to his right. As both the Russell levers travelled in the same slot as the point lever, it followed that the latter had to be reversed before either of the signals could be pulled. Fig. 36 shows the assembly of a pair of "Russell" levers, notes on the drawing being as follows:—

a. *Point lever.*
b. *Catch box of point lever.*
e & f. *"Russell" signal levers.*
j & k. *"Russell" lever catch bolts.*
l & l'. *Ribs on quadrant plate.*
m. *Recess for "Russell" lever catch bolts. (Reverse.)*
n & n'. *Recess for point lever catch box. (Reverse.)*

Plate 166.

The large 'Brighton' lever frame at Gatwick Airport (formerly Gatwick Racecourse). Note the long travel of the levers, and the 'safety tread' on the segments between the levers. The steel supports that appear at intervals along the frame, support the metal frame at the back of the levers, to which are bolted the electrical lever locks and circuit controllers, an addition made by the Southern Railway. Another S.R. alteration involves the lever plates. The old ones have been removed, and those in the picture are of Southern Railway pattern. The frame at this box is long enough to qualify for two illuminated track diagrams, between which can be seen a row of Train Describers of the 'Magazine' type.

Photo E. J. White.

Plate 167.

The interior of Borough Green Signal Box, showing the L.C. & D.R. lever frame, with levers at 4¼ inch centres. Compare the short travel of these levers with those of the L.B. & S.C.R. frame at Gatwick Airport (Plate 166). This frame is of interest in that one of the locking trays contains L.C. & D.R. locking, and the other Saxby locking of the type used in many L.B. & S.C.R. boxes. The two levers nearest the camera, painted in black-and-white chevrons, operate emergency detonator placers on the main lines, the one with the chevrons pointing upwards applying to the Up line, and the nearest one, with chevrons pointing downwards, applies to the Down line. These levers, when pulled, slide two detonators onto the crown of the rail, where they are exploded if the wheels of any rail vehicle run over them, making a loud report to attract the driver's attention. They are pulled over whenever the signalman receives 'Obstruction Danger' or any such emergency bell signal from an adjoining box, or whenever it becomes necessary to stop a train quickly owing to an obstruction on the line, or a defect in the train itself. It should be noted that comparatively few Southern boxes are equipped with this apparatus, and where it is provided, it is usually a recent addition. Unlike the neighbouring G.W.R., who fitted emergency detonator placers in most of their boxes, the levers operating them either being next to the running signals for each direction, or two separate small levers located at each end of the lever frames, the S.R. always put the levers next to each other at one end of the frame.

Photo B. L. Jackson.

Plate 168.
The Saxby & Farmer frame at Horsted Keynes, formerly on the L.B. & S.C.R., and now the property of the 'Bluebell Railway.' It contains 40 levers, and at the time of writing, has the distinction of being the largest lever frame on a privately operated railway in Britain. Frames of this pattern were standard equipment on the 'Brighton' for many years, and a number are still in operation. The levers are at 5-inch centres—wider than most other types—a feature that tends to make the installation seem larger than it actually is.

Photo B. L. Jackson.

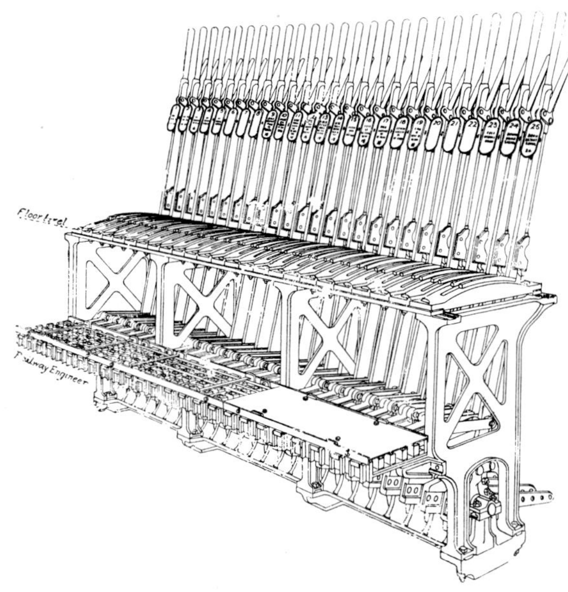

Fig. 37.
After 1888 Saxby and Farmer ceased the manufacture of frames with tumbler locking, and developed the "Duplex Locking" frame—the first type to combine catch-handle and straight lever locking. This pattern, illustrated in the above drawing, was adopted as standard by the L.B. & S.C.R. and a number of other railways. The levers have a stroke of 3 feet and a radius of 7 feet.

Plate 169.

As already mentioned in the text, ground-level signal boxes were generally fitted with what are descriptively called 'Knee' frames, the levers being much shorter than those in an 'elevated' frame to allow for the locking being installed above floor level. This photograph shows the 'Knee' frame at Falmer, (near Brighton), which was installed by the Southern Railway in September 1929 to replace the original box. The short levers, and the steel case containing the mechanical locking, can clearly be seen. Several makes and patterns of 'knee' frame were in use on the S.R. system, differing slightly in detail such as the centre-to-centre measurement between the levers but otherwise very much alike.

Photo B. L. Jackson.

Plate 170.
A rarity that has survived into the age of power signalling—the Dutton lever frame at Wadhurst. Dutton equipment was never a common sight on the railways of Southern England, and this is now the only one in service. Note that the levers at each end of the frame have been sawn off by four inches, a convenient method of conveying to the signalman that the signals they control are power operated, (in this case, colour lights), and there is therefore no need to give a heavy pull.
Photo B. L. Jackson.

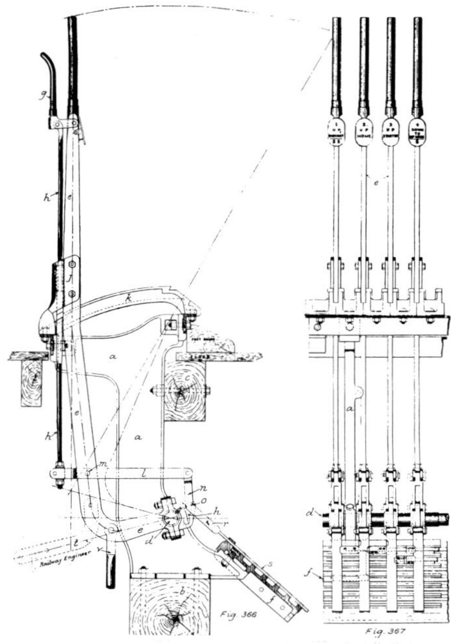

Fig. 38.
Drawings of Dutton's patent locking frame, as shown in the above photograph. Unlike other frames, these were not fixed directly to the signal box floor but supported by cast-iron standards spaced at regular intervals. As with the Saxby and Farmer "Duplex" frame, catch-handle and lever locking were combined. Lever tails, (t) were provided only for those levers working signals, point rodding connections being made as shown at "v".

Plate 171 *(left).*
The Westinghouse 'A2' lever frame, adopted by the Southern Railway as standard for all new boxes. These frames are fitted with catch-handle locking, and lend themselves to the addition of refinements such as electrical circuit controllers and lever locks.
Photo The Westinghouse Brake and Signal Co. Ltd.

Plate 172 *(above).*
Rear view of the Westinghouse 'A2' frame in Millbrook Box, showing the steel girder to which are bolted the metal cases housing the electrical lever locks and circuit controllers. The large catch-handles associated with this pattern of frame can also clearly be seen. (Lever No. 1 is out of use, hence the disconnection of the catch-handle).
Photo E. J. White.

Plate 173.
The complexities of mechanical interlocking on a Westinghouse frame. The lever tails are at the top of the picture.
Photo The Westinghouse Brake and Signal Co. Ltd.

Plate 174.
A typical Southern Railway interior in Tulse Hill signal box. The lever frame is of the Westinghouse 'A2' type. Sykes' "Lock and Block" instruments are in evidence at each end of the shelf, and there is also a set of rotary train describers near the far end. The track diagram is of the older Westinghouse pattern, with two small round lights for each indication.
Photo courtesy National Railway Museum, York.

THE WESTINGHOUSE ALL-ELECTRIC LOCKING FRAME — STYLE "L"

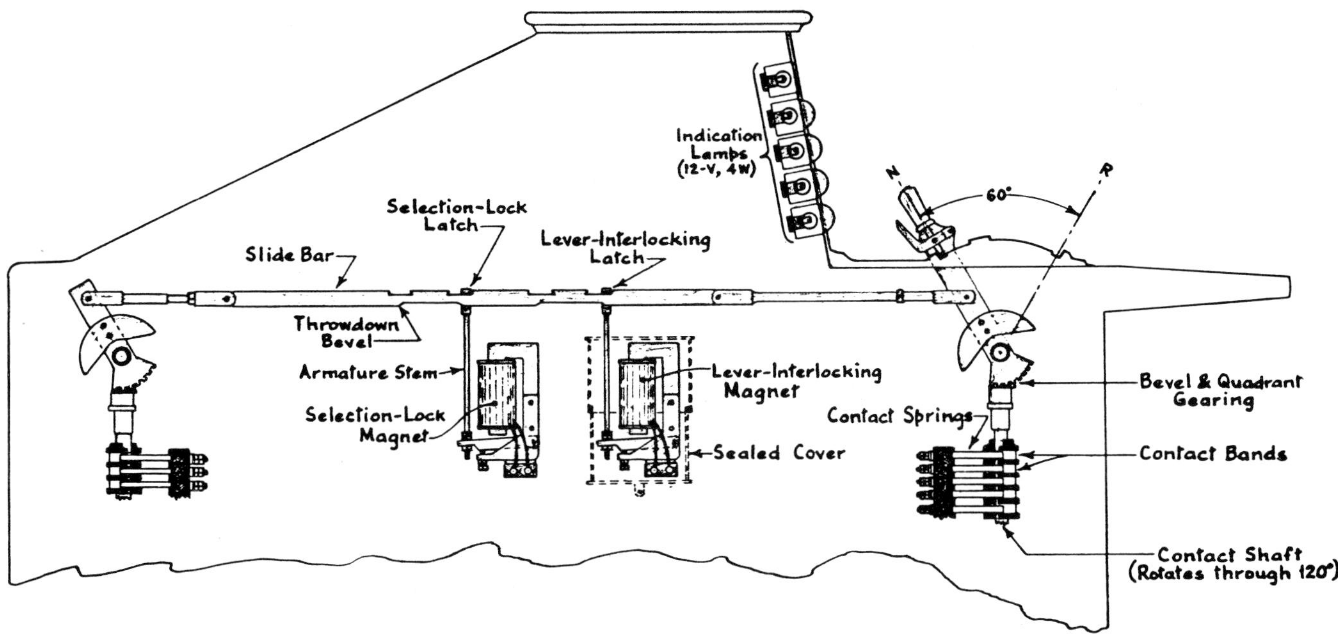

Fig. 39. *Official instructional drawing of the Westinghouse 'Style L' miniature-lever power frame with electrical locking.*

NOTES ON THE OPERATION OF POINTS ETC.

Many years ago, it was only considered possible to operate points mechanically up to a distance of 200 yards from the signal box. For this reason, many older layouts required two signal boxes (or a ground frame in addition to the signal box). However, with the development of the anti-friction roller for the support of point rodding, and the better understanding of mechanics in general, the limit was later increased to 350 yards. Providing that points and rods are well maintained and regularly oiled, they can be pulled without undue effort on the part of the signalman, particularly where the rod-run is reasonably direct. It is obvious that many yards of steel rodding are subject to a fair amount of expansion and contraction according to the out-door temperature, and to prevent the movement so caused having an effect on the position of the point blades, it is necessary to insert compensator cranks into the run. One type of crank is illustrated in plate 176.

The wires controlling signals are likewise subject to temperature changes, but these can be regulated by the Signalman. For signals situated 400 yards or more from the box, it is necessary to provide a ratchet wheel or other approved apparatus in the signal box for the purpose of taking up or letting out the wire, but this facility is also often provided for signals much nearer.

Points that are facing in the direction of travel, such as at junctions and the entrance to loop lines, must be securely held whilst a train is passing over them, as the slightest movement of the blades could result in derailment at high speed. This, of course, applies to all points that connect with a single line of railway, as these are bound to become facing for either 'Up' or 'Down' trains. This is achieved by fitting a Facing Point Lock, (F.P.L.), to the points concerned. A second stretcher bar is fixed between the blades, in which two notches are cut to correspond with the normal and reverse lie of the points. A plunger lock enters one or other of these notches, thereby locking the blades firmly in position. It follows that, should the blades be slightly open, the plunger will not line up with the notch, and the Signalman will therefore be unable to reverse his F.P.L. lever.

Perhaps the terms 'normal' and 'reverse', as applied to points and levers in a locking frame, call for clarification. For points, it is determined by the lie of the operating lever in the box. When a lever is back in the frame it is said to be 'normal', and when pulled over, 'reverse'.

Plate 175.
Close-up view of a Black's Economical facing point lock ("Butterfly" pattern). This specimen, photographed in 1923, was on number 12 points at Pulborough.
Note: Drive via Fouling Bar from signal box on left. Drive to Trap Points on right.
Photo The late E. Wallis.

Plate 176.
The rods leading from signal boxes to points are sometimes of considerable length, and, being made of iron, expand and contract according to the temperature. To avoid the movement so caused affecting the position of the point blades, "Compensator Cranks" have to be inserted in the run of rodding. The photograph below shows one of the "flat" type, at Cranleigh.
Photo The late E. Wallis.

RUNNING SIGNAL DETECTION

Schematic

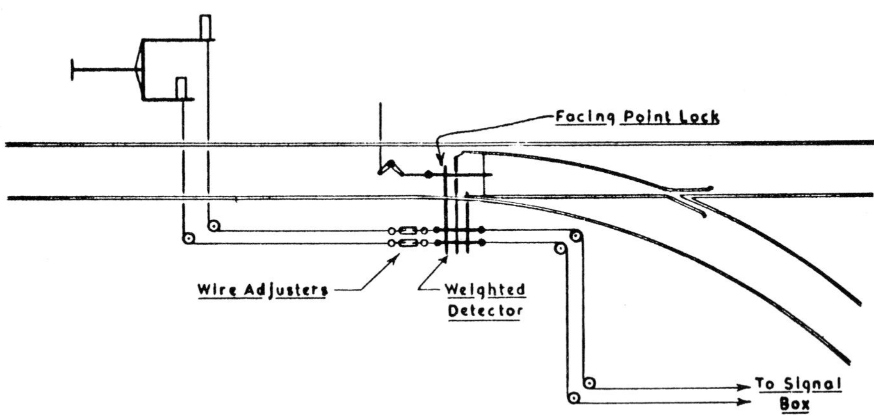

SHUNT SIGNAL DETECTION

Schematic

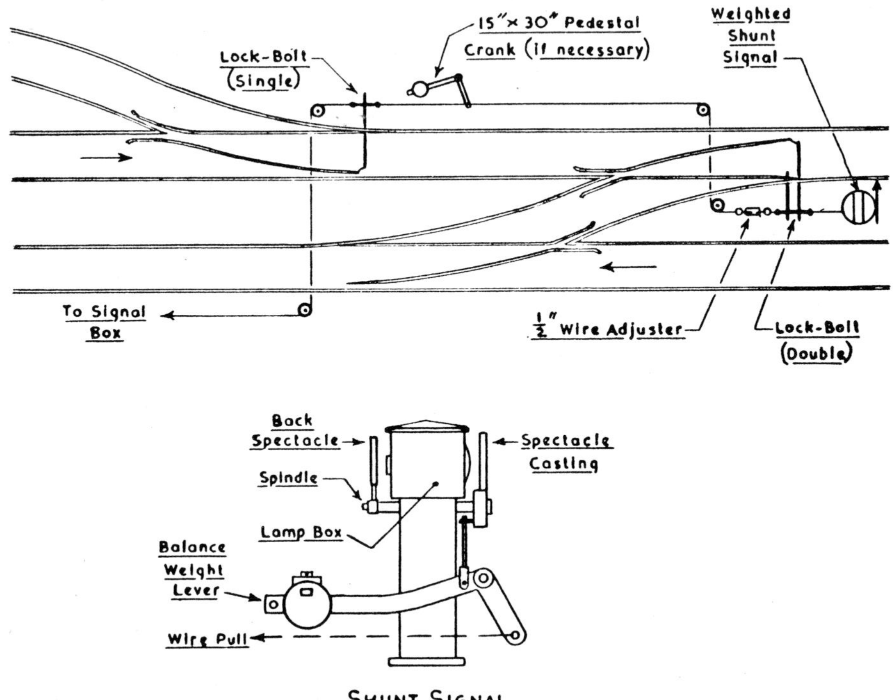

Fig. 40.
Official schematic sketches showing the layout of mechanical detection for running and shunting signals. Detection is provided to prevent a signal being 'cleared' unless the points are correctly set for the movement, with the blades firmly in position. The Southern frequently uses electrical detection, which greatly simplifies the layout of signal wires on the ground.

CLAYTON'S FOGGING MACHINE

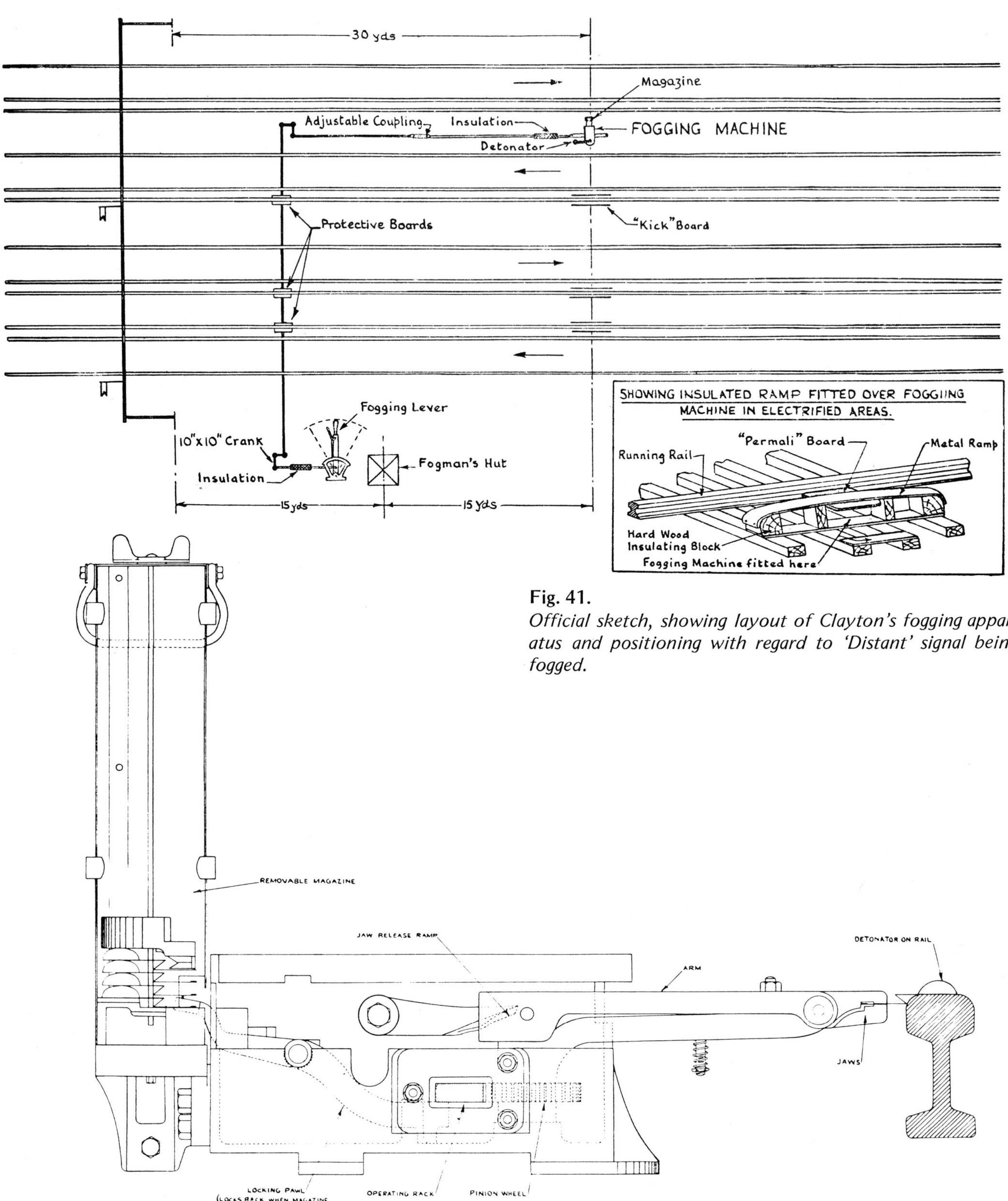

Fig. 41.
Official sketch, showing layout of Clayton's fogging apparatus and positioning with regard to 'Distant' signal being fogged.

Fig. 42.
In areas with light traffic, it is possible for a man engaged on fog-signalling to place his detonators on the rail by hand after the passage of each train, but this cannot easily be done where trains run every few minutes, particularly where four tracks are involved. To overcome this difficulty, Clayton's Fogging Machines are provided. These are fitted with a magazine of detonators, and operated by a ground lever adjacent to the Fogman's hut. This sketch shows such a machine, with detonator in position on the crown of the rail. *From official drawings.*

DETONATOR PLACER

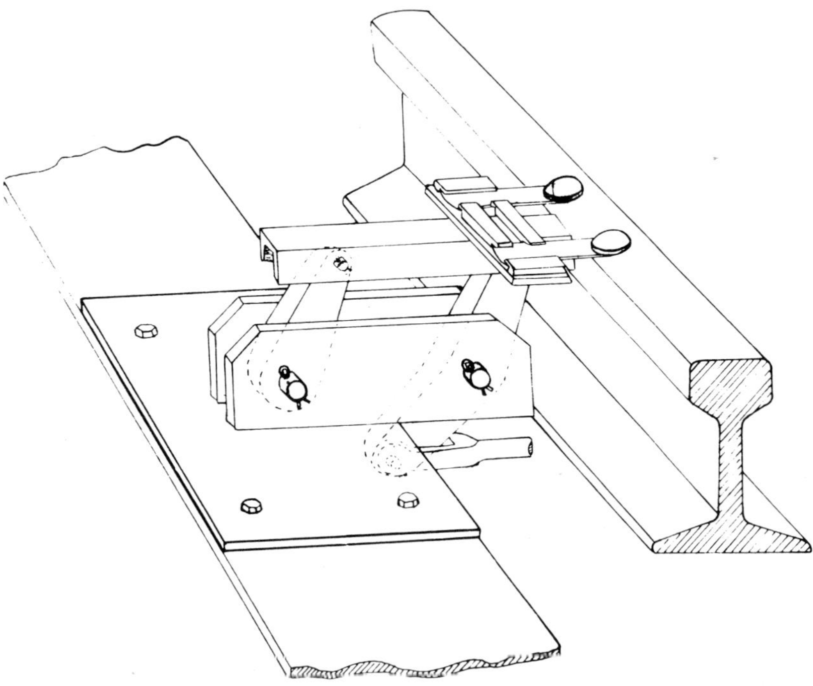

Fig. 43.
The SR standard two-shot emergency detonator placer. Two detonators are provided in case one fails to explode, as the chances of both failing are very remote.

SCOTCH BLOCK

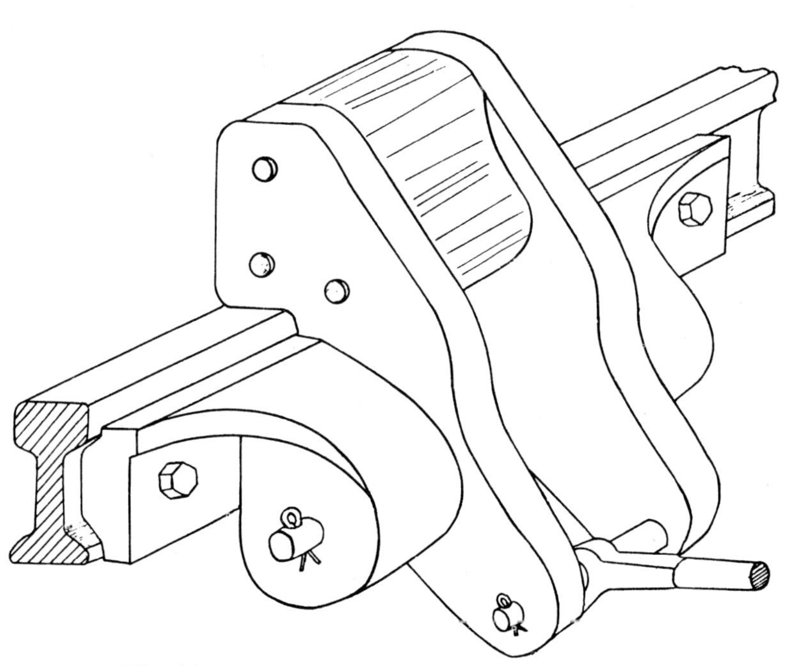

Fig. 44.
Detail of a signal box operated scotch block. These blocks are often used at the outlet of sidings instead of the more conventional 'Trap' points, particularly in cramped locations where points cannot be accommodated.

CODE OF TERMS AND REGULATIONS APPLICABLE TO BLOCK TELEGRAPH WORKING ON DOUBLE LINES OF RAILWAY.
BELL SIGNALS.

Regulation Number.	Description of Signal.	How to be given.
1	Call Attention Signal ...	1
3 & 4	Is Line Clear for Passenger Train or Breakdown Van Train not going to clear the Line. — Main Line ...	3 pause 1
	— Branch ...	1 pause 3
	Is Line Clear for Breakdown Van Train going to clear the Line, or Light Engine going to assist disabled Train. — Main Line ...	2 pause 2
	— Branch ...	4 pause 4
	Is Line Clear for Fish, Meat, Fruit, Horse, Cattle, Milk or Perishable Train composed of coaching stock. — Main Line ...	4 pause 2 pause 2
	— Branch ...	2 pause 2 pause 4
	Is Line Clear for Empty Train ... — Main Line ...	2 pause 2 pause 1
	— Branch ...	1 pause 2 pause 2
	Is Line Clear for Goods or Through Ballast Train or Engines and Brakes — Main Line ...	3 pause 2
	— Branch ...	2 pause 3
	Is Line Clear for Light Engine or Light Engines coupled together ... — Main Line ...	4 pause 1
	— Branch ...	1 pause 4
3, 4 & 8	Is Line Clear for Ballast Train requiring to stop in Section or Goods Train Working at intermediate Sidings ...	5 consecutively
3, 4 & 9	Is Line Clear for Trolley requiring to pass through Tunnel ...	2 pause 2 pause 2
3, 4 & 9A	Is Line Clear for Power-worked Inspection Car or mechanically or power-worked Trolley. — Through ...	1 pause 2 pause 1
	— Required to stop in Section	1 pause 3 pause 1
3	Train Entering Section ... — Main Line ...	2 consecutively
	— Branch ...	4 consecutively
5	Section Clear but Station or Junction Blocked ...	3 pause 5 pause 5
6	Bank Engine in Rear of Train ...	1 pause 4 pause 1
10 & 12	Train Out of Section or Obstruction Removed ...	2 pause 1
10A	Engine Arrived ...	2 pause 1 pause 3
	Train Drawn Back Clear of Section ...	3 pause 2 pause 3
11	Train an Unusually Long Time in Section ...	6 pause 2
12	Obstruction Danger ...	6 consecutively
13	Blocking Back ... — Inside Home Signal ...	2 pause 4
	— Outside Home Signal ...	3 pause 3
17	Stop and Examine Train ...	7 consecutively
18	Cancelling "Is Line Clear ?" or "Train Entering Section" Signal ...	3 pause 5
	Last Train Signalled Incorrectly Described ...	5 pause 3
19	Train Passed Without Tail Lamp ... — To Box in Advance ...	9 consecutively
	— To Box in Rear... ...	4 pause 5
20	Train Divided ...	5 pause 5
21	Shunt Train for Following Train to Pass ...	1 pause 5 pause 5
22	Vehicles Running Away on Wrong Line ...	2 pause 5 pause 5
23	Vehicles Running Away on Right Line ...	4 pause 5 pause 5
24	Opening of Signal Box ...	5 pause 5 pause 5
	Closing of Signal Box ...	7 pause 5 pause 5
27	Testing Block Indicators and Bells ...	16 consecutively
34A	Shunting between Signal Boxes within Station Limits in Right Direction. — Is Line Clear for Shunt Movement on Down Line ...	4 pause 2
	— Is Line Clear for Shunt Movement on Up Line ...	4 pause 3
	— Shunt Movement Entering Section ...	2 consecutively
	— Shunt Movement out of Section ...	2 pause 1
	— Release Slot for Shunting ...	2 pause 1 pause 2
	— Replace Slot—Shunting Completed ...	3 consecutively
	— Cancelling "Is Line Clear for Shunt Movement" or "Shunt Movement Entering Section" signal.	3 pause 5 pause 1
34B	Shunting between Signal Boxes within Station Limits in Wrong Direction. — May Shunt Movement be made on Wrong Line ...	1 pause 2
	— Wrong Line Shunt Movement clear of Section at Box in rear.	2 pause 3 pause 2
	— Wrong Line Shunt Movement clear of Section at Box in advance.	2 pause 1

Signalmen 'speak' to each other by using a set of bell codes. This is not only quicker than a telephone message, but illuminates the chance of a misunderstanding, which could easily occur if one of the men was a little careless in his choice of words. The list given above is the standard Southern one, and those who are familiar with the bell codes of other companies will quickly detect a number of differences. However, all the 'emergency' codes, such as 'Obstruction Danger' and 'Stop and Examine' are the same as used by other railways.

PREECE'S ONE- OR THREE-WIRE, TWO-POSITION, BLOCK INSTRUMENT

Preece's instruments were widely used on the L. & S.W.R., and remain in use at some boxes today, although rapidly being replaced by standard three-position equipment. The main snag with these, and indeed all two-position instruments, is that the 'Normal' and 'Train on Line' indications are the same, the only positive indication being when the arm is lowered to show 'Line Clear'. The signalman at a busy box therefore had to have a good memory, or keep his Train Register right up to date, in order to know the exact state of the line.

Plate 177 *(above).*
A Preece's two-position Block Instrument, with Switch Handle to the right, in Aldershot 'B' Box.
Photo B. L. Jackson.
For operating instructions see next page.

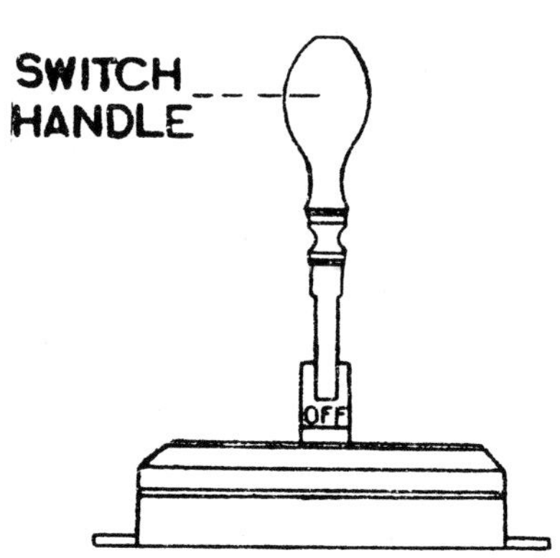

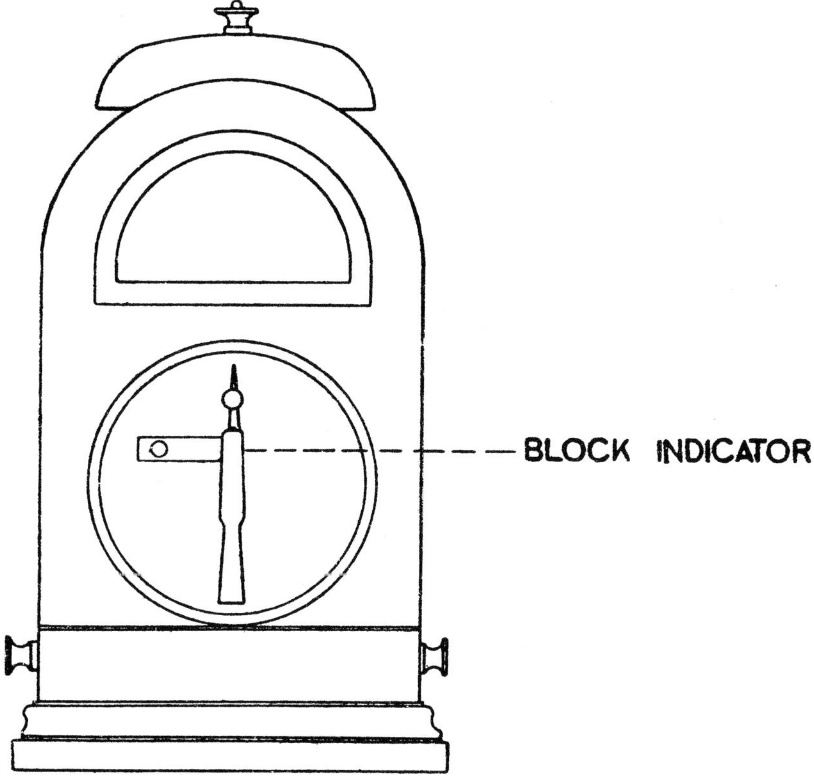

Mode of Signalling.—" A," " B " and " C," represent three consecutive Block Signal Boxes, and the process of signalling a Train is as follows :—

Three-Wire Instruments.

(a) Prior to the despatch of a Train from " A," the Signalman there, provided he has received the **Train Out of Section** Signal for the previous Train, and the Block Indicator is in its normal position, must call the attention of " B," and having obtained it, must give the proper **Is Line Clear** Signal ; if the Line be clear at " B," the Signalman there must acknowledge the Signal and place the Switch handle to the " Off " position, which will lower the Block Indicator at " A " to the **Line Clear** position.

(b) On the Train leaving " A," the Signalman there must send the **Train Entering Section** Signal to " B," who must acknowledge the Signal and place his Switch handle to the " On " position, which will raise the Block Indicator at " A " to the **Line Blocked** position.

(c) " B " must then, provided he has received the **Train Out of Section** Signal for the previous Train and the Block Indicator is in its normal position, call the attention of " C," and having obtained it must give the proper **Is Line Clear** Signal to " C." If the Line be clear " C " will give permission for the Train to approach. As soon as the Train has arrived at or passed " B," or been shunted clear of the Main Line at " B," the Signalman there must give the **Train Out of Section** Signal to " A " which " A " must acknowledge.

One-Wire Instruments.

The method of Signalling a Train under the One-Wire System will be the same as that detailed above for the Three-Wire System, except that the movement of the Switch Handle on the One-Wire System does not raise or lower the Block Indicator at the Distant Station, as in the case of the Three-Wire System. For example, to raise the Block Indicator at " A " it is necessary for the Signalman at " B " to first place his Switch Handle to the " on " position and then send the required bell code. To lower the Block Indicator at " A " it is necessary for the Signalman at " B " to first place his Switch Handle to the " off " position and then send the required bell code, after which the Signalman at " A " must send a special bell signal of one beat to " B."

METHOD OF SIGNALLING USING PREECE'S INSTRUMENTS

Plate 178.
The instruments in Aldershot 'B', showing a train accepted in both directions. The arm is lowered, indicating that 'Line Clear' has been given by Farnham for a Down Train, and the Switch Handle is in the 'Reverse' position, showing that Aldershot 'B' has also given 'Line Clear' to Farnham for an Up Train.

Photo B. L. Jackson.

WALKER'S ONE-WIRE, TWO-POSITION, BLOCK INSTRUMENT

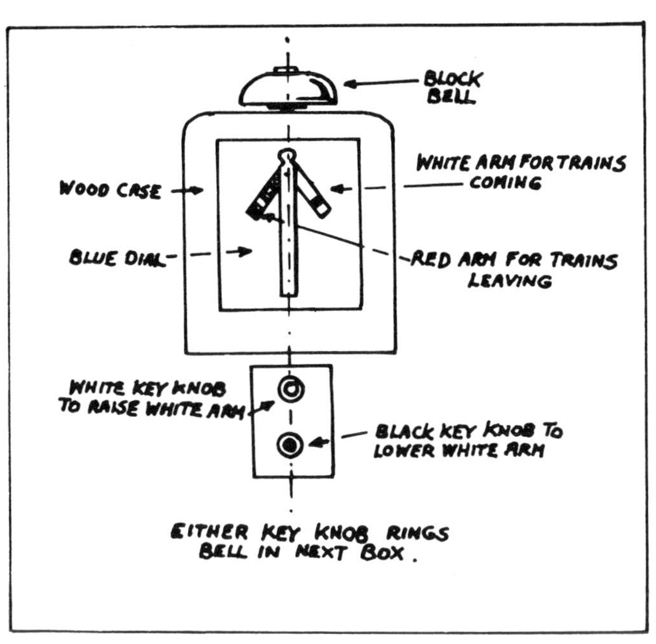

Walker's Instrument as originally introduced in 1864.

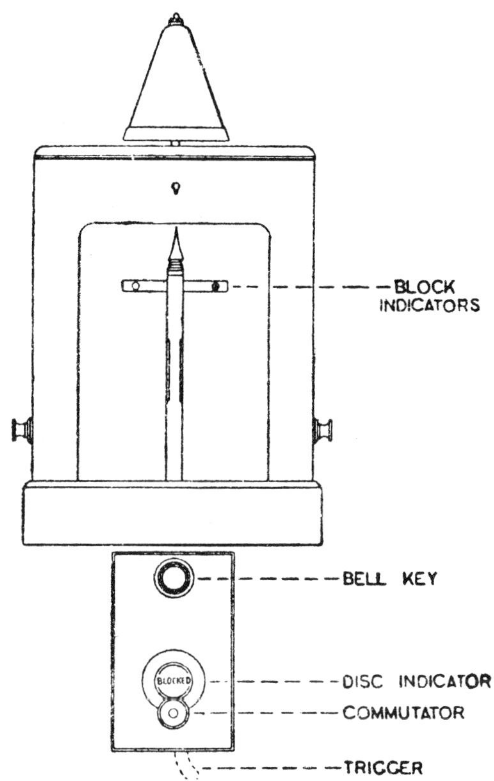

Later modifications, (as still in use) to commutator and bell key.

Mode of Signalling.—" A," " B " and " C " represent three consecutive Block Signal Boxes, and the process of signalling a Train is as follows :—

(a) Prior to the despatch of a Train from " A," the Signalman there, provided he has received the **Train Out of Section** Signal for the previous Train, and the Block Indicator is in its normal position, must call the attention of " B," and having obtained it, must give the proper **Is Line Clear** Signal. If the Line be clear at " B " the Signalman there must turn the commutator to the right, which will show " clear " on the Disc Indicator at " B," and acknowledge the **Is Line Clear** Signal which will lower the white semaphore arm at " B " and the red arm at " A " to the **Line Clear** position.

(b) On the Train leaving " A," the Signalman there must send the **Train Entering Section** Signal to " B " who must turn his commutator to the left to show **Train in Section** on his Disc Indicator, and acknowledge the Signal, which will raise the white arm at " B " and the red arm at " A " to the **Line Blocked** position.

(c) " B " must then, provided he has received the **Train Out of Section** Signal for the previous Train and the Block Indicator is in its normal position, call the attention of " C," and having obtained it must give the proper **Is Line Clear** Signal to " C." If the Line be clear " C " will give permission for the Train to approach. As soon as the Train has arrived at or passed " B," or been shunted clear of the Main Line at " B," the Signalman there must place the Disc Indicator to the normal position by means of the trigger and give the **Train Out of Section** Signal to " A," which " A " must acknowledge.

NOTE.—At certain places, slides (operated mechanically) have been fitted to Walker's Instruments, and these slides, when pushed to the right, prevent the Commutator from being turned.

The slides must be made use of by the Signalman when, in consequence of obstruction or exceptional occupation of the Line, it is necessary to refuse acceptance of a Train.

Working instructions for Walker's block instruments.

HARPER'S ONE-WIRE, TWO-POSITION, BLOCK INSTRUMENT

Plate 179 *(right).*
Detail of lower part of Harper's Instrument, Arundel Junction.

Photo C. Lambert

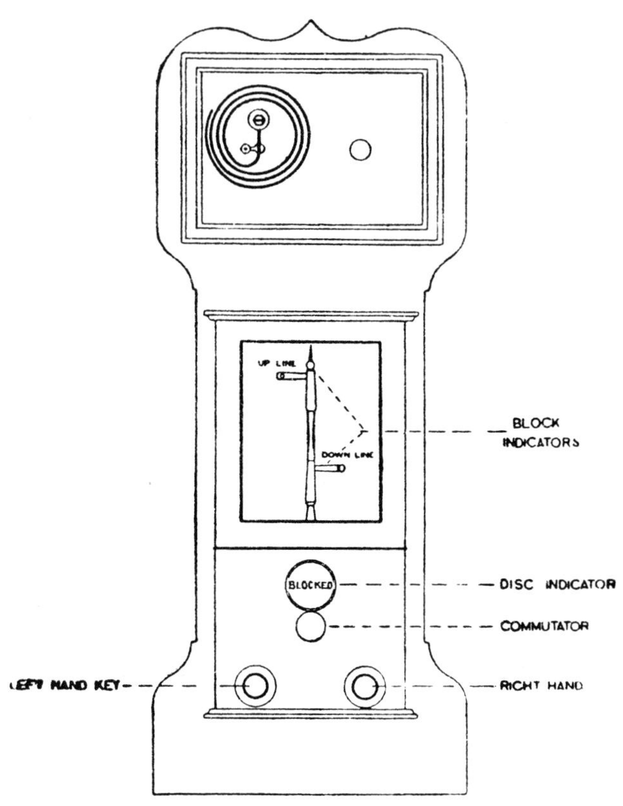

Mode of Signalling.—" A," " B " and " C " represent three consecutive Block Signal Boxes, and the process of signalling a Train is as follows :—

(a) Prior to the despatch of a Train from " A," the Signalman there, provided he has received the **Train Out of Section** Signal for the previous Train, and the Block Indicator is in its normal position, must call the attention of " B " on the left-hand key, and having obtained it, must give the proper **Is Line Clear** Signal on the left-hand key. If the Line be clear at " B " the Signalman there must turn the commutator to the right which will show **" Line Clear "** on the Disc Indicator at " B " and acknowledge the **Is Line Clear** Signal on the right-hand key, which will lower the white semaphore arm at " B " and the red arm at " A " to the **Line Clear** position.

(b) On the Train leaving " A," the Signalman there must send the **Train Entering Section** Signal to " B," on the left-hand key. " B " must turn his commutator to the left to show **Train on Line** on his Disc Indicator, and acknowledge the Signal on the left-hand key, which will raise the white arm at " B " and the red arm at " A " to the **Line Blocked** position.

(c) " B " must then, provided he has received the **Train Out of Section** Signal for the previous Train, and the Block Indicator is in its normal position, call the attention of " C," and having obtained it, must give the proper **Is Line Clear** Signal to " C," on the left-hand key. If the Line be clear, " C " will give permission for the Train to approach. As soon as the Train has arrived at or passed " B," or been shunted clear of the Main Line at " B," the Signalman there must turn the commutator to the left which will restore the Disc Indicator to the normal position, and give the **Train Out of Section** Signal to " A," on the left-hand key, which " A " must acknowledge.

NOTE.—When the white semaphore arm is lowered, all ringing for Trains on the opposite line must be done on the right-hand key.

SYKES' ONE-WIRE, TWO-POSITION, LOCK AND BLOCK INSTRUMENTS, WITH DOUBLE-ARM BLOCK INDICATOR

Plate 180.
W. R. Sykes introduced his 'Lock and Block' system in 1874, being granted the patent the following year. There was a general spread of this equipment after 1878. The set of instruments in the photograph are in Canterbury East Box.

Photo B. L. Jackson.

Mode of Signalling.—" A," " B " and " C " represent three consecutive Block Signal Boxes and the process of signalling a Train is as follows :—

(a) Prior to the despatch of a Train from " A " the Signalman there, provided he has received the **Train Out of Section** Signal for the previous Train and the Block Indicator is in its normal position, must call the attention of " B " and having obtained it must give the proper **Is Line Clear** Signal. If the Line be clear at " B " the Signalman there must turn his Commutator to lower his own Block Indicator and acknowledge the Signal, which will lower the Block Indicator at " A." He must then press in the Plunger firmly which will cause his own lower Tablet to change from **Blank** to **Train On,** unlock the leading signal at " A " and change the upper Tablet there from **locked** to **free.** The Signalman at " A " may then, if the Line is clear, lower his Signals for the Train to leave " A."

(b) On the Train leaving " A " the Signalman there must send the **Train Entering Section** Signal to " B " and the Signalman at " B " must place his Switch Hook over the Plunger, turn his Commutator to raise his own Block Indicator, and acknowledge the Signal which will raise the Block Indicator at " A."

(c) " B " must then, provided he has received the **Train Out of Section** Signal for the previous Train and the Block Indicator is in its normal position, call the attention of " C " and having obtained it must give the proper **Is Line Clear** Signal. On receiving permission from " C " for the Train to approach " B " may lower his Signals which will change his upper Tablet from **free to locked.**

(d) When the **Train passes** over the Treadle (where provided) fixed beyond the Home, Starting or Advanced Starting Signal at " B," it will change the upper Tablet there to **free** and enable the Signalman to replace the relevant Signal. The action of replacing the signal lever will restore the upper Tablet to **locked** and the lower Tablet to **blank ;** " B " must then remove the Switch Hook from the Plunger and give the **Train Out of Section** Signal to " A," which " A " must acknowledge.

(e) If the Line be not clear, or if from any cause the Signalman is not in a position to give permission for a Train to approach when the Signalman in the rear forwards the **Is Line Clear** Signal, that Signal must not be acknowledged but the Switch Hook must be turned over the Plunger. When the Line is again clear and the Signalman is in a position to give permission for a Train to approach the Switch Hook must be removed from the Plunger.

Note.—*Line Blocked Tablets have been fitted to certain of the Sykes' Instruments for the purpose of securing the Switch Hook over the Plunger and must be made use of by the Signalman when, in consequence of obstruction or exceptional occupation of the Line, it is necessary to refuse acceptance of a Train.*

Plate 181.
A Tyer's two-position Block Instrument, of the type installed by the 'Brighton' in 1874, in Christ's Hospital signal box.
Photo B. L. Jackson.

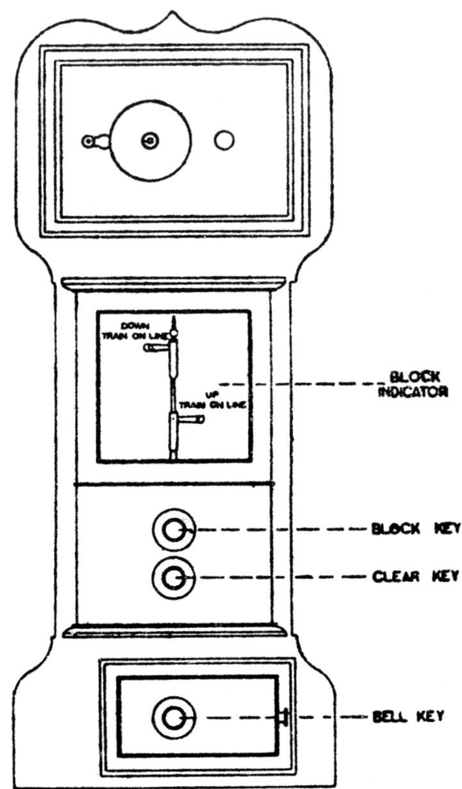

Mode of Signalling.—" A," " B " and " C " represent three consecutive Block Signal Boxes, and the process of signalling a Train is as follows :—

(a) Prior to the despatch of a Train from " A," the Signalman there, provided he has received the **Train Out of Section** Signal for the previous Train and the Block Indicator is in its normal position, must call the attention of " B " on the Bell Key, and having obtained it must give the proper **Is Line Clear** Signal on the Bell Key. If the Line be clear at " B " the Signalman there must acknowledge the Signal on the Clear Key which will lower the white semaphore arm at " B " and the red arm at " A " to the **Line Clear** position.

(b) On the Train leaving " A " the Signalman there must send the **Train Entering Section** Signal on the Bell Key to " B," who must acknowledge the Signal on the Block Key which will raise the white arm at " B " and the red arm at " A " to the **Line Blocked** position.

(c) " B " must then, provided he has received the **Train Out of Section** Signal for the previous Train and the Block Indicator is in its normal position, call the attention of " C," and having obtained it must give the proper **Is Line Clear** Signal to " C." If the Line be clear " C " will give permission for the Train to approach. As soon as the Train has arrived at or passed " B," or been shunted clear of the Main Line at " B," the Signalman there must give the **Train Out of Section Signal** to " A " on the Bell Key, which " A " must acknowledge.

TYER'S ONE-WIRE, THREE-POSITION, BLOCK INSTRUMENT

Plate 182.
Tyer's three-position block instrument.

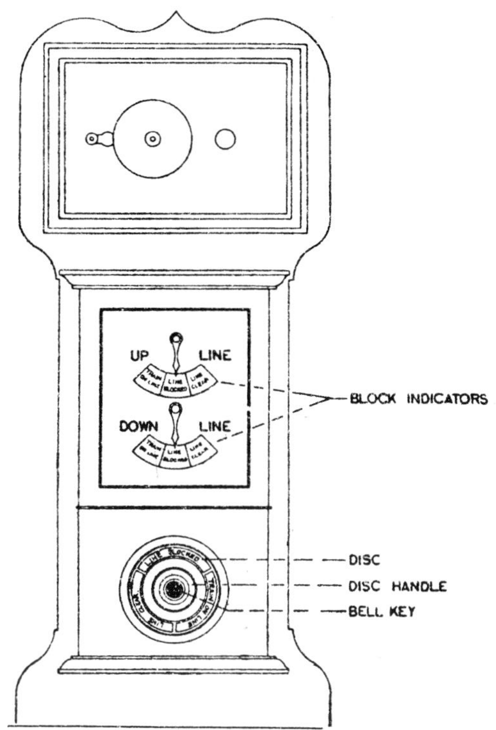

Mode of Signalling.—" A," " B " and " C " represent three consecutive Block Signal Boxes, and the process of signalling a Train is as follows :—

(a) Prior to the despatch of a Train from " A," the Signalman there, provided he has received the **Train Out of Section** Signal for the previous Train and the Block Indicator is in its normal (**Line Blocked**) position, must call the attention of " B " and having obtained it must give the proper **Is Line Clear** Signal to " B." If the Line be clear at " B," the Signalman there must turn the Disc to the **Line Clear** position and acknowledge the Signal which will place his own lower Block Indicator and the Upper Block Indicator at " A " to the **Line Clear** position.

(b) On the Train leaving " A " the Signalman there must send the **Train Entering Section** Signal to " B." " B " must turn the Disc to the **Train on Line** position and acknowledge the signal, which will place his own lower Block Indicator and the upper Block Indicator at " A " to the **Train on Line** position.

(c) " B " must then, provided he has received the **Train Out of Section** Signal for the previous Train and the Block Indicator is in its normal position, call the attention of " C," and having obtained it must give the proper **Is Line Clear** Signal to " C." If the Line be clear, " C " will give permission for the Train to approach. As soon as the Train has arrived at or passed " B " or been shunted clear of the Main Line at " B," the Signalman there must turn the Disc to the normal (**Line Blocked**) position and give the **Train Out of Section** Signal to " A," which will restore the Block Indicators in both Boxes to the normal (**Line Blocked**) position. " A " must acknowledge the signal.

NOTES.—(i) *It is necessary, in connection with all movements of the Block Indicators, that the disc should be turned* **before** *the Bell Signals are sent.*

(ii) *In connection with the opening of a Signal Box where Switches are provided, if a Train or Engine should be in progress on one or both lines of rails the Signalmen concerned must so advise the Signalman at the Opening Box, and give the position of their Indicators and Discs working with the Opening Box. The Signalman at the Opening Box must then place or maintain his Discs to corresponding positions, and after having put the Switch to the* **In Circuit** *position, give the* **Opening** *Signal, which must be acknowledged in the usual manner.*

Official instructional drawing and operating instructions for Tyer's one-wire three-position block instruments. These were first introduced about 1880, when they were installed on the Brighton main line south of Balcombe Station.

Photograph Courtesy the National Railway Museum, York.

SYKES' THREE-WIRE, TWO-POSITION, LOCK AND BLOCK INSTRUMENT

Plate 183.
Instruments old and new at East Croydon. The "Lock and Block" instruments are on the left, with separate sending and receiving units. To the right can be seen a magazine-type train describer, and on the woodwork above, a variety of repeaters for signals, a back-lock, and a lamp.

Photo E. J. White.

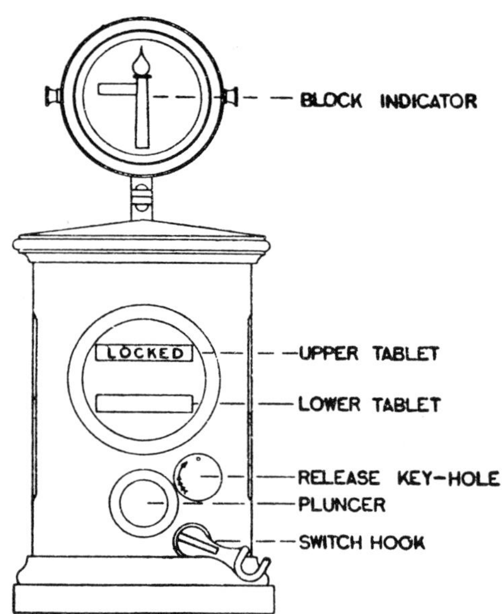

Note:—The Sykes' Lock and Block two-position instruments, although similar in appearance, are arranged to work in two different ways, i.e. —

(i) As used on the Central and Eastern Sections (normal position of block indicator being lowered).

(ii) As used on the Western Section (normal position of block indicator being raised).

Mode of Signalling—Central and Eastern Sections.—" A," " B," and " C " represent three consecutive Block Signal Boxes and the process of signalling a Train is as follows :—

(a) Prior to the despatch of a Train from " A " the Signalman there, provided he has received the **Train Out of Section** Signal for the previous Train and the Block Indicator is in its normal position, must call the attention of " B " and having obtained it must give the proper **Is Line Clear** Signal. If the Line be clear at " B " the Signalman there must acknowledge the Signal and press in the Plunger firmly which will cause his own lower Tablet to change from **Blank to Train On,** unlock the leading signal at " A," change the upper Tablet there from **locked to free** and raise the Block Indicator at " A." The Signalman at " A " may then, if the Line be clear, lower his Signals for the Train to leave " A."

(b) On the Train leaving " A " the Signalman there must send the **Train Entering Section** Signal to " B " and the Signalman at " B " must thereupon place his Switch Hook over the Plunger and acknowledge the Signal.

(c) " B " must then, provided he has received the **Train Out of Section** Signal for the previous Train and the Block Indicator is in its normal position, call the attention of " C " and having obtained it must give the proper **Is Line Clear** Signal. On receiving permission from " C " for the Train to approach " B " may lower his Signals which will change his upper Tablet from **free** to **locked.**

(d) When the Train passes over the Treadle (where provided) fixed beyond the Home, Starting or Advanced Starting Signal at " B," it will change the upper Tablet there to **free** and enable the Signalman to replace the relevant Signal. The action of replacing the Signal Lever will restore the upper Tablet to **locked** and the lower Tablet to **blank** ; " B " must then remove the Switch Hook from the Plunger (which will lower the Block Indicator at " A ") and give the **Train Out of Section** Signal to " A " which " A " must acknowledge.

(e) If the Line is not clear, or if from any cause the Signalman is not in a position to give permission for a Train to approach when the Signalman in the rear forwards the **Is Line Clear** Signal, that Signal must not be acknowledged but the Switch Hook must be turned over the Plunger which will lock the Plunger and raise the Block Indicator at the Box in the rear. When the Line is again clear and the Signalman is in a position to give permission for a Train to approach the Switch Hook must be removed from the Plunger which will lower the Block Indicator at the Box in rear.

NOTES.—At certain Boxes in the London Area of the Eastern Section, Needle Instruments are provided in place of Bell Keys.

Line Blocked Tablets have been fitted to certain of the Sykes' Instruments for the purpose of securing the Switch Hook over the Plunger and must be made use of by the Signalman when, in consequence of obstruction or exceptional occupation of the Line, it is necessary to refuse acceptance of a Train.

Mode of Signalling—Western Section.—" A," " B " and " C " represent three consecutive Block Signal Boxes, and the process of signalling a Train is as follows :—

(a) Prior to the despatch of a Train from " A," the Signalman there, provided he has received the **Train Out of Section** Signal for the previous Train and the Block Indicator is in its normal position, must call the attention of " B," and having obtained it, must give the proper **Is Line Clear** Signal. If the Line be clear at " B " the Signalman there must acknowledge the Signal, remove the Switch Hook from the Plunger (which will lower the Block Indicator at " A ") and press in the Plunger firmly, which will cause his own lower Tablet to change from **Blank** to **Train On,** unlock the leading signal at " A " and change the upper Tablet there from **Locked** to **Free.**

(b) On the Train leaving " A," the Signalman there must send the **Train Entering Section** Signal to " B." " B " must thereupon place his Switch Hook over the Plunger (which will raise the Block Indicator at " A "), and acknowledged the Signal.

(c) " B " must then, provided he has received the **Train Out of Section** Signal for the previous Train and the Block Indicator is in its normal position, call the attention of " C," and having obtained it must give the proper **Is Line Clear** Signal to " C." If the Line be clear " C " will give permission for the Train to approach which will unlock the leading Signal at " B," change the upper Tablet there from **Locked** to **Free,** and lower the Block Indicator at " B." " B " may then lower his Signals, which will change his upper Tablet from **Free** to **Locked.**

(d) On the Train leaving " B," the Signalman there must send the **Train Entering Section** Signal to " C." " C " will thereupon place his Switch Hook over the Plunger (which will raise the Block Indicator at " B ") and acknowledge the Signal.

(e) When the Train passes over the Treadle fixed beyond the Home, Starting or Advanced Starting Signal at " B," it will change the upper Tablet there to **Free** and enable the Signalman to replace the relative signal. The action of replacing the appropriate signal lever will restore the upper Tablet to **Locked** and the lower Tablet to **Blank.** " B " must then give the **Train Out of Section** Signal to " A," which " A " must acknowledge.

NOTE.—Line Blocked Tablets have been fitted to certain Sykes' Instruments for the purpose of securing the Switch Hook over the Plunger, and must be made use of by the Signalman when, in consequence of obstruction or exceptional occupation of the Line, it is necessary to refuse acceptance of a Train.

Plate 184.

Standard S.R. closing switch at Hamworthy Junction. it would obviously be very expensive in terms of wages, if every signal box had to be open whenever a train was required to run. At times of light traffic, such as at night and on Sundays, many intermediate boxes can be done without. When the Signalman pulls the switch, an arm carrying a series of contacts moves forward, breaking the contacts with the instruments and bells at his box and making with others to form a through circuit by-passing that particular box. The boxes on either side are then in direct communication with each other, whilst the block bells and instruments at the box where the switch has been pulled, become inoperative. The action of pulling the switch revolves, by means of a small cog wheel, the brass tablet below, to read "out".

Photo B. L. Jackson.

SYKES' THREE-WIRE, THREE-POSITION, LOCK AND BLOCK INSTRUMENT

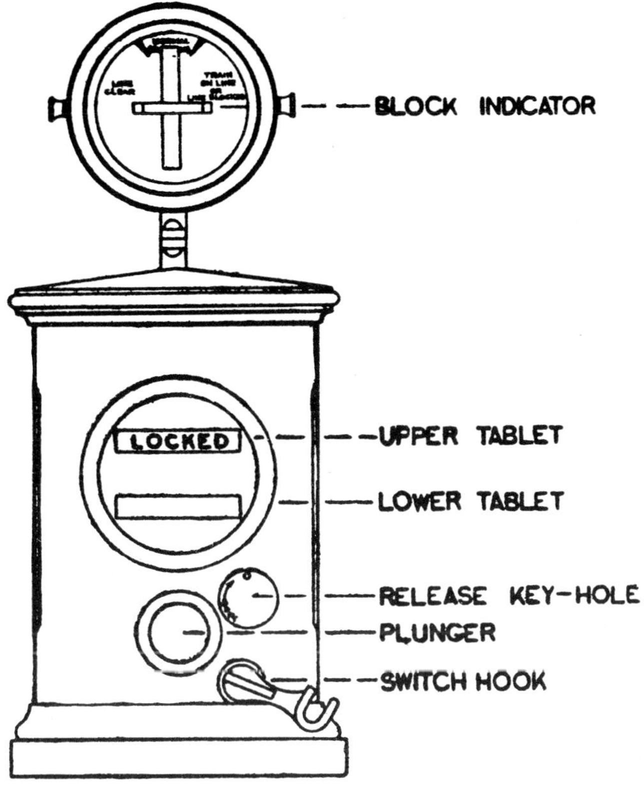

Mode of Signalling.—" A," " B " and " C " represent three consecutive Block Signal Boxes, and the process of signalling a Train is as follows :—

(a) Prior to the despatch of a Train from " A " the Signalman there, provided he has received the **Train Out of Section** Signal for the previous Train and the Block Indicator is in its normal position, must call the attention of " B," and having obtained it, must give the proper **Is Line Clear** Signal. If the Line be clear at " B " the Signalman there must acknowledge the Signal and press in the Plunger firmly, which will cause his own lower Tablet to change from **Red** to **Train Accepted,** unlock the leading Signal at " A," change the upper Tablet there from **Locked** to **Free,** and place the Block Indicator at " A " to the **Line Clear** position.

(b) On the Train leaving " A " the Signalman there must send the **Train Entering Section** Signal to " B." " B " must acknowledge the Signal and place the Switch Hook over the Plunger which will change the Block Indicator at " A " to **Train on Line** and will also in certain cases alter the indication on the lower Tablet at " B " to **Train On.**

(c) " B " must then, provided he has received the **Train Out of Section** Signal for the previous Train and the Block Indicator is in its normal position, call the attention of " C," and having obtained it must give the proper **Is Line Clear** Signal to " C." If the Line be clear " C " will give permission for the Train to approach, which will unlock the leading Signal at " B," change the upper Tablet there from **Locked** to **Free** and place the Block Indicator at " B " to the **Line Clear** position. " B " may then lower his Signals which will change his upper Tablet from **Free** to **Locked.**

(d) When the Train passes over the Treadle fixed beyond the Home, Starting or Advanced Starting Signal at " B " it will change the upper Tablet there to **Free** and enable the Signalman to replace the relative Signal. The action of replacing the appropriate signal lever will restore the upper Tablet to **Locked** and the lower Tablet to **Red,** " B " must then remove the Switch Hook from the Plunger which will place the Block Indicator at " A " to normal, after which the **Train Out of Section** Signal must be given to and acknowledged by " A."

Note.—*Line Blocked Tablets have been fitted to certain Sykes' Instruments for the purpose of securing the Switch Hook over the Plunger, and must be made use of by the Signalman when, in consequence of obstruction or exceptional occupation of the Line, it is necessary to refuse acceptance of a Train.*

Official instructional drawing and operating instructions for Sykes' three-wire three-position block instruments.

STANDARD THREE-WIRE, THREE-POSITION, BLOCK INSTRUMENT

Plates 185 and 186.
The "standard" instrument (left), and an exploded view (right), showing commutator contacts.

Photos B. L. Jackson.

The Southern Railway, faced with such a tremendous variety of Block Instruments inherited from the pre-grouping companies, quickly designed a more up-to-date three-position instrument. In the 'exploded' view, (above, right), can be seen the commutator drum, to which are attached a number of brass contacts. Other spring contacts mounted alongside made or break with the contacts on the commutator according to whether it is placed in the 'Normal', 'Line Clear' or 'Train on Line' position, and can be used for a number of purposes. For instance, in many places, the Distant and Home signals must be proved 'ON', and the approach track circuit 'clear' before the commutator can be turned to the 'Line Clear' position. Many other such circuits, designed to reduce the risk of accidents caused by errors on the part of the Signalman, can be proved through these instruments. A useful feature is that the upper dial can be turned to any desired angle, to afford the Signalman a view at a glance of the state of the section ahead—a great asset in a large box with a long lever frame. The upper dials can also be detached, and used separately as indicators at intermediate level crossings which are not 'Block Posts', so that the crossing-keeper can note at once the state of the section, and thereby decide whether it is safe to open the gates.

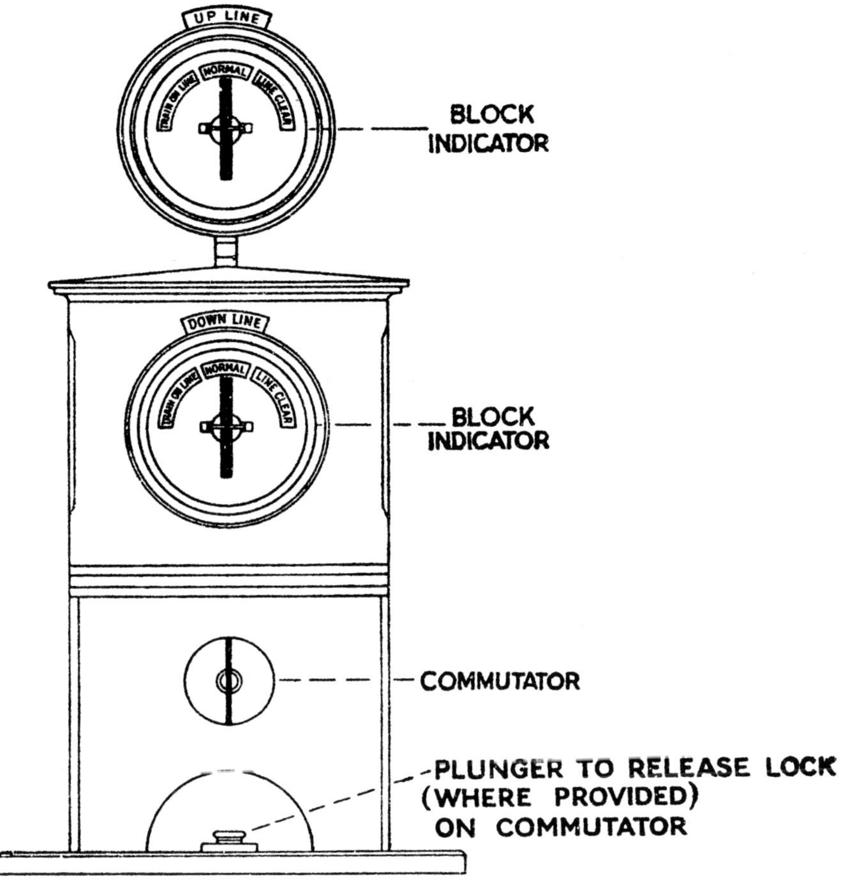

NOTE.—The Plunger to release the Lock on the Commutator will require to be operated only when the Commutator is turned from **" Normal "** *to* **" Line Clear."**

Mode of Signalling.—" A," " B " and " C " represent three consecutive Block Signal Boxes, and the process of signalling a Train is as follows :—

(a) Prior to the despatch of a Train from " A," the Signalman there, provided he has received the **Train Out of Section** Signal for the previous Train, and the Block Indicator is in its normal position, must call the attention of " B," and having obtained it, must give the proper **Is Line Clear** Signal ; if the Line be clear at " B," the Signalman there must acknowledge the Signal and turn his Commutator to the right which will change his lower Block Indicator from **" Normal "** to **" Line Clear "** and at the same time change " A's " upper Block Indicator to **" Line Clear."**

(b) On the Train leaving " A," the Signalman there must send the **Train Entering Section** Signal to " B," and the Signalman at " B " must acknowledge the Signal and turn his Commutator to the left, which will change his lower Block Indicator and " A's " upper Block Indicator to **" Train on Line."**

(c) " B " must then, provided he has received the **Train Out of Section** Signal for the previous Train, and the Block Indicator is in its normal position, call the attention of " C," and, having obtained it, must give the proper **Is Line Clear** Signal to " C." If the Line be clear, " C " will give permission for the Train to approach. As soon as the Train has arrived at, or passed " B," or been shunted clear of the Main Line at " B," the Signalman there must place the Block Indicator to its normal position, and give the **Train Out of Section** Signal to " A," which " A " must acknowledge.

Cancelling Arrangements. Standard Three-Position Closed Block Apparatus.—At certain Signal Boxes special apparatus is provided whereby when the Block Commutator has been turned to **" Line Clear "** and back to **" Train on Line "** or **" Normal "** it cannot again be turned to **" Line Clear "** until the relevant Home Signal has been lowered, a Train has operated a Treadle or Track Circuit ahead of the Home Signal and such Signal has been replaced to Danger.

In the event of a Train being cancelled the Signalman acknowledging the **Cancelling** Signal in accordance with Block Regulation 18 must turn the Commutator to **" Normal."** He must then telephone to the Box in rear and arrange with the Signalman there for the Push Button Releases at both Boxes to be depressed simultaneously which will release the Lock on the Commutator so that it can be placed to **" Line Clear "** when the next Train on the Line affected is accepted.

Should the Signal at the rear Box controlling the entrance to the Section ahead have been lowered and the **Train Entering Section** Signal sent and acknowledged before the Train is cancelled, the Back-lock of such Signal will be released by the placing of the Block Indicator to **" Train on Line "** and this Signal must be replaced to Danger before the **Cancelling** Signal is given. If the **Train Entering Section** Signal has not been sent the operation of the Release Buttons will release the Back-lock of the leading Signal.

Instructions for the operation of standard Southern Railway Three-position Block Instruments.
Note: At some time, the position of the plunger to release the commutator lock was moved from that shown in the above drawing, to a more convenient position immediately to the left of the commutator.

Plate 187.

Walker's Rotary Train Describer, (sending instruments), at North Kent West Junction. It would perhaps be more appropriate to call them 'Destination Describers', as that is the information they convey, and not a description of the type of train. For this reason it is necessary to supplement them with block bells, the advantage being that only one set of bell codes is required. From the number of places named on the dial, it is easy to see how many special 'route' codes would be needed if such instruments were not provided. The method of working the describers is best illustrated by a quote from the L.B. & S.C.R. rules:— 'The lever at the description required must be pulled forward, and the lever where the pointer is then resting put back; the pointer will then move forward to the description required, and remain there until the next train is described.'

Photo C. Lambert.

Plate 188.

Sykes' One-wire two-position 'Lock and Block' instruments built into the panel above the power frame in Maidstone East signal box.

Photo B. L. Jackson.

Plate 189.

Instruments of L.B. & S.C.R. vintage preserved by the 'Bluebell Railway' in Horsted Keynes box. On the left is a 'Train Waiting' indicator and bell, to warn the Signalman when a train arrives at the Home Signal. To the right are two 'Brighton' pattern signal repeaters.

Photo B. L. Jackson.

Plate 190 *(above).*
Typical L. & S.W.R. Block Shelf at Fulwell Junction showing, from right to left, a closing switch, three Preece's two-position block instruments and associated switch handles, and a pair of Sykes treadle release instruments. The brass bell plungers and signal repeaters are mounted along the front of the shelf. The track diagram is of the non-illuminated old style, including a table of the mechanical locking.

Photo C. Lambert.

Plate 191 *(left).*
Occasionally it was found necessary to add a lever to the frame, particularly when 'Intermediate' signals were installed to shorten the section. However, here at Liss the frame could not be extended, so a pull-out pistol grip lever was attached to the end of the Block Shelf, and numbered as 'Lever 22'. The assembly also incorporates a signal repeater at the top.

Photo P. D. Rutter.

PART THREE – THE TRAIN REGISTER BOOK

At most signal boxes, the Signalmen are required to maintain what is known as a 'Train Register'—a specially printed book or sheet upon which must be recorded all bell signals sent or received by means of the Block bell, together with details of any messages affecting the working of traffic, or unusual occurrences. The keeping of these records is known to Signalmen as 'Booking', and a good Signalman will ensure that it is kept with care, entries being inserted as quickly as possible.

Train Registers are important for a number of reasons. Firstly, they provide a reminder to the Signalman of exactly what trains are in his Block Sections, a matter over which he could easily become confused at a very busy box, or a box controlling four lines or a junction. They can be looked upon as a 'diary' of day-to-day events at the signal box, and as such, can frequently furnish valuable evidence at enquiries into railway accidents. For instance, an Inspector can tell by looking at the times recorded in the book, whether a certain train was travelling at excessive speed over a given section of line, simply by taking the interval between the time the 'Train Entering Section' signal was received, and the time the train passed the box. If that particular class of train normally took six minutes to run through the section, but on the occasion of the accident covered the distance in four minutes, 'dangerous driving' is immediately indicated. By knowing the distance between boxes, the exact speed of the train can be worked out.

The sample 'page', reproduced by permission of British Rail, (Southern Region), is an extract from the register of Broad Clyst Signal Box, four miles out of Exeter on the former main line to Waterloo. The block sections on either side are to Pinhoe, (1 mile, 1,511 yards), in the direction of Exeter, and to Whimple, (3 miles, 1,163 yards), in the direction of London. Although this box was small, the register is of interest for a number of reasons, but before looking at these, the layout of the book should be explained.

It will be noted that a day's work actually occupies two pages of the book, so printed that when it is opened flat on the desk, the page on the Left is for 'Down Line' entries, and that on the Right for 'Up Line'. Columns are provided for all regular bell signals, leaving the Signalman to enter the details of the trains concerned and the times. No columns are provided, however, for any of the 'Emergency' signals, or for such things as Opening and Closing signals, and entries of this nature must be written across the page. In addition, all Signalmen must sign the Register when taking or leaving duty, and any visiting official, such as a Station Master or Area Inspector, must also sign it adding the time of his visit, as a witness to the fact that he has visited the box and found the working in order and the Register up to date.

Looking at our sample page, a number of interesting facts emerge. Most obvious is the fact that, although the Signalman signs on duty at 6.45 a.m. he does not open the Signal Box until 9.05. There is also a further period in the afternoon, from 1.56 p.m. to 3.29 p.m. when the Box is switched out. This is a true reflection of life at a small Southern country station at that time, where the Signalman was often expected to do far more than operate the signal box. At Broad Clyst, the first part of the turn was spent in the Ticket Office, and the afternoon period of closure allowed the Signalman to trim and fill the station oil lamps, weed the flower-beds, and assist the 'Leading Porter' with the goods traffic. Such staff economies were widely practised on the Southern, although not all Signalmen could be used in this way. It was possible to do so at Broad Clyst because the Block Section to Pinhoe was very short, and such a short section was not required during the slacker periods of the day. It is interesting to note that, on both occasions that the box was opened, a train was already in the section. No time is therefore shown in the 'Regulation 4' column, but the letters 'T.I.S.' (Train In Section), are inserted instead. It is perfectly in order to open a box with trains in the section, but closure cannot take place until the sections are clear of traffic, and all Block Indicators in the 'Normal' position.

Because of the shortness of the section in the direction of Pinhoe, the 'Is Line Clear?' signal was transmitted forward to Whimple immediately on receipt for Up trains not stopping at Pinhoe or Broad Clyst. If this was not done, such trains would be likely to miss the Up Distant, causing them to lose considerable time.

An intriguing entry will be found on the Down page:—'Shunt Move. 4-2'. This special code was provided for in the 'Special Instructions' for the box, and was used as follows. The West Crossover Points at Whimple were situated beyond the Starting Signal, and were therefore released by the Block, the Whimple Signalman having to obtain a 'Line Clear' from Broad Clyst before he could pull the points. When the movement was completed, and the points again restored to 'Normal', the Whimple Signalman would withdraw the move by sending the special bell code '3 Consecutively', upon receipt of which, the Signalman at Broad Clyst would restore his Block Instrument to 'Normal' and repeat the bell signal.

Pads of tear-off sheets are now standard on the Southern Region in place of Train Register Books. With this method of booking, a carbon copy is made, and at the end of the day the sheets are torn off, the top copy being sent to the Divisional Offices, and the carbon copy being retained in the Signal box.

B.R. 24847

DOWN

Broad Clyst. Signal Box

Mon day, 1st day of November 1964

Description of Train	REAR SECTION: Is Line Clear: Received but not accepted	Accepted under— Regulation 5(3-5-5) or Permissive (2-4-2 or 4-3)	Regulation 4	Train approaching Signal received	Train entering Section received	Train out of Section sent	Time description received	Train arrived	Train departed or passed	Line	ADVANCE SECTION: Is Line Clear: Offered but not accepted	Accepted under— Regulation 5(3-5-5) or Permissive (2-4-2 or 4-3)	Regulation 4	Train approaching Signal sent	Train entering Section sent	Train out of Section received	Time description sent	Remarks
		—		Clock	correct	@	9.5 AM					—						
7.50 Yeovil Town.			9.6		11	17		16	16½				9 11		17	24		
4 50 S'oton Docks ft			17		21	28			28				24		28	32		
6 30 Wilton Stone Etys.			37		44	49			49				44		49	53		
B B Signal 2-4			49		c/R	10 15												
8.10 Salisbury			10 15		21	26			26				10 21		26	28		
11/12 Honiton Engine			11 17		23	28			28				11 23		28	31		
Shunt Move. 4-2			55		Canc.	58												
10.57 Whimple ft.			58		12 0	14		10			To	Down	Sidings					
Sidmouth Goods.			12 14		14	21			21				12 14		21	26		
8 30 Yeovil Jc. ft.			21		26	34			34				26		34	38		
9 0 Waterloo			34		37	41			41				38		41	44		
10 57 Whimple ft.			Ex	Down	Sidings				44				44		44	49		
10 50 Salisbury			59		1 5	10		9	9½				1 5		10	15		
Engine.			1 18		23	29			29				23		29	33		
1 10 Salisbury			T.I.S.		—	3.29		3 27	28				T.I.S		—	3.32		
1 20 Salisbury ft.			3 29		33	39			39				33		39	42		
3 40 Sidmouth			4 2		8	14		12½	13½				4 8		14	18		
1.00 Waterloo			22		27	30			30				27		30	32		
4.00 Honiton.			30		38	45		44	45				38		45	49		

— [illegible] A. Dyer off Duty 6.45 PM. —

B.R. 24847

Broad Clyst. Signal Box

Mon day, 1st day of November 1964

UP

Description of Train	REAR SECTION — Is Line Clear — Received but not accepted	Accepted under— Regulation 5(3-5-5) or Permissive (2-4-2 or 4-3)	Regulation 4	Train approaching Signal received	Train entering Section received	Train out of Section sent	Time description received	Train arrived	Train departed or passed	Line	ADVANCE SECTION — Is Line Clear — Offered but not accepted	Accepted under— Regulation 5(3-5-5) or Permissive (2-4-2 or 4-3)	Regulation 4	Train approaching Signal sent	Train entering Section sent	Train out of Section received	Time description sent	Remarks
— C J A Pryer on Duty 6.45 AM. —																		
Opening signals to Pinhoe & Whimple 9.1 AM.																		
00 Plymouth.			T.I.S	—		9 3		9.1	·2				T.I.S	—		9.12		
00 Exmouth Jc ft			9.3		6	50		13	·	Shunt Up sidings, then to Down sidings.								
50 Plymouth.			10 17		19	·21	——	·	21				10.17		21	28		
30 Exeter.			43		46	48			48				43		48	56		
Engine.			48		51	56		55		To Up Sidings. (Pilot for 09 00 Ex Jc ft)								
00 Exmouth Jc ft			— Ex Up Sidings —						11 1				11 00		11. 1	45		
5 Torrington.			11 59		12.2	·06		05	05½				12.2		·06	13		
55 Plymouth.			12 33		38	40			40				12 33		40	45		
7 Exeter St. Davids.			1 22		·25	·29		·28	28½				1 25		·29	36		
5 Exmouth Jc ft			38		43	47			·47				38		47	56		
—— Closing signals to Pinhoe & Whimple 1 56 PM. ——																		
—— Opening signals to Pinhoe & Whimple 3 29 PM. ——																		
B Signal 2 4			——										3 29		O/R	38		
5 Meldon Stone			3 30		36	40			39				38		39	46		Check.
8 Exeter.			53		·57	4 1		59½	4 0				57		4 0	4.7		
50 Plymouth.			4 32		·37	·39			·39				4 32		39	46		
35 Exeter.			39		43	47		45	·46				46		46	·55		
—— Closing signals to Pinhoe & Whimple 4 56 PM. ——																		

8. Control of Single Lines

Safe working over single lines needs additional controls to those required for double line block working as already described. Not only must it be impossible for the Signalman at either end of the section to admit a second train until the previous one has cleared the box in advance, but the opposite direction must also be 'locked up' to prevent trains from meeting head-on in the middle of the section. Therefore all types of Tablet and Token instruments have common features; once a Tablet or Token has been withdrawn from an instrument, the Signalman cannot withdraw another until it has either been inserted in the instrument at the other end of the section, or restored to his own instrument. The action of withdrawing the Tablet or Token also electrically locks the instrument at the other end of the section, making it impossible for the Signalman there to withdraw one to permit a conflicting movement.

In all instances, the Tablet or Token travels with the driver of the train. If a train is double-headed or banked by an engine in rear through the section, the Driver of the first engine is shown the Tablet, and it is given to the Driver of the second engine. The one exception to this rule is where 'Train Staff and Ticket' working is in use. With this system, should two trains be following in the same direction before anything is to come the opposite way, the Driver of the first train is shown the Staff, and given a specially printed 'Ticket' as his authority to occupy the single line. The Staff is given to the Driver of the second train. As with Tablets, Tokens, etc, the Driver must surrender the Ticket to the Signalman at the other end of the section. An example of a single-line 'Ticket' is illustrated below. The security of the section is safeguarded by the fact that there is only ONE staff, the end of which is formed into a key for unlocking the box of tickets. A Signalman cannot therefore gain access to a ticket unless he is also in possession of the Staff, and it will be noted from the wording of the Ticket, that as an additional precaution against forced locks or other irregular means of working, the Driver must SEE the staff before accepting a ticket from the Signalman.

The simplest form of single line control is the 'One Engine In Steam' method (today called 'One Train' working). This dispenses with the need for signals, and controls of any kind are minimal, perhaps consisting only of a mechanical lever lock on the points giving access to the single line. As with 'Staff and Ticket' working, only one train staff is provided, but in this case there are no 'Tickets' or any other provision for admitting a second train until the Signalman who issued the Train Staff has it back in his possession.

Today, new forms of operating single lines have been introduced. Along with Tablets, Tokens, Staves, and the other 'Traditional' ideas, we now have 'Tokenless Block', a device which secures the section by the electrical interlocking of the block instruments. Of recent origin, it is outside the scope of this book. The use of Interlocking Levers and Track Circuits is not a new idea, but until recent years it was confined to very short sections of single track, chiefly because of the cost of providing long stretches of continuous track circuiting. However, as power signalling spreads, and with it the use of track circuits, this system is now occasionally used over fairly long single lines, such as between Romsey and Eastleigh.

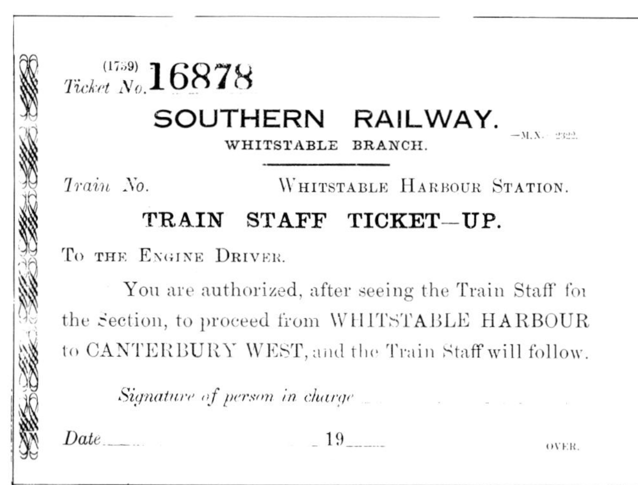

(1759) Ticket No. 16878

SOUTHERN RAILWAY.

WHITSTABLE BRANCH.

Train No. WHITSTABLE HARBOUR STATION.

TRAIN STAFF TICKET—UP.

To the Engine Driver.

You are authorized, after seeing the Train Staff for the Section, to proceed from WHITSTABLE HARBOUR to CANTERBURY WEST, and the Train Staff will follow.

Signature of person in charge

Date 19

OVER.

This Ticket must be given up by the Engine Driver, immediately on arrival, to the person in charge of the Staff working at the place to which he is authorized to proceed to be cancelled and dealt with as the latter may be instructed by the Chief Operating Superintendent.

Figs. 45 and 46.
A single-line Ticket, as used in 'Train Staff and Ticket' working. The left-hand plate shows the front of the ticket, and the right-hand one the reverse.

Produced by courtesy of British Rail, Southern Region.

Another system that dispenses with the need for signals, but offers a greater degree of freedom in operating the traffic, is the 'No Signalman' key token. With these, two or more trains can be allowed to work on the branch at a time, subject to certain specially provided safeguards, as illustrated below.

Plate 192.
Shows the 'No Signalman' token instrument in Hamworthy Junction Box, used for working the branch to Hamworthy Goods. On withdrawing a token from the instrument the Signalman must insert it in the lever lock shown below in **Plate 193**, *and turn it to lock the lever 'Normal', before handing it to the Driver. By this means, he is prevented from setting the points to let another train onto the branch until either the Token has been inserted in the instrument at the opposite end of the line, (Located in the Goods Office), which allows him to withdraw a second token, or the train has returned with the same token. No bell signals are used with this mode of working, but a tablet, showing 'Locked' or 'Free' is fitted to the instrument. When a Token is withdrawn from either end, the tablet shows 'Locked', and the word 'Free' only appears when no keys are out. Whilst the tablet shows 'Free', the person at either end may withdraw a token, which action electrically locks opposing moves.*
Photos B. L. Jackson.

*The Electric Key Token instrument is without doubt the simplest of the many systems designed for the control of single lines, and offers flexible working. On the Southern, Tyer's Key Token Instruments were the most widely used, and the working instructions for these are given below. The photograph (*Plate 194*) shows the Tyer's Instrument in Hamworthy Junction signal box, used to control the section from there to Broadstone.*

Photo Author's Collection.

ELECTRIC TRAIN KEY-TOKEN INSTRUMENT.

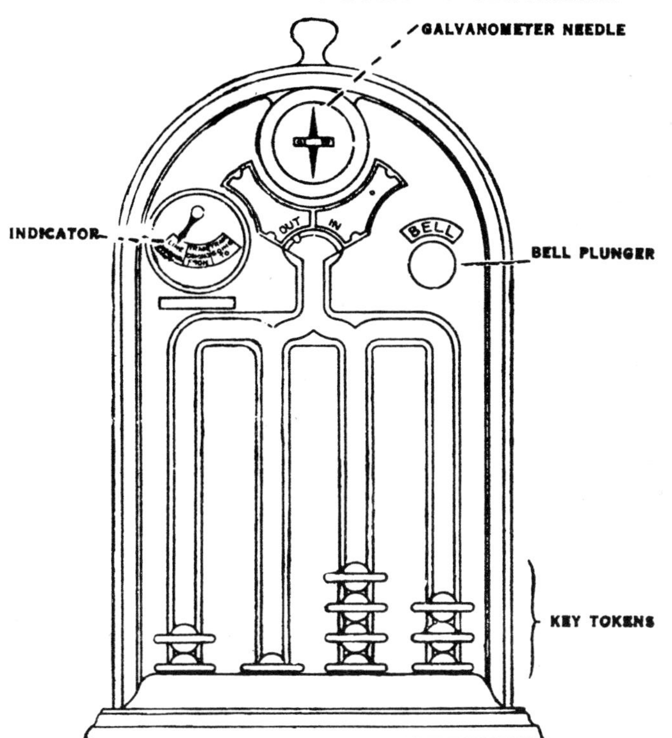

Mode of Signalling.—" A " and " B " represent two Signal Boxes and the process of signalling a Train is as follows :—

Prior to the despatch of a Train from " A " the Signalman there, provided he has received the **Train Out of Section** Signal for the previous Train and permission has not been given for a Train to approach in the opposite direction, and provided the Key-Token Indicator is in the **Line normal** position, must give the prescribed **Is Line Clear** Signal to " B." If the Line be clear at " B " the Signalman there, if he is prepared to receive the Train, must acknowledge the Signal and hold in his Bell Plunger on the last beat until the Galvanometer Needle, which will be deflected to the left, momentarily returns twice to the upright position, which will indicate that a Key-Token has been withdrawn at " A."

When the Signalman at " A " observes the Galvanometer Needle deflected to the left after the acknowledgment of the **Is Line Clear** Signal, he must place a Key-Token on the Pin and give it two half turns to the left, which will place his Indicator to the **Train going to** position. The Key-Token can then be withdrawn from the Instrument. When the Galvanometer Needle has again returned to the upright position after " B " has released the Plunger, " A " must give one beat to " B," which will change " B's " Indicator to the **Train Coming from** position.

The Signalman at " A " will then lower his Signals for the Train to leave and hand the Key-Token in the pouch, where provided, to the Driver. On the Train leaving " A " the Signalman there must send the **Train Entering Section** Signal to " B " and the Signalman at " B " must acknowledge the Signal.

On arrival of the Train at " B " the Signalman must obtain the Key-Token from the Driver and deposit it in the Instrument by placing it on the Pin and giving it two half turns to the right. He must then give " A " the **Train Out of Section** Signal, which will change " A's " Indicator to the **Line normal** position and the acknowledgment of the **Train Out of Section** Signal will place " B's " Indicator to the **Line normal** position.

If necessary, a Key-Token can be replaced in the Instrument from which it was withdrawn, after which the **Cancelling** Signal must be sent which will place the Indicator at the opposite end to **Line normal**, and upon this Signal being acknowledged the Indicator in the **Cancelling Box** will be placed to the **Line normal** position.

Plate 195 *(left).*
The Signalman at Waddon Marsh prepares to withdraw a Train Staff for the single-line section to Beddington Lane.
Photo B. L. Jackson.

ELECTRIC TRAIN STAFF INSTRUMENT.

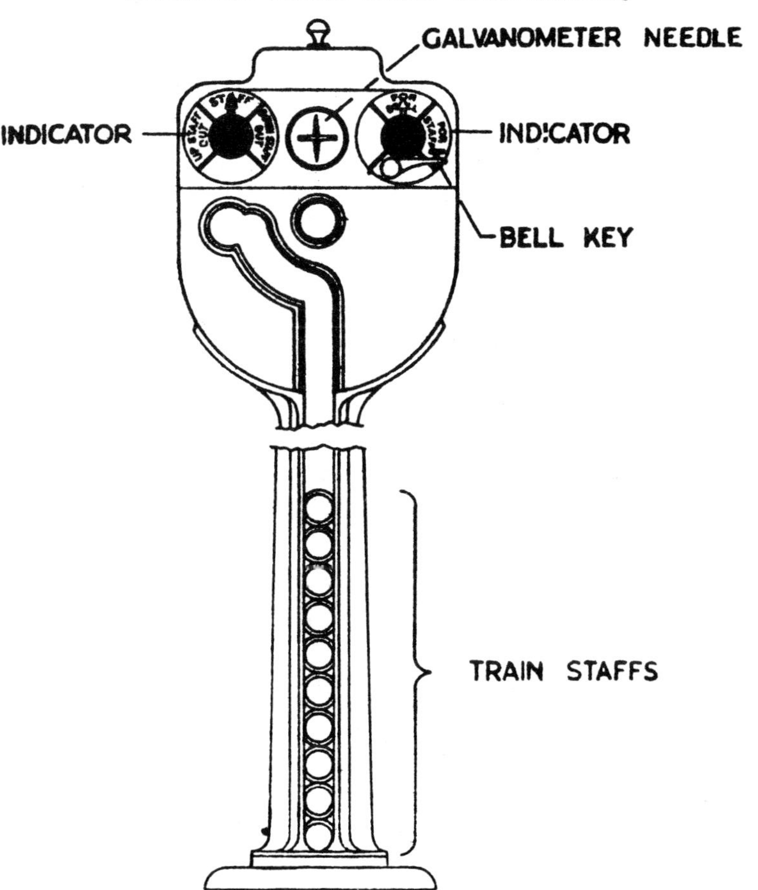

Mode of Signalling.—" A," " B " and " C " represent three consecutive Block Signal Boxes and the process of signalling a Train is as follows:—Prior to the despatch of a Train from " A " the Signalman there, provided he has received the **Train Out of Section** Signal for the previous Train and permission has not been given for a Train to approach in the opposite direction, must give the prescribed **Is Line Clear** Signal on the Bell Key. If the Line be clear at " B " the Signalman there must acknowledge the Signal, and on giving the last beat must hold down the Bell Key, and continue to hold it down until the Needle returns to its upright position.

The holding down of the Bell Key by " B " will cause the needle in " A's " Instrument, as well as in his own, to be deflected to a slanting position, and, on seeing the Needle assume that position, " A " must point his right-hand Indicator to **For Staff** and take out a Staff, the actual withdrawal of which will mechanically repoint his right-hand Indicator to **For Bell.** When the right-hand Indicator is thus repointed to **For Bell** it will cause the Bell in that Instrument to ring but this must not be taken for a Signal from the other end of the Section. As soon as " A " has taken out a Staff, he must turn the Pointer of his left-hand indicator to **Down Staff Out,** if it is a Down Train, or **Up Staff Out** if it is an Up Train, and **press it hard in.** This will cause the Needle to return to its upright position in both Signal Boxes, and will indicate to " B " that a Staff has been withdrawn at " A " and the left-hand pointer there turned; " B " must also turn his left-hand pointer to **Up Staff Out** or **Down Staff Out** as the case may be.

When the Staff has been withdrawn, the Starting Signal may be lowered, and the Train allowed to proceed, after the Staff has been handed to the Driver, the **Train Entering Section** Signal being given to and acknowledged by " B." " B " must then, provided he has received the **Train Out of Section** Signal for the previous Train, and permission has not been given for a Train to approach in the opposite direction, give the prescribed **Is Line Clear** Signal to " C "; on receiving permission from " C " for the Train to approach, " B " may lower his Signals for the Train to proceed to " C " and hand the Staff to the Driver. On arrival of the Train at " B," the Signalman there must obtain the Staff (for the Section " A " to " B ") from the Driver, insert the Staff in his Instrument and give the **Train Out of Section** Signal which " A " must acknowledge. Both " A " and " B " must then repoint their left-hand Indicators to **Staff In** and their Instruments will again be in the normal position, ready for another Train in either direction.

The Indicator on the left-hand side of the Instrument is provided for the Signalman to remind himself of the state of the Section. Its normal position must be at **Staff In.**

Putting Staff Back in Instrument.—Communication with other end of Section unnecessary.—A Staff can be put back in either Instrument at any time without any communication being made with the opposite end of the Section.

NOTE.—Certain of these Instruments are not equipped with right-hand Indicators.

Plate 196 *(above).*
Line-up of Train Staff instruments in the signal box at Waddon Marsh, which doubles as the booking office, hence the cash register to the left of the picture. The instruments are as follows, (left to right)—Large Staff to West Croydon. (Goods Line). Miniature Staff to W. Croydon. (Passenger Line). Large Staff to Beddington Lane.
Photo B. L. Jackson.

Plate 197 *(right).*
Close-up of the Railway Signal Company miniature Train Staff instrument, (Config. 'B'), at Waddon Marsh.
Photo B. L. Jackson.

Note: The independent Goods Line between Waddon Marsh and West Croydon 'B' box, was taken out of use in February 1976, and the miniature staff instruments were removed.

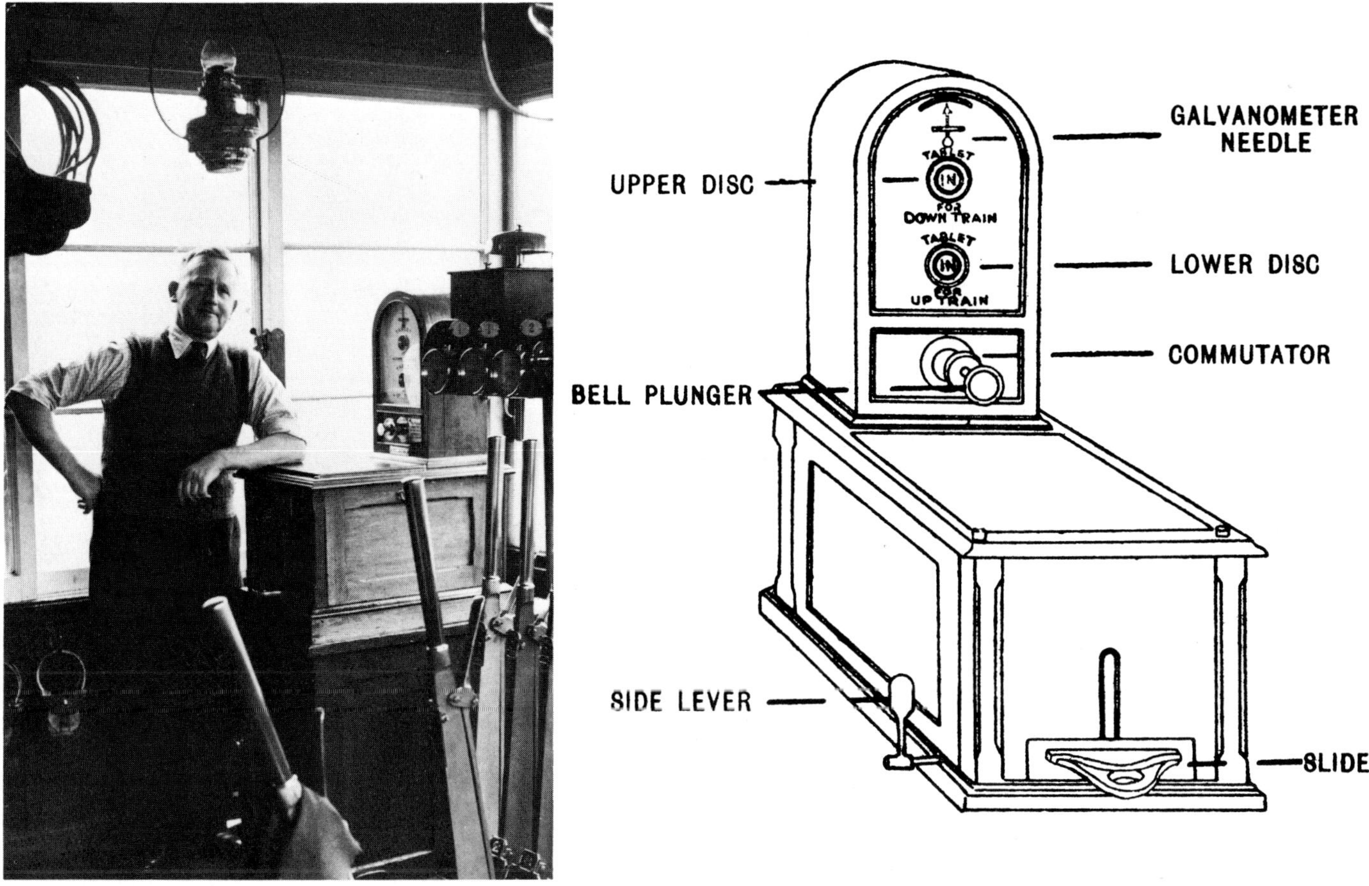

Official instructional drawing for No. 3 and No. 6 Tablet Instruments.

Plate 198 *(above left).*
The Signalman at Midford, on the former Somerset & Dorset line, poses proudly beside his Tyer's No. 6 Tablet Instrument for the single line section from there to Bath Junction.

Photo Ivo Peters.

No. 3 Instruments.

Mode of Signalling.—" A," " B " and " C " represent three consecutive Block Signal Boxes, and the process of signalling a Train is as follows :—

Prior to the despatch of a Train from " A " the Signalman there, provided he has received the **Train Out of Section** Signal for the previous Train and permission has not been given for a Train to approach in the opposite direction, and provided the Tablet Indicators show Tablet " In," must give the prescribed **Is Line Clear** Signal. If the Line be clear at " B " the Signalman there must, if he is prepared to receive the Train, acknowledge the Signal. The Signalman at " A " upon receiving the repetition of the **Is Line Clear** Signal, indicating that the Signalman at " B " is prepared to accept the Train, must hold in his Plunger for three seconds to allow the Signalman at " B " to lift the side lever, withdraw an empty Slide, and turn his Commutator from right to left, which will change his lower Disc from " In " to " Out." When the Signalman at " B " observes the Galvanometer Needle at zero he must hold in the plunger for three seconds, which will change the upper disc at " A " from " In " to " Out " and enable the Signalman at " A " to withdraw the Slide containing the Tablet. The Signalman at " A " must then give one beat to " B " to denote that the Tablet is out of the Instrument. " A " will then lower his Signals for the Train to leave, and hand the Tablet in the pouch to the Driver. On the Train leaving " A " the Signalman there must send the **Train Entering Section** Signal to " B," and the Signalman at " B " must acknowledge the Signal. " B," provided he has received the **Train Out of Section** Signal for the previous Train, and permission has not been given for a Train to approach in the opposite direction, and provided the Tablet Indicators show Tablet " In," must then give the prescribed **Is Line Clear Signal** to " C."

On receiving permission from " C " for the Train to approach " B " may lower his Signals for the Train to proceed to " C " and hand the Tablet in the pouch to the Driver. On arrival of the Train at " B," the Signalman there will receive the Tablet (for the Section " A " to " B ") from the Driver and place it in the Slide of the Instrument; he will then give " A " the **Train Out of Section** Signal. " A " will acknowledge the Signal and hold in for three seconds on the last beat. " B " will then replace the Slide and turn Commutator from left to right, which will change his lower Disc to " In "; after he observes the Galvanometer Needle at zero he must hold in the plunger for three seconds, replacing the upper Disc at " A " to " In," and enabling the Signalman at " A " to return his Slide to normal; when the Galvanometer Needle at " A " has returned to zero the Signalman there will give one beat to " B " and both Instruments are again ready for use.

No. 6 Instruments.

Mode of Signalling.—" A," " B " and " C " represent three consecutive Block Signal Boxes, and the process of signalling a Train is as follows :—

Prior to the despatch of a Train from " A " the Signalman there, provided he has received the **Train Out of Section** Signal for the previous Train and permission has not been given for a Train to approach in the opposite direction, and provided the Tablet Indicators show Tablet " In," must give the prescribed **Is Line Clear** Signal to " B." If the Line be clear at " B " the Signalman there must, if he is prepared to receive the Train, acknowledge the Signal and hold in his Plunger for about three seconds on the last beat. This will enable " A " to turn the Commutator to the left, and the Indication " Out " will appear on the lower Disc of his Instrument; he will then withdraw the Slide (leaving it out) and obtain the Tablet and send one beat to " B," which will change " B's " upper Disc to " Out " which " B " will acknowledge by one beat. " A " will then lower his signals for the Train to leave, and hand the Tablet in the pouch to the Driver. On the Train leaving " A " the Signalman there must send the **Train Entering Section** Signal to " B," and the Signalman at " B " must acknowledge the Signal. " B," provided he has received the **Train Out of Section** Signal for the previous Train, and permission has not been given for a Train to approach in the opposite direction, and provided the Tablet Indicator shows Tablet " In," must then give the prescribed **Is Line Clear** Signal to " C." On receiving permission from " C " for the Train to approach, " B " may lower his Signals for the Train to proceed to " C " and hand the Tablet in the pouch to the Driver. On arrival of the Train at " B " the Signalman must obtain the Tablet (for the Section " A " to " B ") from the Driver, lift his side lever, withdraw his empty Slide, and after inserting the Tablet in the Slide, push the Slide home, lift the side lever, withdraw the Slide empty, and again push it home. He will then give " A " the **Train Out of Section** Signal (pausing on the last beat for about three seconds to enable " A " to reverse his Commutator). " A " will turn his Commutator to the right, push his Slide home, and then acknowledge the **Train Out of Section** Signal. This will reverse the upper disc at " B " from " Out " to " In " and prove to " B " that " A " has replaced his Slide; " B " will then give one beat to " A," which will place the lower Disc at " A " to " In " and show that both Instruments are again ready for use.

To restore a Tablet which has been withdrawn for shunting purposes (Regulation 13) or in connection with the **Cancelling** Signal (Regulation (18a)), the following procedure must be followed:—

The Signalman at " A " will place the Tablet in the Slide, push the Slide home and hold it in. He will then turn the Commutator to the right, lift the side lever, withdraw the empty Slide and again push the Slide home. The **Shunting Completed—Tablet or Staff Replaced (2 pause 5)** or the **Cancelling** Signal **(3 pause 5)** as the case may be, must then be given to and acknowledged by " B." This will reverse the lower disc at " A " from " Out " to " In," and " A " will give one beat to " B " which will place the upper disc at " B " to " In."

Note: No. 3 Instruments are 'Non-returnable', which means that, once a Tablet is withdrawn, it cannot be re-inserted in the instrument from which it was drawn, but must travel through the section. No. 6 Instruments are 'Returnable', which allows the Tablet to be restored to the issuing instrument if required.

TYER'S NO. 7 ELECTRIC TRAIN TABLET INSTRUMENT.

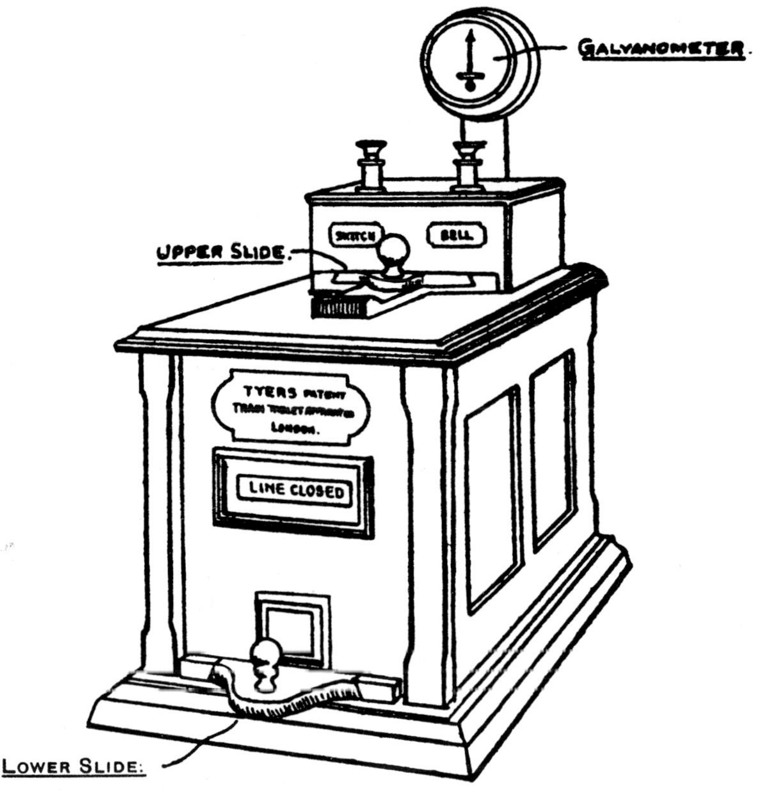

Mode of Signalling.—" A," " B " and " C " represent three consecutive Block Signal Boxes and the process of signalling a Train is as follows :—

Prior to the despatch of a Train from " A " the Signalman there, provided he has received the **Train Out of Section Signal** for the previous Train, and permission has not been given for a Train to approach in the opposite direction, and provided the Tablet Indicator shows " Line Closed " must give the prescribed **Is Line Clear** Signal to " B." If the Line be clear at " B " the Signalman there must, if he is prepared to receive the Train, acknowledge the signal by repeating it. The Signalman at " A," upon receiving the repetition of the **Is Line Clear** Signal indicating that the Signalman at " B " is prepared to accept the Train, must then hold down his Bell Plunger for a few seconds, which will ring the Bell at " B," and the man at " B " must depress his switch plunger with his left hand, and at the same time withdraw his lower Slide (which will then only come halfway out) with his right hand. The partial withdrawal of this Slide will reverse the commutator in the Instrument, and will bring the signal **Up Train Approaching** into view at " B." The Signalman at " B " will then depress his Bell Plunger, holding it down for a few seconds, which will ring the Bell at " A," and the man at " A," upon receipt of this Signal, will hold down his switch plunger with his left hand and withdraw his lower Slide to its full extent with his right hand, which will then bring the Signal **Up Train on Line** in to view at " A." The Signalman at " A " will then give one beat to " B " to denote that the Tablet is out of the Instrument, remove the Tablet from the recess in the Slide, lower his signals for the Train to leave, and hand the Tablet in the pouch to the Driver. On the Train leaving " A," the Signalman there must send the **Train Entering Section** Signal to " B," and the Signalman at " B " must acknowledge the Signal.

" B," provided he has received the **Train Out of Section** Signal for the previous Train, and permission has not been given for a train to approach in the opposite direction, and provided the Tablet Indicator shows " Line Closed," must give the prescribed **Is Line Clear** Signal to " C." Upon receiving permission from " C " for the Train to approach, " B " may lower his Signals for the Train to proceed to " C " and hand the Tablet in the pouch to the Driver. On arrival of the Train at " B " the Signalman must obtain the Tablet (for the Section " A " to " B ") from the Driver, withdraw the upper Slide of his Instrument, and after inserting the Tablet in the Slide, push the Slide home. The passing of the Tablet into the Cylinder will unlock the Instrument, and the Signalman at " B " must then push in the lower Slide, which will restore the Indicator of his Instrument to " Line Closed." He will then give to " A " the **Train Out of Section Signal**, pausing on the last beat for a few seconds. The Signalman at " A " will, upon receipt of the **Train Out of Section** Signal, depress his switch plunger and push home his lower Slide, which will at the same time restore his Indicator to " Line Closed," and he must then acknowledge the Signal to " B."

When a Train is required to be despatched from " C " to " A," the above instructions will apply, except that the Signal **Down Train Approaching** or **Down Train on Line** will appear on the Tablet Instruments.

To restore a Tablet which has been withdrawn for shunting purposes (Regulation 13) or in connection with the Cancelling Signal (Regulation 18a) the following procedure must be followed :—

The Signalman at " A " will withdraw the upper Slide of the Instrument, and after inserting the Tablet in the Slide, push the Slide home. He will then push in the lower Slide which will restore the Indicator in his Instrument to " Line Closed."

He will then give to the Signalman at " B " the **Shunting Completed—Tablet or Staff Replaced** Signal (2 pause 5), or the **Cancelling** Signal (3 pause 5), as the case may be, pausing on the last beat for a few seconds.

The Signalman at " B," upon receipt of the **Shunting Completed—Tablet or Staff Replaced** Signal or **Cancelling** Signal, must depress his Switch Plunger and push home his lower Slide, which will restore his Indicator to " Line Closed," and he must then acknowledge the signal to " A."

Official operating instructions for Tyer's No. 7 tablet instruments.

Plate 199.

A type of instrument that has long vanished from the scene—the Tyer's No.1 Tablet. This picture was taken at Wells 'A', (Somerset and Dorset), and shows the instrument controlling the single line to Glastonbury. The last survivor of this type was also on the S. & D. covering the Shillingstone-Sturminster Newton section, and was replaced in 1950. The Southern Railway book of Signalling Regulations as re-printed in 1945 makes no mention of No.1 tablets, so it must be assumed that they were already extremely rare by that date.

Author's Collection.

Plate 200.

The number of single lines which are still controlled by staff or tablet instruments is now quite small, as many such routes have been closed completely or converted to sidings for goods traffic only, whilst others that still carry a passenger service are now worked under 'One Train' regulations. In **Plate 200**, *(below), the signalman at Instow, on the line from Barnstaple Junction to Torrington, adopts the time-honoured stance ready to exchange tablets with the driver of a light engine, en route for Torrington to collect the milk train.*

Photo I. L. Shorter.

Closing switches are provided in many signal boxes on double lines of railway, but this facility is something of a rarity on single lines. There are a number of reasons for this. Firstly, as the security of the single line section must be ensured, and locking provided to guard against possible conflicting movements, far more is required than the straightforward 'Block Switch'. In most cases, two sets of Tablet or Token instruments have to be provided, one for the 'Long Section', and the other for the 'Short Section', with quite complex electrical circuits between the two to prevent both instruments being in use at the same time. The mechanical locking in the lever frame is also made more complicated by the need to lock certain signals whilst the box is in circuit, and free them to allow it to close. Single lines, taken as a whole, carry little or no night traffic, and lack the traffic 'peaks' found on main lines, so it is not usually considered worth the expense of installing so much specialised equipment in order to vary the traffic capacity of the line. Single lines are usually either open or closed, and all the signal boxes along the route are open whilst traffic is passing, and closed at other times.

However, there are exceptions. The section of the old Somerset & Dorset between Templecombe Junction and Blandford, though single track, was subject to great fluctuations in the volume of traffic passing over it, to the extent that it was necessary to provide a crossing loop about halfway between Shillingstone and Blandford. This additional crossing loop would have been an expensive luxury indeed if it had to be manned on Sundays and during other periods of light traffic, so closing facilities were provided.

The instructions on the next page give some idea of the complexities caused by long and short section working, and it is easy to see why such arrangements never became a common feature on the average country branch line.

Plate 201.
McKenzie and Holland 'Square Tablet', used for 'Long Section' working between Shillingstone and Blandford, when the intermediate box at Stourpaine was not in circuit.
Photo B. L. Jackson.

Fig. 47.

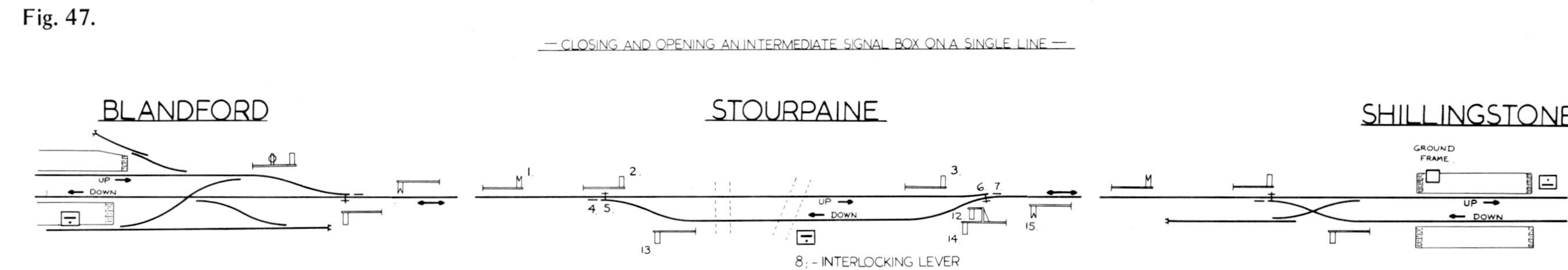

BLANDFORD

To Close Stourpaine

When asked by Stourpaine to plunge, plunge on Tyer's Tablet Instrument, pressing plunger until galvanometer needle goes to 'Zero'. When informed by Stourpaine that closing is effected, turn switch to 'Long Section'. Exchange signals with Shillingstone on long section Tablet Instrument.

To Open Stourpaine

When asked by Stourpaine to plunge, press down tapping key on Long Section Tablet Instrument, holding down until galvanometer needle goes to 'Zero'. When informed by Stourpaine that opening is effected, turn switch to 'Short Section'. Exchange signals with Stourpaine on Tyer's Tablet Instrument.

STOURPAINE

To set road for long section working, the following levers must be pulled over;— 8 Half-way, 4, 6, 7, 3, 2, 1, 12, 15 and 8-second half.

To close

Ask Blandford and Shillingstone if they are ready to close section. If so, turn short key for closing. Phone Blandford and Shillingstone and ask them to plunge. When indicator shews 'Lock Off', turn key as far as possible, withdraw it, and take it to lever frame, inserting it in lock on Interlocking Lever, (No. 8), and turning it. Pull No. 8 to middle position, then pull over point and signal levers for through working. Pull Interlocking Lever No. 8 right over, and withdraw long key. Put key in 'Long Section' and turn as far as possible. Phone to Blandford and Shillingstone that closure is effected, and tell them to turn their switches to 'Long Section'.

To open

Ask Blandford and Shillingstone if they are ready to open section. If so, turn long key for opening. Phone Blandford and Shillingstone, and ask them to plunge. When Indicator shews 'Lock Off' turn switch as far as possible and withdraw key. Take key to lever frame and insert it in lock on Interlocking Lever No. 8, and turn it. Push No. 8 to the middle position, then return all points and signals to normal. Return Interlocking Lever No. 8 to normal, and withdraw short key. Put key in 'Short Section', and turn as far as possible. Phone to Blandford and Shillingstone that opening is effected, and tell them to turn their switches to 'Short Section'. Exchange signals with Blandford and Shillingstone on Tyer's Tablet Instruments.

SHILLINGSTONE

To Close Stourpaine

When asked by Stourpaine to plunge, plunge on Tyer's Tablet instrument, pressing plunger until galvanometer needle goes to 'Zero'. When informed by Stourpaine that closure is effected, turn switch to 'Long Section'. Exchange signals with Blandford on Long Section Tablet Instrument.

To open Stourpaine

When asked by Stourpaine to plunge, press down tapping key on Long Section Instrument, holding down until the galvanometer needle goes to 'Zero'. When informed by Stourpaine that opening is effected, turn switch to 'Short Section', and exchange signals with Stourpaine on Tyer's Tablet Instrument.

NOTE: Long section, Blandford-Shillingstone. McKenzie & Holland square tablet.
Short sections, Blandford-Stourpaine and Stourpaine-Shillingstone. Tyer's No. 6 Tablet.

Copy of Instructions issued by L. & S.W.R. at Waterloo, on Feb. 9th, 1905.

9. Level Crossings

The level crossing is perhaps the most expensive feature of railway operation, as they not only cost a considerable sum in maintenance, but often require more staff to be employed than would otherwise be necessary. Indeed, the additional expenses are so high, that lines where level crossings are numerous, such as between Barnstaple and Ilfracombe and along the coast from Portsmouth to Brighton, are seldom able to cover their operating costs. In the case of the first named line, the abundance of crossings was almost certainly the deciding factor when closure was contemplated, and the latter, although quite heavily patronised, needs a Government grant in order to keep going.

For these reasons there has been a massive 'purge' on level crossings in recent years, the once familiar gates being dispensed with wherever possible. They are usually replaced by lifting barriers which are electrically operated, either under the control of an adjacent signal box, or worked automatically by the trains passing over treadles. Many other crossings have been closed altogether, the road being diverted to a new under or over bridge. Others have been reduced to 'Occupation' status, serving the needs of a nearby farm or factory only, in which cases the gates are secured across the roadway by chains and padlocks, a key being issued to the authorised user.

As already stated, where gates are in use at a public level crossing, the railway company is faced with increased staff costs. Many signal boxes that would not otherwise be required to work the traffic at off-peak times, such as at night or on Sundays, have to be manned continuously solely to work the gates. The Southern found a way of reducing this expense to a minimum by providing block switches at locations where road traffic was light, the crossing being worked by a resident crossing-keeper during the hours that the signal box was out of circuit. When the Signalman operated the switch, the block instruments and bells were rendered inoperative, the box becoming a 'ground frame' for the control of the gates and protecting signals only.

The high cost of maintenance has always been aggravated by the fact that motor vehicles are frequently in collision with the gates, particularly where they are situated at the foot of a steep hill or around a sharp bend in the road. Because of this, very few examples of pre-grouping gates remain today. Occasionally, it is a train that demolishes crossing gates, but this is a less frequent occurrence.

The level crossing is a thing of infinite variety, and although they are all similar in principle, they differ widely in detail. The relative width of the road to that of the railway, and the angle at which the road crosses, have a strong influence over the design, and it is therefore impossible to give all the possible configurations in a book of this size. However, it is hoped that the drawings and photographs which follow will serve to give some idea of the design and working of these fast-vanishing items of railway equipment.

There remains one last point to be made about level crossings in general. Where the gates are under the control of a signal box, their nomal position is across the railway. Although on the face of it, a set of gates with vehicles passing between forms an obstruction upon the railway, it is not considered as such for the purposes of block working. The 'obstruction' is under the direct control of the Signalman, and he can therefore accept trains from the box on either side even if the crossing lies within his 'Clearing Point'. At some intermediate crossings controlled by crossing-keepers, particularly where vehicular traffic is light, the gates stand normally across the road, and are placed across the railway only when necessary to permit road traffic to pass. Many crossings of this type have hand operated gates.

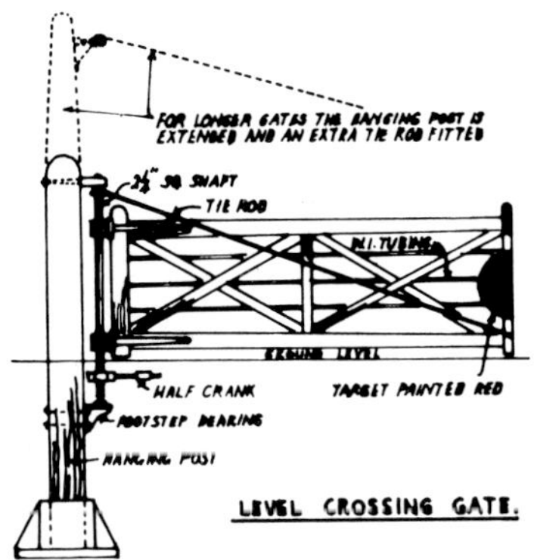

Fig. 48.
The components of a level crossing gate. These vary greatly in detail, and the 'W.I. Tubing' is replaced in many cases by heavy wire mesh.

Drawing G. Bowring.

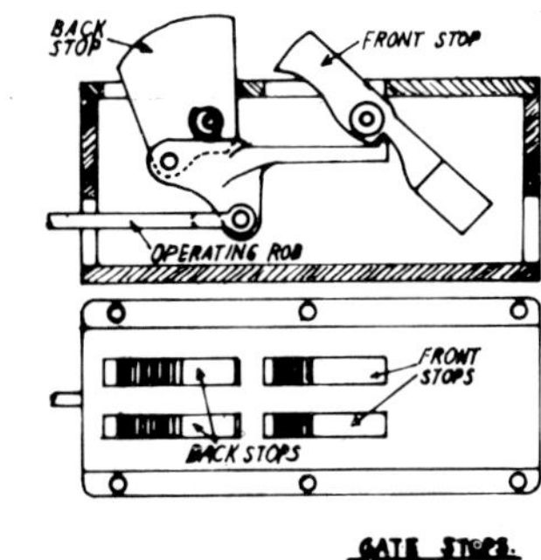

Fig. 49.
When a set of gates have been closed across the road, it is necessary to hold them in that position. For this reason, Gate Stops are provided. They are controlled by the action of the gates, and so arranged through escapement cranks that they will not rise until the movement of the gates is almost completed, otherwise they would form an obstruction on the road that is almost invisible to the drivers of motor vehicles. Gate Stops actually perform two functions—the back stop prevents the gates over-running, and the front stop, which is depressed as the toe of the gate passes over it, provides a positive lock. If this were not done, a strong wind could easily blow the gates into the path of an approaching train.

Drawing G. Bowring.

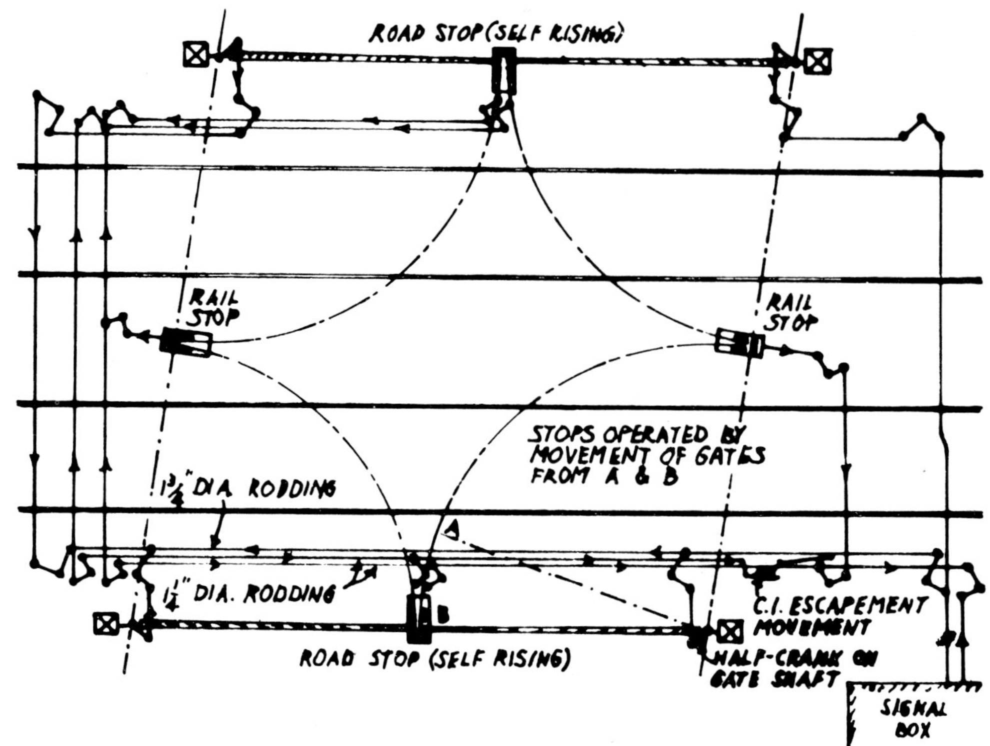

Fig. 50.

Diagram of the mechanical connections to a four-gate lever crossing on a double line of railway, operated by a wheel in the signal box.

Drawing G. Bowring.

Plate 202.

Part of the Stevens Frame at Cosham, showing the standard pattern of level crossing gate wheel used by the L. & S.W.R.

Photo G. Kinsey.

Plate 203.
Standard 'Southern' gates, constructed of timber and stout wire mesh, at Wallsend Crossing.

Photo J. P. Morris.

Plate 204.
South Eastern design of level crossing gate box at Rye. This is not a block post, the gates being released by the station signal box. The gates themselves are of the standard 'Southern' type, hung on concrete posts.

Photo B. L. Jackson.

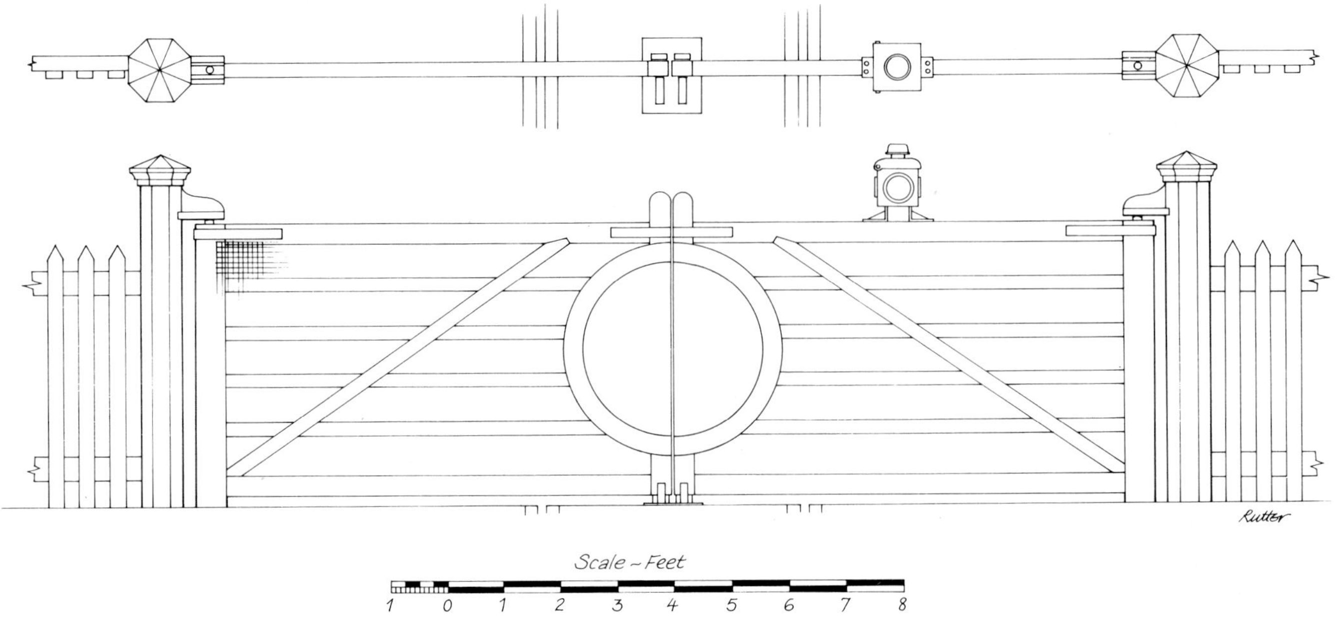

Fig. 51.
Scale drawing of a pair of gates for single line. These are of Saxby & Farmer design, with cast iron hanging posts, modelled on a set on the Hayling Island branch, L.B. & S.C.R.

Drawing P. D. Rutter.

Plate 205.
Unusual gate arrangement at Billingshurst. The roadway is of 'single' width, and at first glance the crossing appears to be fitted with two single gates. However, four gates are provided to enclose the double-line railway when the crossing is open to road traffic, two of them swinging back parallel to the line for the passage of trains. Part of one such gate can be seen to the left of the gate-post.

Photo B. L. Jackson.

Plate 206.
L. & S.W.R. gates on concrete hanging posts, near Braunton, on the line to Ilfracombe. Note the small side gates, called 'Wickets', for the use of pedestrians.

Photo B. L. Jackson.

Plate 207.
Crossing gates at Braunton, showing a 'South Western' gate, (nearest to the camera), and one of Southern design. It was common to find odd gates at level crossings, as they were rather accident-prone, and frequently had to be renewed and patched up.

Photo B. L. Jackson.

10. Unusual Signals

Plates 208 and 209.
Slotted-post semaphore of the three-phase time interval type, at the racecourse platform, Esher. When the platforms were in use, the indicators were as above. (The left-hand plate shows the arm at "danger", and the right-hand one at clear.) However, during the lengthy spells when the platforms were not in use, the arm was dropped into the slot, (the original "clear" position), and pinned in.

Photos Lens of Sutton.

Plates 210 and 211.

Chain-operated Weighbridge signal at Herne Hill sidings. The arm, applying to movements in both directions, is a single unit pivoted in the centre, and is therefore both an upper and lower quadrant, depending on direction of approach. When the arm is 'On' (left) a red glass covers the double sided lamp to give the "Stop" signal after dark. When 'Off' the glass, which is worked from the arm by a rod, is lifted clear of the lamp, displaying a white "clear" indication.

Photos Lens of Sutton.

Plate 212.

Lattice post semaphore signals with the arms removed, leaving only the spectacle plates operative. They are, in effect, mechanical colour-light signals. These signals, the platform starters (Sutton Line) at Wimbledon 'B' with lower distants for Wimbledon 'C', are located under a lengthy overbridge, and are in semi-darkness even on bright days. When the arms were attached, they were barely visible, so it was decided to dispense with them altogether.

Photo D. B. Clayton.

Plate 213.

Marshalling yards were often happy hunting grounds for those seeking the oddities of the signalling world. On the extreme right of this view can be seen the double-arm signal governing movements in and out of the sidings at Faversham yard. The loco engaged in shunting is No. 31256.

Photo R. C. Riley.

Plate 214.

Although the signal itself is a perfectly standard "South Western" structure with an SR arm, it is seldom that one finds part of the station lighting attached to a signal. Here at Clatford, in the rural charm of the now-closed Andover to Romsey line, the starting signal sprouted an oil lamp of genuine L. & S.W.R. vintage.

Photo G. Kinsey.

Plate 215.
Details of arms and top of signal post.

Plate 216.
General view of signal, showing unusual crossing gates.

Edinburgh Road Crossing, Portsmouth Dockyard Railway, provides us with the last surviving example of this early form of semaphore signal. Although of no great age, it is an exact copy of signals which have stood on the site for nearly one hundred years, and has about it features associated with the original naval semaphore telegraph. There is no interlocking of any sort, the arms being controlled by hand levers attached to the base of the post.

Photos B. L. Jackson.

Plate 217.
Rail-built rarity. Junction signal with splitting distants at Gloucester Road Junction, made up of three independent posts instead of the conventional gantry.

Photo courtesy National Railway Museum, York.

Plate 218.

The Southern's grand 'Farewell' to the era of Mechanical Signalling—Weymouth Signal Box. Opened in 1957, and containing a 116-lever Westinghouse 'A3' frame, it was to be the last LARGE mechanical box to be installed on the Southern. Several small ones were erected later, notably between Salisbury and Exeter, but most of these were abolished when that line was singled. Weymouth still remains, albeit with simplified track layout and reduced train service.

Photo British Railways, Southern Region.

Appendix 1

SOUTHERN RAILWAY HEADCODES — LOCO-HAULED SERVICES

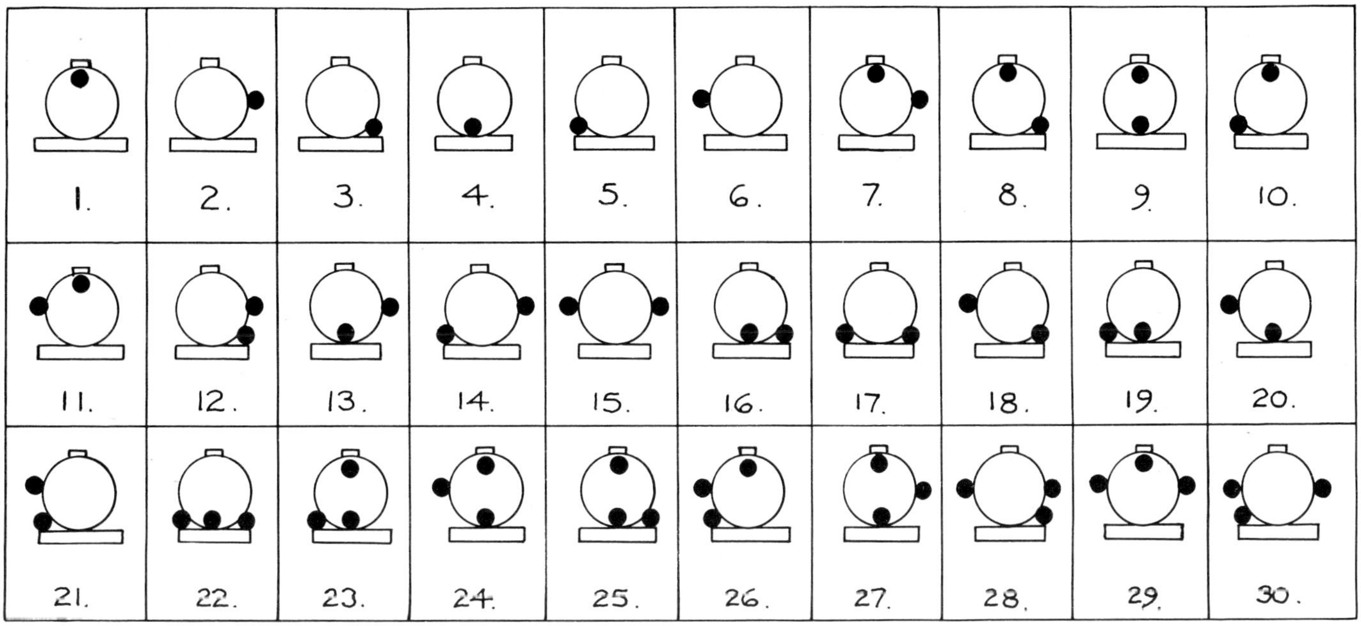

1.	2.	3.	4.	5.	6.	7.	8.	9.	10.
11.	12.	13.	14.	15.	16.	17.	18.	19.	20.
21.	22.	23.	24.	25.	26.	27.	28.	29.	30.

NOTE: Codes indicated by the positioning of white enamel discs, (or lamps by night), as shown.

Code No	*Service or Route*
1	Victoria & Dover via Chatham Victoria & Norwood Yard via Selhurst Loughborough Sidings & Holborn Viaduct Eastleigh & Bulford, via Chandlers Ford & Andover Andover & Hastings Reading & Margate via Redhill Southampton Terminus & Brockenhurst or Weymouth via Wimborne Plymouth Friary & Tavistock Woking & Reading via Virginia Water West Curve Exeter Central & Ilfracombe Bodmin & Wadebridge Exeter Central & Exmouth
2	Victoria or Clapham Jc. & Holborn Low Level London Bridge or Bricklayers Arms to Portsmouth via Quarry Line & Horsham Via Mid-Kent line and Beckenham Jcn. Ashford & Eastbourne direct Waterloo or Nine Elms & Southampton Terminus direct. (Other than boat trains) Willesden & Feltham Yard via Gunnersbury Waterloo or Nine Elms & Windsor via Twickenham Southampton Central & Lymington Yeovil Jcn. & Yeovil Town Seaton Jcn. & Seaton Barnstaple Junction & Torrington Halwill & Bude
3	Victoria or Clapham Jcn. & Holborn London Bridge or Bricklayers Arms & Brighton via Quarry Line Tonbridge & Brighton via Eridge Hastings via Mid Kent Line, Oxted, Crowhurst Jcn, and Tonbridge Dunton Green & Westerham Ashford & Margate via Canterbury West Lydd Branch Folkestone Jcn. & Folkestone Harbour Crowhurst & Bexhill West Swanley Junction & Gravesend West Sittingbourne & Sheerness Deal & Kearsney Gravesend Central & Allhallows-on-Sea or Port Victoria All stations to Feltham (except via Mortlake) Weymouth & Portland & Easton (goods trains) Bournemouth West & Brockenhurst via Wimborne
4	Victoria or Battersea Yard & Brighton via Redhill Oxted & Eastbourne via Eridge London Bridge & New Cross via Bricklayers Arms Jcn. Horsham & Brighton Alton & Fareham Bentley & Bordon Salisbury & Bulford Axminster & Lyme Regis Tipton St John's & Exmouth Wareham & Swanage Brockenhurst & Lymington Pier Bere Alston & Callington

5 Victoria or Stewarts Lane & Clapham Jcn.
Oxted & Tunbridge Wells West via East Grinstead H.L.
Pulborough, Midhurst & Chichester
Havant & Hayling Island
London Bridge & Bricklayers Arms
Tonbridge & Maidstone West
Ashford (Kent) & Dover via Minster and Deal
Stewarts Lane & Victoria
Southampton Docks & Nine Elms via Main Line (market goods, fruit or potato trains)

6 London Bridge or Bricklayers Arms to Dover or Ramsgate via East Croydon, Oxted & Tonbridge
Tonbridge & Hawkhurst
Battersea Yard & Kensington
Waterloo or Nine Elms & Reading, via Twickenham
Willesden & Feltham Yard via Kew East Jcn.
Exeter Central & Sidmouth
Plymouth Friary & Turnchapel
Eastleigh or Southampton & Fawley
Bournemouth Central & Brockenhurst via Wimborne
Torrington & Halwill

7 Victoria or Battersea Yard & Portsmouth via Quarry Line & Horsham
Via Maidstone East Line to Victoria or Holborn
Waterloo or Nine Elms & Southampton Docks via Brentford, Chertsey, and Woking

8 London Bridge or Bricklayers Arms & Eastbourne or Hastings via Quarry Line
Victoria or West London Line & Ramsgate via Herne Hill, or Catford Loop
London Bridge or Bricklayers Arms & Hastings via Chiselhurst & Tunbridge Wells Central
West London Line & East Croydon via Crystal Palace L.L.
Special Boat Train Waterloo to Southampton Docks via Northam
Special Boat Train Southampton Docks to Waterloo via Millbrook
Southampton & Andover via Redbridge

9 Victoria or Battersea Yard to Eastbourne or Hastings via Quarry Line
London & Hither Green Sidings
Victoria & Folkestone Harbour, or Dover Marine, via Swanley, Otford & Tonbridge
Waterloo or Nine Elms & Plymouth
Bournemouth Central & Dorchester (goods trains)
Battersea Yard & Brent via New Kew Jcn.
Southampton Terminus & Portsmouth Harbour via Netley

10 London Bridge or Bricklayers Arms & Portsmouth via Redhill and Horsham
Victoria or Battersea Yard & Norwood Yard via Crystal Palace L.L.
London Bridge and New Cross Gate to Eardley Sidings via Peckham Rye
Deptford Wharf & New Cross Gate
London Bridge or Bricklayers Arms & Folkestone or Dover via Chiselhurst, Tonbridge & Ashford
Dover & Margate via Deal and Minster Loop
Special Boat Train Waterloo to Southampton Docks via Millbrook
Feltham to Durnsford Road via Chertsey

11 Victoria or Battersea Yard & Portsmouth via Redhill & Horsham
Via Dartford Loop Line
Victoria or Holborn & Hastings line via Orpington Loop and Tunbridge Wells Central
Bricklayers Arms & Guildford via Leatherhead & Effingham Jcn.
Waterloo or Nine Elms & Southampton Terminus via Alton
Salisbury & Bournemouth West via Wimborne
Fareham & Gosport
Ballast train to Meldon Quarry from Exeter Central and stations west thereof

12 Victoria or Battersea Yard & Portsmouth via Mitcham Jcn.
London Bridge or Bricklayers Arms & Eastbourne or Hastings via Redhill
Victoria, Stewarts Lane, or Holborn to North Kent Line via Nunhead Line
Nine Elms & Feltham via Mortlake
Exeter Central to Nine Elms (market goods and fish trains)
Down Main Line goods terminating at Woking
Southampton Docks & Salisbury via Eastleigh

13 London Bridge or Bricklayers Arms & Brighton via Redhill
Three Bridges & Tunbridge Wells West
West London Line to Norwood Yard via Thornton Heath
Victoria or Holborn to Dover via Nunhead line, and Maidstone East
Parcels & Empty trains Waterloo to Clapham Jcn. (Kensington Sdgs)
Feltham Yard & Neasden via Kew East Jcn.
Portsmouth Harbour or Portsmouth & Southsea to Fratton Loco Shed
Exeter Central & Exmouth Jcn
Bournemouth West to Dorchester
Southampton & Salisbury via Redbridge

14 London Bridge & Portsmouth via Mitcham Jcn
London Bridge, Oxted and Tunbridge Wells West via Hever
Oxted & Lewes or Seaford or Eastbourne via Haywards Heath & Keymer Jcn. (Change to h/codes No. 5 or 21 at Lewes)
London Bridge or Bricklayers Arms & Dover via Chiselhurst Loop & Maidstone East
Waterloo or Nine Elms & Brockenhurst & Bournemouth West via Sway

15 Via Bexleyheath Line
Victoria or Stewarts Lane or Holborn via Nunhead line & Bexleyheath
Oxted & Brighton via Haywards Heath
Waterloo or Nine Elms & Reading via loop line
All trains terminating at Portsmouth & Southsea (Trains from Salisbury to carry Headcode 17 to Eastleigh)
Exeter Central & Padstow
Light engines Bournemouth Central or Bournemouth West to Bournemouth Central via triangle to turn
Light engines Eastleigh Loco to Portsmouth & Southsea
Light engines to Guildford Loco via Woking, except via Staines

16 London Bridge or Bricklayers Arms & Portsmouth via West Croydon
Victoria or Battersea Yard & Eastbourne or Hastings via Redhill
Oxted & Brighton via Eridge
London Bridge or Bricklayers Arms & Ramsgate via Tonbridge and Canterbury West
Waterloo or Nine Elms & Woking via Richmond and Chertsey
Milk and Empty trains to Clapham Jcn via Byfleet Curve & Richmond

17 London Bridge or Bricklayers Arms & Tonbridge or Reading via East Croydon & Redhill (Also Tonbridge & Reading)
Brighton & Hove via Preston Park spur
Three Bridges & Eridge
Victoria or Holborn & Folkestone or Dover via Orpington Loop, Tonbridge and Ashford
London Bridge or Bricklayers Arms & Gillingham, Faversham, Ramsgate or Dover via Chiselhurst Loop and Chatham
Waterloo or Nine Elms & Clapham Jcn. (Empty trains and light eng)
Passenger trains Bournemouth Central & Weymouth

18 London Bridge or Bricklayers Arms & Dover, Ramsgate or Hastings via Chiselhurst, Swanley, Otford, and Sevenoaks
Victoria, Oxted, and Tunbridge Wells West via Hever
Holborn & Ramsgate via Herne Hill or Catford Loop
Light engines and trains requiring to run to Up Main Loop at Clapham Jcn. from stations westward
Southampton & Andover via Eastleigh
Light engines, or engines with vehicles attached, running round the triangle at Bournemouth West to turn

19 Victoria or Battersea Yard & Brighton via Quarry Line
London Bridge or New Cross Gate & Norwood Yard
Tunbridge Wells West & Eastbourne
Victoria or Holborn & Ramsgate, Dover or Hastings via Nunhead Line and Tonbridge
Horsham & Guildford
Waterloo or Nine Elms & Southampton Docks via East Putney
Salisbury & Portsmouth Harbour via Eastleigh
Portsmouth & Southsea to Salisbury via Eastleigh

20 Victoria, Stewarts Lane or Holborn to Ramsgate via Nunhead line Chiselhurst and Chatham
London Bridge or Bricklayers Arms & North Kent Line via Greenwich
Via Streatham Spur
Feltham Yard & Brent via Kew East Junction
Clapham Junction & Kensington
Portsmouth & Southsea & Salisbury via Redbridge
Salisbury & Portsmouth Harbour via Redbridge

21 Victoria & Newhaven Harbour
Victoria or Holborn to Ramsgate via Nunhead Line & Maidstone East
Waterloo or Nine Elms & Portsmouth via Woking & Guildford
Light engines from all stations to Feltham Loco
Light engines from all stations west of Basingstoke to Eastleigh Loco

22 Waterloo & Portsmouth Harbour via Eastleigh
Feltham & Brent via Richmond
SR and WR trains Hither Green Sidings, Stewarts Lane, or South Lambeth to Old Oak Common
LM (Western Division) trains between Willesden and Redhill via Clapham Junction
LM (Midland Division) and ER (GN) trains to or from Hither Green Sidings
WR trains Norwood Yard to Old Oak Common
WR trains Cattewater Junction & Plymstock

23 Nine Elms & Willesden via New Kew Junction
Brighton & Salisbury via Southampton Central
Eastleigh & Micheldever or Basingstoke (light engines for testing)
Windsor & Hastings excursion trains
Windsor & Margate or Dover excursion trains, or between Windsor and Redhill
WR trains to South Lambeth
ER trains to or from Lower Sydenham

24 Waterloo & Guildford via Leatherhead (except light engines Nine Elms to Raynes Park)
Southampton & Willesden via Richmond and Gunnersbury
Southampton or Salisbury & Willesden via Chertsey & Kew East Jcn. (or from Basingstoke)
Reading to Willesden via Feltham

25 Nine Elms and Brent via New Kew Junction
Kingston & Shepperton
Brighton & Salisbury. Through trains via Eastleigh
Windsor & Bognor Regis excursion trains
To LMR via West London Line

26 Brighton & Bournemouth
Waterloo & Wimbledon Park Sidings via East Putney (empty trains and light engines)
Merstham & Staines Moor via Guildford, Byfleet Jcn and Staines
Victoria (E or C), Stewarts Lane, Clapham Jcn. or Holborn & Eardley Sidings via Herne Hill

27 Hither Green Sidings & Feltham via Brentford
Feltham to Wimbledon West Yard
London Bridge or Bricklayers Arms & Brighton via Oxted, Eridge & Lewes

28 Hither Green Sidings & Feltham via Richmond
London Bridge or Bricklayers Arms & Brighton via Oxted, East Grinstead and Lewes

29 Plumstead & Feltham via Brentford
Victoria or Battersea Yard & Brighton via Oxted, Eridge, & Lewes

30 Plumstead & Feltham via Richmond
Victoria or Battersea Yard & Brighton via Oxted, E. Grinstead & Lewes

Plate 219.
Up train, carrying headcode 9, pulls out of Devonport King's Road hauled by rebuilt Bulleid Pacific No. 34104 Bere Alston. *White enamel discs were used during the day, and lamps at night.*

Photo R. C. Riley.

Appendix 2

PERMANENT WAY DEPARTMENT TROLLEYS PASSING THROUGH TUNNELS. (BLOCK REGULATION 9)

As a general rule, these hand-propelled trolleys are not worked under the Block System, but protected by a flagman stationed at a sufficient distance, (originally ¾ mile but now increased to 1 mile), to the rear of the work. The ganger in charge of the "trolley gang" consults the Signalman as to a suitable margin between trains, but thereafter the flagman is responsible for safe working.

However, tunnels present added difficulties and sources of potential danger, and many of them, (though by no means all), are designated as coming under the provisions of Block Regulation 9. Length of the tunnel seems to have little bearing on whether or not this additional safeguard is required. It is more likely to apply to a very short tunnel built on a curve, or having approaches giving limited visibility, than to a straight bore of greater length.

The bell code for such a trolley (under SR Block) was 2-2-2, and the Signalman receiving this signal was authorised to accept it under "Regulation 5" or the "warning arrangement". If the trolley was removed from the rails after passing through the tunnel, but before arriving at the box in advance, the ganger had either to walk to the next box ahead and advise the Signalman there, who could then send the "train out of section signal", or back to the box in rear. If he adopted the latter course, that Signalman would clear the line by sending the "Cancelling" signal (3 pause 5).

A list of tunnels on the Southern Railway where this Regulation applied is given below.

SOUTH EAST SECTION

Tunnel	*Between Signal Boxes*	*Miles*	*Yards*
Charing Cross to Dover Marine (via Tonbridge)			
Chelsfield	Chelsfield & Knockholt		597
Polhill	Knockholt & Polhill	1	851
Sevenoaks	Sevenoaks 'B' & Weald Intermediate	1	1693
Sandling	Westenhanger & Sandling		100
Saltwood	Sandling & Cheriton		954
Abbotscliffe	Abbotscliffe & Shakespeare	1	182
Shakespeare	Shakespeare & Archcliffe Jcn.		1387
Tonbridge 'B' to Hastings			
Wells	Tunbridge Wells Central Goods & Grove Jcn.		823
Wadhurst	Wadhurst & Stonegate		1205
Mountfield	Robertsbridge 'B' & Battle Road Crossing		526
Bopeep (Up line only)	Hastings & Bopeep Jcn.		1318
Hastings (Down line only)	Bopeep Jcn. & Hastings		788
Swanley to Ashford 'B'			
Eynsford	Swanley & Eynsford		828
Preston Hall 'A'	West Malling & Barming		33
Preston Hall 'B'	West Malling & Barming		54
Wheeler Street	Maidstone East & Bearsted		358
Faversham to Dover Marine & Archcliffe Jcn.			
Selling	Selling & Chartham Crossing		405
Lydden	Shepherds Well & Kearnsey	1	609
Charlton	Buckland Jcn. & Dover Priory		264
Dover Harbour	Dover Priory & Hawkesbury Street Jcn.		648
Paddock Wood to Hawkhurst			
Horsmonden	Paddock Wood & Horsmonden		86
Badgers Oak	Cranbrook & Hawkhurst		178
Ashford 'D' to Hastings			
Ore (Up line only)	Doleham Sidings & Ore		1402
Mount Pleasant	Ore & Hastings		230

Tunnel	*Between Signal Boxes*	*Miles*	*Yards*
Grove Jcn. (Tunbridge Wells) & Tunbridge Wells West 'B'			
Grove (Frant Road) (to Grove Jcn. direction only)	Grove Jcn. & Tunbridge Wells West 'B'		183
North Kent East Jcn. to Maidstone West (via Greenwich)			
Greenwich College (Down line; up line when Maze Hill box closed)	North Kent East Jcn. & Maze Hill		450
Charlton	Charlton Lane Crossing & Sand Street Crossing		154
Mount Street	Charlton Lane Crossing & Sand Street Crossing		121
Greenhithe	Greenhithe & Northfleet		253
Higham	Higham & Strood Tunnel		1531
Strood	Higham & Strood Tunnel	1	569
St Johns to Charlton			
Blackheath	Blackheath 'B' & Angerstein Jcn.		1681
Blackheath 'B' to Crayford Creek Jcn. & Slade Green			
Kidbrooke	Blackheath 'B' & Kidbrooke		437
Parks Bridge Jcn. to Selsdon			
Woodside	Woodside & Selsdon		266
Park Hill	Woodside & Selsdon		122
Coombe Lane	Woodside & Selsdon		157

CENTRAL SECTION

Tunnel	*Between Signal Boxes*	*Miles*	*Yards*
London Bridge to Brighton			
Merstham	Star Bridge & Merstham	1	71
Keymer Crossing to Eastbourne & Ore			
Lewes	Lewes West & Hamsey Crossing		369
Bopeep (Up line only)	Hastings & Bopeep Jcn.		1318
Hastings (Down line only)	Bopeep Jcn. & Hastings		788
Mount Pleasant	Hastings & Ore		230
Bricklayers Arms Jcn. to Arundel Jcn. (via Mitcham Jcn.)			
Knights Hill	Knights Hill Sidings & Tulse Hill		331
South Croydon to Grove Jcn. (Tunbridge Wells Central) (via Edenbridge Town)			
Riddlesdown	Sanderstead & Upper Warlingham		837
Oxted	Woldingham & Oxted	1	501
Limpsfield	Oxted & Hurst Green Jcn.		551
Grove (Frant Road)	Tunbridge Wells West 'B' & Grove Jcn.		183
Hurst Green Jcn. to Ashurst Jcn. (via East Grinstead)			
East Grinstead No 1	East Grinstead 'B' & Forest Row		78
East Grinstead No 2	East Grinstead 'B' & Forest Row		48
Redgate Mill Jcn. to Polegate 'A'			
Heathfield	Mayfield & Heathfield		265
Peckham Rye 'C' to Battersea Park Jcn. (South London line)			
Grove (Up South London line only)	Denmark Hill & Peckham Rye 'C'		132
Balham to Beckenham Jcn.			
Leigham Court (Streatham Hill)	Streatham Hill & Leigham Jcn.		443
Crystal Palace	Gipsy Hill & Crystal Palace 'A'		746
Purley to Tattenham Corner 'A'			
Kingswood	Kingswood & Tadworth		310

Tunnel	Between Signal Boxes	Miles	Yards
WESTERN SECTION			
Waterloo (Main lines) to Weymouth			
Litchfield	Waltham & Roundwood		198
Popham No 1 (Down line only)	Roundwood & Micheldever		265
Popham No 2 (Down line only)	Roundwood & Micheldever		199
Wallers Ash	Wallers Ash & Winchester Jcn.		501
Southampton	Tunnel Jcn. & Southampton Central		528
Bincombe	Dorchester Jcn. & Upwey & Broadwey		814
Woking to Portsmouth Harbour			
Chalk (Up line only)	Shalford Jcn. & Guildford South		845
St. Catherines	Guildford South & Shalford Jcn.		132
Buriton (Up line only)	Idworth Crossing & Buriton Siding		485
Worting Jcn. to Devonport Jcn.			
Fisherton	Tunnel Jcn. & Salisbury East		443
Gillingham	Gillingham & Templecombe		742
Crewkerne	Crewkerne & Hewish		206
Honiton	Honiton Incline & Honiton		1345
Blackboy	Exmouth Jcn. & Exeter Central 'A'		263
St Davids	Exeter Central 'B' & Exeter St. Davids West		184
Shillamill	Tavistock North & Bere Alston		603
Ford	St Budeaux Victoria Road & Devonport Kings Road		373
Devonport Park	St Budeaux Victoria Road & Devonport Kings Road		531
Brookwood to Winchester Jcn. (via Alton)			
Foxhills	Brookwood & Ash Vale Jcn.		418
Eastleigh West to Portcreek Jcn. & Farlington Jcn.			
Fareham No 1 (Single line)	Knowle Jcn. & Fareham East		56
Fareham No 2 (Single line)	Knowle Jcn. & Fareham East		553
Barnstaple Jcn. 'B' to Halwill			
Land cross	Bideford & Torrington		196
Meldon Jcn. to Padstow			
Trelill	Port Isaac Road & St Kew Highway		352
Point Pleasant Jcn. to Wimbledon 'A'			
East Putney	East Putney & Cromer Road		311
Ryde Pier Head to Ventnor			
Ryde Esplanade	Ryde Pier Head & Ryde St. Johns Road		391
Ventnor	Wroxhall & Ventnor		1312
Ryde St Johns to Cowes			
Newport	Havenstreet & Newport		73
Mill Hill	Newport & Cowes		208

W

Index

Plate 220.
The end of an era at Moreton, Dorset. Following the automation of the level crossing, contractors demolish the ex-L. & S.W.R. signal box in the summer of 1972.

Photo Evan Jones.

PLATFORM